BUILDING POWER

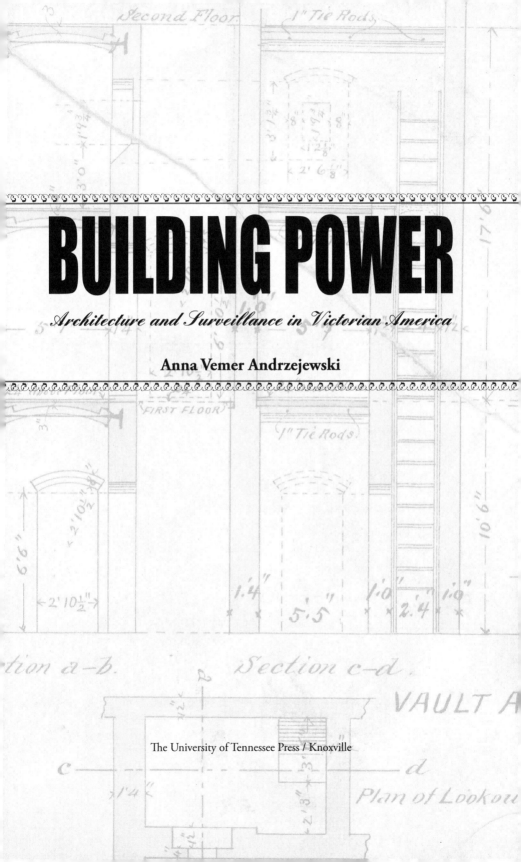

BUILDING POWER

Architecture and Surveillance in Victorian America

Anna Vemer Andrzejewski

The University of Tennessee Press / Knoxville

Copyright © 2008 by The University of Tennessee Press / Knoxville.
All Rights Reserved. Manufactured in the United States of America.
First Edition.

This book is printed on acid-free paper.

Library of Congress Cataloging-in-Publication Data

Andrzejewski, Anna Vemer.
  Building power : architecture and surveillance in Victorian America / Anna Vemer
Andrzejewski.
    p. cm.
  Includes bibliographical references.
  ISBN-13: 978-1-57233-631-5 (hardcover : alk. paper)
  ISBN-10: 1-57233-631-5
  1. Space (Architecture)—Social aspects—United States—History—19th century.
  2. Space (Architecture)—Social aspects—United States—History—20th century.
  3. Architecture—Human factors—United States—History—19th century.
  4. Architecture—Human factors—United States—History—20th century.
  5. Social control—United States—History—19th century.
  6. Social control—United States—History—20th century.
  I. Title.
    NA2543.S6A525 2008
    720.1'03097309034+dc22   2008005351

For the two Elizabeths

CONTENTS

ILLUSTRATIONS

PREFACE

$\mathscr{I}$t has become a truism to say that the world changed on September 11, 2001. The immediate aftermath of the terrorist attacks on the World Trade Center in New York City and the Pentagon in Washington was marked by expressions of grief and anger. Not long afterward, however, the U.S. government (and American citizens) took up efforts to prevent further attacks. David Lyon has argued that the post-9/11 world is marked by what he terms the phenetic fix, which he characterizes as a type of surveillance that suspends privacy to classify, sort, and otherwise glean knowledge with the hopes of preserving values of freedom that are at the heart of democratic society.[1] If one might view our contemporary "surveillance society" as the ultimate realization of the kind of dystopia envisioned by George Orwell in *1984* or prophesized in Philip K. Dick's 1968 book, *Do Androids Dream of Electric Sheep?* (the basis of the 1982 Hollywood blockbuster *Bladerunner*), surveillance of everyday life certainly is not new. Anyone familiar with the burgeoning field of surveillance studies knows that the post-9/11 world, with its omnipresent cameras, identity cards, CCTV, and ever-expanding use of GPS technology, represents part of a much longer history.[2]

This book, focusing on what I call the architecture of surveillance during the late nineteenth and early twentieth centuries, tells parts of this history while being mindful of our present condition. Looking to buildings in the past reminds us that surveillance has influenced the lives of everyday Americans for centuries, if in ways less ominous or pernicious than twenty-first-century technology allows. Far beyond merely a means to discover and apprehend delinquents—be they prisoners, terrorists, or otherwise—surveillance has long been enlisted for all kinds of purposes. Today we are constantly reminded that surveillance measures improve our lives in numerous ways. We are told that such provisions can help make us more efficient, preserve and enact hierarchies between people (when appropriate), and, perhaps when at their most productive, enhance a feeling of community by making us feel safe. Evidence in the historical built environment helps us understand the varied uses to which surveillance has been and continues to be put. It also prompts us to think about why those in power hold faith in surveillance as a tool to shape behavior of people and groups.

Although today's technologies would have been unimaginable to those living in the period covered by this book, concerns motivating surveillance in the past continue to drive its implementation today, including concerns about discipline, efficiency, hierarchy, and fellowship that provide the basis for the chapters in this book. Thus even if the means by which surveillance is implemented have changed, motivations behind it have not. Moreover, as much as we claim to live in a virtual world, our bodies still occupy real spaces, and surveillance measures, even if realized less in built form today than in the past, still seek to control our physical movement in a very real way. As scholars working in surveillance studies know, surveillance in our contemporary culture affects how we move through spaces (virtual or otherwise). Thus looking to the built environment provides clues for examining the myriad ways that surveillance has influenced our daily lives.

When I first drafted this preface (in 2005), an alert flashed across my computer screen (undoubtedly released by some cookie on the Internet) that the terror alert level had been raised because of an imminent threat to interests within the continental boundaries in the United States. We were subsequently told that new surveillance measures in airports, public buildings, and transportation facilities have been put in place to help prevent this (or any) terror attack. This was very much part of American culture at this moment, and it constantly impinged on how we lived our daily lives in the wake of 9/11. I remember recent air flyovers at sporting events; airplane travel increasingly being laden with security measures; as recently as 2005 and 2006 we were still being warned that we were supposed to be ever vigilant about looking for terrorists on trains or subways as well as at the grocery store, the mall, and the playground. Our twenty-first century experience of these spaces—part of our everyday culture— is part of the history of surveillance as much as it is of terrorism, and this book contributes to that history.

ACKNOWLEDGMENTS

Although the process of writing a book can be lonely at times, I have been fortunate to have the support and encouragement of many people throughout the last decade as this book came to fruition. Two dissertation fellowships—a McNeil fellowship from the Research Fellowship Program, Winterthur Museum and Country Estate, and a Henry Belin DuPont fellowship from the Hagley Museum and Library—jump-started my research on this topic in the late 1990s. Time in residence at Hagley and Winterthur also allowed me to receive critical feedback from other fellows and staff at both institutions, which greatly shaped my thinking. The Chipstone Foundation of Fox Point, Wisconsin, supported me through the final phases of editing the manuscript and provided financial support for the illustrations and for research assistance. I particularly want to thank Chipstone's director, Jonathan Prown, for his unfailing support of my academic efforts, and Nancy Sazama for her administrative finesse. Meghan Doherty has proved to be a reliable and skillful research assistant who helped me gather image permissions and produce publication-quality reproductions when she herself was immersed in her own scholarly work. The Graduate School and the College of Letters and Sciences at the University of Wisconsin–Madison provided financial assistance that helped me at several critical junctures.

My research has taken me to archives and libraries throughout the country, where I have benefited from the assistance of numerous individuals. At the National Archives I received gracious assistance of staff members in the textual reference division, cartographic division, and the still-pictures division at Archives II in College Park as well as in the reading room and civil reference in Washington, DC. Aloha P. South, supervisory archivist, who administers Record Group 28, Records of the Post Office Department, was particularly helpful as I sorted through some rather unusual materials. I also wish to thank the librarians, archivists, curators, and staff at the Center for the History of Business, Technology and Society at Hagley. At Winterthur I received the assistance of numerous librarians, but particularly that of Eleanor McD. Thompson, without whom I could not have completed the research for chapter 3 (and certainly I would not have enjoyed it as much without her company). My work on camp meetings benefited from several visits to the Methodist Archives at Drew University, as well as to numerous camps. Caretakers and campers at God's Holiness Grove (Selinsgrove, Pennsylvania—now Willow Lake Wesleyan Camp), Highland Park Camp Meeting (Sellersville, Pennsylvania), Elm Grove Camp Meeting Association (Center Valley, Pennsylvania), and Northeast Nazarene Camp (Northeast, Maryland) graciously gave me their time and assistance. Thanks also are owed to staff at the libraries of the University of Wisconsin–Madison; Library of the University of Wisconsin–LaCrosse; Morris Library at the University of Delaware; Penn State University Libraries; the Free Library of Philadelphia; the Library of Congress; Paley Library at Temple University; the Library at the University of Pennsylvania; the Historical Society of Delaware; the Historical Society of Pennsylvania; the Luzerne County Historical Society; and the Columbia County (Pennsylvania) Historical Society. Last minute help from Richard Boardman in the Map Collection at the Free Library of Philadelphia and Denise Carlson at North Coast Indexing helped me complete the book in a timely manner.

Colleagues and friends have read portions of this manuscript in its various iterations, and their ideas have greatly shaped my thinking. Members of the material culture dissertation group at the University of Delaware—Gabrielle M. Lanier, Tom Ryan, Patricia Keller, Cynthia G. Falk, Monique Borque, Ann Kirschner, Jeroen van den Hurk, Louis P. Nelson, Nancy Holst, Karen Sherry, Jeffrey E. Klee, and Pamela Sachant—read early incarnations of my work and helped give shape to the book's wide range of material. Bernard L. Herman patiently guided me through the writing of the dissertation. He has continued to mentor me as my ideas on the book—especially on camp meetings—have changed. Support from students in my seminars at the University of Wisconsin–Madison has shaped my thinking about surveillance in the workplace and in the Victorian house. I particularly wish to thank Andrew M. Sawyer, whose careful editing of the manuscript and his enthusiasm for my research helped give me the courage to send it to the press. I also appreciate the feedback and assistance I have received on this project at various points from Ann Smart Martin, Arnold Alanen, William Littmann, Thomas Carter, Gigi Price, Roger Horowitz, Philip Scranton, Gary Kulik, Dell Upton, Damie Stillman, David L. Ames, Nancy Rose Marshall, Marsely Kehoe, Christine Long, Kenneth J. Basalik,

Quitman E. Phillips, Abby Van Slyck, Ellen Weiss, Paula Lupkin, Rebecca Sheppard, Scott E. Casper, Cristina Bishop Klee, Carolyn L. White, Gretchen Buggeln, Thomas Andrew Denenberg, Marilyn M. Mehaffy, Carla Yanni, Kenneth O. Brown, James A. Jacobs, Arijit Sen, Annmarie Adams, Sally A. McMurry, and several anonymous readers for the University of Tennessee Press. I also wish to thank Scot Danforth, Gene Adair, and others at UT Press for bringing this book to fruition in such a timely and expeditious manner.

Friends and family have patiently supported me throughout my academic career, especially through the painstaking process of writing a book. I would like to thank my colleagues in the Department of Art History and the Material Culture Program at the University of Wisconsin—Madison for their support since my arrival on campus, my friends and collegues involved in the Buildings-Landscapes-Cultures program at UW–Madison and UW–Milwaukee, and my students—past and present—who continue to stimulate my thinking. In addition, Virginia Sapiro, Julia K. Murray, and Beverly Gordon lent an ear at critical times; their academic excellence goes hand-in-hand with their generosity and kindness. Without Nancy Rose Marshall's encouragement, critical feedback, and friendship, the last eight years would have been a lot more stressful and much less fun. To her I can only say *namaste*. Though my family still does not quite understand what I study or why I study it, they have never wavered in their support of me. I only wish that my mother, Elizabeth Nelson Vemer, might have lived to see this book published. Though our fields of study differed greatly, my mom's interest in humanity and social welfare undoubtedly shaped some of my thinking as I wrote this book. Her example as a mother and a scholar set a high standard—one that I aspire to live up to.

Finally, thanks go to my husband, Matt, for teaching me the value of following dreams. As he knows too well, one of my dreams has been to study buildings. Another is to watch the curiosity of my daughter grow as she matures. Elizabeth has complained at times—"another building, mom?"—but her own insatiable curiosity, about birds, rocks, planets, or swimming, consistently reminds me of the value of pursuing knowledge that continues to motivate me.

INTRODUCTION

The practice of placing individuals under "observation" is a natural extension of a justice imbued with disciplinary methods and examination procedures. Is it surprising that the cellular prison, with its regular chronologies, forced labour, its authorities of surveillance and registration, its experts in normality, who continue and multiply the functions of the judge, should have become the modern instrument of penality? Is it surprising that prisons resemble factories, schools, barracks, hospitals, which all resemble prisons?

—Michel Foucault, *Discipline and Punish: The Birth of the Prison,* 1975

*I*n his 1975 book, *Discipline and Punish: The Birth of the Prison,* the French philosopher, historian, and social theorist Michel Foucault proposed a complex relationship between surveillance, architecture, and modernity. Despite the book's subtitle, the author's chief concern revolved less around providing a historical account of the development of the prison than explaining a disciplinary mechanism that Foucault felt lay behind the institutions of modern culture—a mechanism defined by its reliance on continuous, if often unremarked, power relations. According to Foucault, surveillance lay at the heart of the disciplinary mechanism. Enlisting Jeremy Bentham's 1791 design for the panopticon as an interpretive metaphor, Foucault contended that the potential for continuous, uninterrupted surveillance lying behind the panopticon's design informed—in varying degrees—the organization and operation of all kinds of modern institutional spaces, including asylums, schools, hospitals, and the workplace.

In these institutions, Foucault argued, any deviation from correct behavior ascertained via surveillance had consequences ultimately punitive in nature. These consequences were comparable in scope, if not in degree:

> At the heart of all disciplinary systems functions a small *penal mechanism* . . . The workshop, the school, the army were subject to a whole micro-penality of time (latenesses, absences, interruptions of tasks), of activity (inattention, negligence, lack of zeal), of behaviour (impoliteness, disobedience), of speech (idle chatter, insolence), of the body ('incorrect' attitudes, irregular gestures, lack of cleanliness), of sexuality (impurity, indecency). . . . It was a question both of making the slightest departures from correct behaviour subject to punishment, and of giving a punitive function to the apparently indifferent elements of the disciplinary apparatus: so that, if necessary, everything might serve to punish the slightest thing; each subject finds himself caught in a punishable, punishing universality.[1]

For Foucault the disciplinary mechanism at work in all of these spaces prescribed that subjects under watch submit to expectations of their superiors, both through responding to the omnipresent gaze and through a kind of internal policing because they were perpetually subject to its scrutiny. Thus through a reciprocal process the disciplinary apparatus functioned continuously, assuring its perpetual operation. Because the gaze-as-action placed restrictions on human behavior (specifically through constraints on bodily freedom to move in space) regardless of context, Foucault saw the operation of surveillance in all of these settings as inherently disciplinary in a punitive sense. Thus he concluded the third section of *Discipline and Punish* with a potent rhetorical question: "Is it surprising that prisons resemble factories, schools, barracks, hospitals, which all resemble prisons?"[2]

However tantalizing and compelling Foucault's arguments may seem, his book is not without its problems. Previous writers have criticized Foucault's approach to history, the issue of where (if anywhere) agency lies in Foucault's account, and the place (or lack thereof) for resistance in Foucault's history of power.[3] Many have taken issue with Foucault's interpretations of prisons, particularly his lack of attention to the realities of prison building, prison life, and the history of punishment.[4] Several scholars have sought particularly to revisit and revise Foucault's findings about architecture, particularly prisons, hospitals, and workplaces.[5] Yet despite these efforts, writers have not yet critically delved into Foucault's provocative, if problematic, contention that concerns about surveillance underlie the organization of the modern built environment. Nor has anyone explored the range of built spaces organized around surveillance concerns, seemingly assuming that provisions for surveillance are confined to institutional buildings. Foucault's finding that a similar, univocal disciplinary mechanism informed design of institutional buildings has also gone relatively unchallenged. For the most part, even among writers who have added nuance to Foucault's findings through detailed discussion of actual buildings and historical evidence, the equation of surveillance with discipline has not been seriously questioned. Ultimately these elisions and omissions lead us to ask how a more detailed and nuanced study of architecture and surveillance would enrich understandings of modern western culture.

This book explores some of the means by which surveillance has been incorporated into the built environment of the United States between the middle decades of the nineteenth century and the early years of the twentieth. In the following chapters, I suggest the different, often complex, ways in which concerns about surveillance structured relationships of people and groups to one another in different kinds of spaces. In contrast to previous historical studies that have looked at surveillance in modern prisons and other institutional settings, this book assumes a wider scope. I discuss a range of building types—prisons, post offices, factories, single-family middle-class houses, and camp meetings—to show how discourses of surveillance informed design and use of all kinds of everyday environments. Those responsible for building and operating these structures took concerns about surveillance into account, but to different degrees and in quite different ways. Through detailed examinations of provisions in these building types for surveillance, this book elucidates its multifarious manifestations in the built environment of the United States during the modern period, thus revealing a more complicated landscape of surveillance than has heretofore been acknowledged.

Exploring buildings reveals surveillance to be infinitely more complex than previous interpretations, such as Foucault's, have suggested. In the environments discussed in this book, we learn that people enlisted surveillance for a range of purposes, just as the forms it took varied considerably. Some forms of surveillance—or what I call gazes—were monocentric and disciplinary, whereas others were dispersed, returned, and contradicted. At religious camp meetings, discussed in chapter 4, for example, gazes were welcomed and completely apparent to those under surveillance. The open nature of the camp-meeting landscape encouraged exchange of visual information between campers as they moved throughout the grounds. Thus as much as individuals used surveillance to discipline in prisons, users in other contexts relied on it to enhance efficiency, to forge and buttress hierarchical divisions between people and groups, and even to bond people united by shared interests, goals, or obligations together in a context of fellowship. As goals for surveillance changed, its manifestation in buildings and the means by which it was to operate through those spaces modified accordingly. When considered collectively, this range of possibilities challenges (and ultimately refines) notions about surveillance as a historical practice tied to the development of modern culture. This book seeks to expand our historical understanding of surveillance as a defining practice of modernism during the late nineteenth and early twentieth centuries, to suggest its ties to our spatial landscape, and in the process to further critical debate about the history of power relations.

Given the loaded nature of terms such as *surveillance, modernity,* and even *architecture* in contemporary scholarly discourse, it is important to define them as used in this book. A good place to begin is to consider what I mean by surveillance, especially since a major goal of this study is to reconsider it in a more comprehensive manner than previous accounts, scholarly and otherwise. According to contemporary popular associations, surveillance refers to a fixed, purposeful, and typically visual act, often offered in stealth, which has a correctional or punitive intent. In our twenty-first century culture, replete with closed-circuit television (CCTV) in stores, schools, casinos, airports, urban streets, and the workplace, wiretaps, high-definition satellite images, and Internet spy software, all of which are prominently promoted through print media, network television, and Hollywood films, it is hardly surprising that many tend to view surveillance as a covert operation of bureaucratic forces.[6] Previous scholarly studies centered on surveillance, including those by Foucault and by the urban historian Mike Davis, also define it along these lines.[7] Although Foucault insists that surveillance is not solely negative, in that it produces knowledge for those who exercise it, surveillance in these terms remains inherently disciplinary in the sense that it ultimately functions as a means of obtaining power by delimiting movement of bodies in space and thus serves principally as a means of control. These forms of surveillance presume and prescribe a set of rules for its subjects under the gaze. Through its exercise, surveillance of this sort aims to recognize transgressions and use this knowledge in order to correct (repression) or to gain information about the subject (production of knowledge). Such a definition implies a voyeuristic, somewhat sexualized, notion of surveillance, since these kinds of gazes are largely hidden and dependent on this concealment as a means of obtaining knowledge and pleasure.[8]

This book treats surveillance in a much more expansive sense and seeks to transcend definitions that equate it with a watchdog form of spying. By surveillance I refer to acts of sustained, close observation of others that have transformation of behavior as their intent. Like sociologist David Lyon, who has examined contemporary modes of data collection outside of a policing context,

I consider surveillance beyond its associations with inherently sinister and surreptitious means by which those in power attempt to affirm and enforce their dominance.[9] An act of surveillance refers to any purposeful act in which information about others is collected for all kinds of transformative purposes, of which punishment is but one. This more flexible definition allows for attentive and purposeful gazes that examine subjects closely but not necessarily with the goal of detecting wrongdoing or condemning behavior relative to a particular expectation or standard. Although surveillance certainly has operated in this way in many institutional settings, it is not limited in aim or practice to this disciplinary purpose. At late-nineteenth- and early-twentieth-century camp meetings discussed in the fourth chapter, for example, surveillance worked in a more affirmative context. Camp-meeting goers gazed on other campers as much to find a model Christian whose behavior they wished to emulate as they did to find a sinner to rebuke. The expansive definition of surveillance offered here also allows for purposeful gazes known, and sometimes welcomed, by those under watch. In workplaces discussed in chapter 2, for example, surveillance was highly visible, and thus known, to workers. What constitutes an act of surveillance in this study revolves around the intentional focus of the gaze, rather than whether it is conducted anonymously, in stealth, or with a disciplinary intent.

Throughout the book I use the term *gaze* to refer to an act of surveillance with a transformative end. Although often and typically visual in nature, gazes need not be so exclusively. As I will suggest, gazes could be (and often were) multisensate, involving auditory as well as visual acts. For Bentham and Foucault, the condition of visibility meant that those under watch were knowable by a variety of means—visual and otherwise. As scholars studying contemporary forms of surveillance have shown, surveillance can take on infinite forms, ranging from the visual and auditory to electronic forms of data collection.[10] In this book I focus on the ways in which surveillants relied on gazes in spaces with a transformative end, through visual and other means. In addition the practice of gazing, as I use the term here, assumes an element of purpose that other kinds of directed acts, visual and otherwise, do not have. Influenced partly by Norman Bryson's important distinction between the "gaze" and the "glance," I distinguish between sustained, purposeful gazes and other kinds of more casual sensorial acts that are more fleeting and passive and thus remain detached from their objects.[11] If gazes are sustained and purposeful, they also may be distinguished by what lies behind them, which is the intent to shape behavior. In this way gazes actively shape the objects of focus, whereas other directed acts, visual or otherwise, lack such a fixed objective.

By engaging with discourses of surveillance, this book also builds on understandings of modernism. For Foucault forms of disciplinary surveillance that he saw embodied in the panopticon were directly linked to an episte-mological shift from the classical age to the modern one, from a premodern society organized around ritual and spectacular performance to a modern one revolving around surveillance, one that he dated to the late eighteenth and early nineteenth centuries.[12] Jonathan Crary has argued for a similar trans-formation through his reading of the collapse of the paradigm of the camera obscura in the second and third decades of the nineteenth century. Crary has discussed how new modes of photography enabled a profound shift toward the subjectivity of the viewer that to him evinced a new technology of power, or what he called a scopic regime.[13] My findings accord with those of Foucault and Crary in that I see the prominence of surveillance in the organization of modern spaces as directly linked with the rise of modern western culture. I use the term *modernism* to refer to the cultural conditions that an assemblage of factors (economic, social, political) spawned beginning toward the end of the eighteenth century and reaching maturity by the mid–twentieth century. Fol-lowing the ideas of cultural historian Daniel Singal, modernism in this sense is distinct from modernization. Singal denotes modernization as a process of economic and social development with origins as far back as the seventeenth century but which flourished in the nineteenth and twentieth, perhaps most often equated with the rise of industrialization and the capitalist economy.[14] As I use the concept here, modernism refers to the cultural conditions or responses to which modernization (as Singal describes it) gave rise—conditions which can vary from processes and phenomena (urbanization and mechanization) to particular artistic responses to it (abstract painting or the international style in architecture).

Building Power seeks to contribute to the historical literature on modern-ism in several interrelated ways. At the most basic level, I examine buildings and landscapes which themselves are products of modern culture. Though cer-tainly previous incarnations of many of these kinds of spaces existed prior to 1800, I focus on the systematized forms these spaces took after the middle of the nineteenth century, when one can speak of them as recognizable types and see their codification through both proliferation of examples and through extensive prescriptive discourse.[15] Understanding these built environments and their relationship to modern culture thus contributes to our ideas about the architecture of modernism. More significant, this study elaborates on the role of surveillance as a defining feature of modern culture. Foucault linked surveil-lance and modernity through the early-nineteenth-century prison, claiming the visual relationships at work there exemplified those that proliferated sub-sequently throughout modern institutions and everyday life. Although I agree with Foucault's contention that surveillance is inextricably linked with the rise of modernity, the panoptic and disciplinary manifestations he described illustrate only one aspect of surveillance. Foucault's coupling of surveillance and modernity is reconsidered and refined in the chapters that follow through discussions about how gazes worked through different kinds of modern spaces outside of a context of discipline. Finally, this study considers how the ideology and practice of surveillance exemplify some of modernity's defining features. By this I mean the notion that surveillance was meant to function as a means by which one attempted to acquire knowledge and confirm authority is a defining modern practice.[16]

This book focuses on a particular period of modernism: the mid–nineteenth to the early twentieth centuries. This is a period that corresponds (though not precisely) with the reign of Queen Victoria in Britain (1837–1901). Despite the obvious problems with using the reign of a foreign monarch to characterize a period of American history, treating the period from the antebellum years through the early twentieth century under the rubric of American Victorianism works well for examining the formation of the architecture of surveillance.[17] The development of the building types that I explore—and the codification of surveillance measures in them—is inextricably bound with Victorian American culture. As Daniel Walker Howe and others have defined it, this culture, the dominant (although certainly not the only) one from the mid–nineteenth century through roughly World War I, sought certainty in a time of rapid change by attempting to fix and establish boundaries of all sorts—including between people and the spaces they occupied—in ways that accorded with a belief system based on a notion of fixed and immutable truths (about race, class, gender, sexuality, religion, and so on). Surveillance was one means among many through which many Americans sought to affirm and define their relationships to others in the face of a rapidly modernizing society that threatened to tear apart dichotomies that the middle-class wanted to preserve.

I examine the Victorian period largely because of its formative impact on modern culture. Across the modern period, surveillance was incorporated on a widespread scale into buildings that middle-class Americans experienced on a regular basis, just as a prolific and distinctive written discourse developed around them that explained their usefulness and pragmatic value. The preoccupation with surveillance that appears in these structures and in prescriptive literature surrounding them helps us understand how middle-class Americans sought to make sense of changes associated with modernization. This study ends with buildings designed during the early twentieth century. By this time Victorian values, already under assault by the later nineteenth century from certain quarters, had become stultifying to most Americans. By the early twentieth century, Singal explains, Americans had come to embrace aspects of culture that had been shunned during the Victorian period, in order "to reconnect all that the Victorian moral dichotomy tore asunder."[18] Part of this shift lay in a general receptiveness to different realms of experience, from technological inventions to modes of life that challenged white, middle-class Protestant values so dominant during the Victorian age. Although debates about the nature and timing of the end of the Victorian period in the United States will continue, most agree that the context for modernism had changed for much of the population by the 1920s, which has critical ramifications for understanding the meanings of surveillance in the American built environment.[19] Concerns about surveillance do not go away. Indeed they become more pronounced as modern culture reaches its apex in the mid–twentieth century, which is tied to shifting power dynamics under the impact of twentieth-century large-scale industrial capitalism. In short, the context for understanding the relationship between architecture, surveillance, and modernity changes significantly after 1920. I plan to explore twentieth-century forms of surveillance in a future book that examines its manifestations in hospitals, white-collar offices, public schools, and postwar middle-class housing developments.

Building Power, meanwhile, focuses firmly on the later nineteenth and early twentieth centuries, using evidence related to buildings as primary source material. Still this is far from a conventional architectural history—both in terms of the kinds of buildings discussed and the ways in which I approach them. Some readers' ideas of what constitutes architecture may be tested, as many of the building types I consider here have not been subject to extensive study by American architectural historians. Many buildings discussed in this book would lie outside of what some might call high style architecture—that is, buildings designed by architects in prevailing styles. But at the same time, most of the buildings treated in this study are not folk buildings either. In many instances designers responsible for buildings in this study are known, and their work follows styles or trends common to the era, even if they are not on the forefront of design. The fact that many of the building types in this study lie somewhere in between high style and folk categories affirms what many today see as the futility of attempting to distinguish between architecture with a capital "A" on the one hand and more ordinary buildings on the other.[20] I define architecture as any shaping of the built environment for human use. In Spiro Kostof's terms, architecture is the art of making places, be they architect-designed and fashionable, or locally designed and conservative.[21] Adopting this flexible definition allows us to dispense with assigning buildings to categories of study derived from critical judgments of their value based on their architect, patron, or style, and instead study their place within the broader historical period of which they are part.

The methods used in this book also might surprise those accustomed to previous studies of American architectural history. Chapters in this book do not revolve around names of well-known architects, stylistic categories, building technologies, or patronage systems. Further, although popular types of buildings and landscapes of the nineteenth and twentieth centuries are treated in this study, the case studies in the chapters that follow are not comprehensive explorations focused on explicating the development of building or landscape types—something previous scholars have already done at least partially. It is not that the methods of traditional architectural history are not useful in examining the architecture of surveillance. Formal and typological analysis is indispensable to this book, and questions of attribution, patronage, and building technology also are treated here as they relate to the major arguments. But these more traditional methods of architectural history function in this study more as tools of description than as means of explanation. In this way this book follows an interdisciplinary turn within the field of architectural history that has been variously called the "new architectural history," the "social history of architecture," or the "vernacular architecture approach."[22] Practitioners of this mode of architectural history focus their attention on buildings and landscapes as evidence, using tools and methods derived from social history, anthropology, folklore, and cultural geography.[23] I consider buildings and landscapes, like all forms of material culture, as forms of evidence that help us better understand the values, beliefs, and ideals of their makers and users.[24] Because surveillance was incorporated into and worked through all kinds of modern environments, buildings and the landscapes they comprise are highly revealing forms of evidence that tell us about the ideology and practice of surveillance during the modern era.

Recognizing the impossibility of comprehensively surveying modern building types that incorporated surveillance into them, this book is organized around a series of case studies. Each chapter aims to illuminate or explain a particular dimension of surveillance by discussing how it was intended to operate through one or more common building types in Victorian America. Within each chapter I discuss surveillance as lying behind the layout and working through the built fabric in a particular way or with a certain dominant intent. In order to stress the focus of each chapter on theme or context rather than the building type, I have titled each of the chapters by the various dimension of surveillance discussed within. While not strictly chronological, the book does proceed in some senses across time. It begins by discussing the emergence of surveillance concerns in prisons, proceeding to the development of building types—namely, workspaces and middle-class houses—that flourished with the rise of industrial capitalism after the Civil War. The final chapter looks at the heyday of camp meetings in the late nineteenth and early twentieth centuries, which can be explained at least partly out of a desire to hold onto aspects of Victorian culture that were by then increasingly threatened. The last chapter thus serves to suggest how modernism pervaded even fringe environments outside of the realm of everyday middle-class life while also indicating that Victorianism held sway in some respects beyond its heyday into the twentieth century. As it proceeds to examine this series of spaces built during the nineteenth and into the twentieth century, the book also moves from exploring the better known aspect of surveillance, that of discipline, through its lesser known or discussed aspects in the contexts of efficiency, hierarchy, and fellowship.

The first chapter explores issues at stake in a context of discipline by reexamining the role of surveillance in prison architecture. Considering the ways that architects and builders designed prisons in nineteenth- and early-twentieth-century America around surveillance offers several insights. At one level it allows us to reconsider the influence of the panopticon on institutional design, particularly its principle of perpetual surveillance. Most prisons made little use of the concept directly, instead incorporating surveillance into prison buildings in other ways. A detailed investigation of prison architecture also shows that surveillance in prisons had limits in a practical sense. The disciplinary gazes enabled through prison buildings were not as comprehensive as Foucault suggested. Prison officials came to rely on other means of discipline to maintain order in the prison landscape. But prisons continued to be designed around surveillance—something that signals that it served functions in this context outside of its obvious role as a strategy of punishment. The chapter concludes by suggesting some of these other functions of surveillance in the penal landscape, which ultimately opens up avenues investigated in subsequent chapters.

Chapter 2 addresses how surveillance was incorporated into the modern workplace as a strategy of work discipline. Beginning with post offices and moving on to other kinds of modern workspaces that emerged in the wake of industrialization, this chapter looks at how workplace surveillance sought to bring method, order, and uniformity to the tasks workers performed—a process of regulation (as opposed to restraint) that aimed to control labor for its productive value. Surveillance in the workplace thus includes a temporal as well as a spatial component. This suggests that even though the gaze of work discipline shared a disciplinary purpose with the gaze in prisons, its manifestations differ because of context. I discuss the place of surveillance within a variety of workplaces, examining its visible and less visible manifestations, through an exploration of different buildings alongside various literature of the efficiency movement that promoted surveillance as a strategy of work discipline. In these workplace settings and others, the imposition of surveillance was motivated partly by fears of potential resistance, which undoubtedly mediated hierarchical relationships between surveillants and those they watched.

The third chapter examines surveillance in a context of hierarchy, focusing on its potential to shape hierarchical relationships between people and groups. If hierarchies were at stake in factories and post offices, they were equally at issue in the domestic realm in the late nineteenth and early twentieth centuries. Here middle-class women seized on surveillance as a means of supervising their live-in female domestic servants. Motivating acts of surveillance in this setting was a fear that servants sought ways to resist the authority of their mistresses. This prompted architects to plan houses with servant spaces organized so that they could be conveniently and completely under watch. Intended to empower mistresses by giving them visual control over their employees, this segregation of servant spaces led mistresses to worry further that servants might grab moments of freedom from their mistress in order to transgress their spatial and social marginalization in the household. Exploring the layout of Victorian houses through pattern books and examining women's advice literature that counseled middle-class women on managing their households shows how middle-class Americans enlisted surveillance as a means of enforcing hierarchies over those who they viewed as fundamentally different from themselves.

Hierarchies at stake in domestic environments were reproduced in other environments in Victorian America, such as at religious camp meetings. However, at these camps, concerns about everyday social and economic hierarchies waned as camp-meeting goers came together as part of a community of like-minded believers. Chapter 4 examines the ways surveillance operated in a context of fellowship to help strengthen social relationships between people who fraternize out of shared goals, interests, or obligations. Camp-meeting grounds were laid out in centralized fashion to enhance a sense of community and to facilitate surveillance on the grounds. From his elevated and centrally located pulpit, the presiding minister could overlook the congregation and focus his attention on those who he felt needed his attention most. Worshippers meanwhile gazed on the minister to experience his preaching and through him the blessings of a higher power. Worshippers on the grounds also exchanged gazes as they moved throughout the densely designed camp-meeting grounds, where contact with other campers was unavoidable. The built environment facilitated all of these complex, and often reciprocal, kinds of surveillance, in part by collapsing boundaries between public and private space. At Methodist and Holiness camps, omnipresent surveillance brought camp-meeting participants together in pursuit of a shared desire to attain religious salvation. This final chapter suggests the potential of surveillance to affirm relationships between people and groups as much as establish differences—something that previous historians of surveillance have minimized by focusing on more divisive, and often disciplinary, manifestations. Moreover, examining surveillance at camp meetings shows the pervasiveness of surveillance in the built environment, which by 1900 had pervaded all kinds of spaces, ranging from the public to the private, the secular to the religious, and the ordinary to the extraordinary.

Taken together, these case studies suggest how evidence from buildings, landscapes, and discourse around them constituted and contributed to a complex culture of surveillance in late nineteenth- and early twentieth-century America. Surveillance shaped the dynamics of the penal landscape, but in ways more complicated than a disciplinary paradigm reveals. In factories and post offices, the use of gazes was meant to instill a sense of efficiency among workers, while in Victorian middle-class homes, mistresses relied on surveillance to enforce hierarchies between themselves and their servants. At camp meetings, meanwhile, directed visual exchanges helped bring together campers as part of a fellowship of believers. Surveillance thus framed all kinds of buildings in the Victorian period, albeit in more complex and less sinister ways than Foucault and others have discussed. Examining these and other myriad instances of surveillance undoubtedly enrich our knowledge of American architectural history. It also helps us better understand the asymmetries of power in American culture and the role of buildings and landscapes in shaping everyday experience.

Chapter 1

DISCIPLINE

On May 22, 1823, workers laid the cornerstone of Eastern State Penitentiary, originally known as Cherry Hill Prison, on an approximately ten-acre plot of land two miles north of City Hall in Philadelphia, Pennsylvania (fig. 1.1). For the citizens of Pennsylvania, particularly members of the Society for Alleviating the Miseries of Public Prisons founded in 1787 (later known as the Philadelphia Prison Society), the event marked the first step in realizing a goal, several decades in the making, of erecting a penitentiary to house a swelling population of prisoners in the commonwealth. The construction of Eastern State also represented a watershed in the history of penology. Eastern State was the first complex designed around the disciplinary regimen that came to be known as the Pennsylvania system of confinement, one of two dominant modes of discipline that held sway throughout the Victorian period in the United States. Solitary confinement was at the core of the Pennsylvania system. Its advocates believed that isolating prisoners in individual cells would encourage inmates on the path to rehabilitation by providing them with time to reflect on and ultimately repent of their crimes.[1]

Surveillance played a critical role in the Pennsylvania system and thus influenced the design of this model penitentiary around it. John Haviland, the architect of the prison, devised the layout around surveillance concerns. In an 1824 description of Eastern State, Haviland explained that his plan helped guards monitor the movements of inmates as they moved throughout the prison:

> [The plan] appears to me to be a form that possesses many advantages in the watching, health and superintendence of the Prison, for by the distribution of the several blocks of Cells forming so many radiating lines to the Observatory or Watch-House . . . a watchman can, from one point, command a view

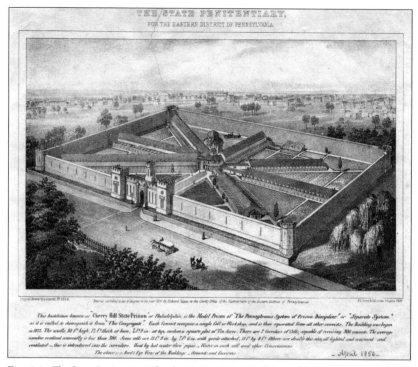

Fig. 1.1. *The State Penitentiary, for the Eastern District of Pennsylvania.* Aerial view, lithograph from drawing by Samuel Cowperthwaite, convict #2954. Philadelphia: P. S. Duval & Co., 1855. Courtesy of The Library Company of Philadelphia.

of the extremity of the passages of the cells, or traverse under cover unobserved by the prisoners and overlook every cell; when they are exercising in their yards, the same watchman, by walking round on a platform three feet wide, to be constructed on the outside of this watch-room, situated on a level with the first floor . . . can see into every yard and detect any prisoner that may attempt to scale the minor walls.[2]

In Haviland's plan the watchhouse, or observation tower, served as the nerve center of the prison. Haviland originally planned for seven single-story cellblocks, each containing two rows of solitary cells positioned on either side of a central corridor, to extend outward from this central point toward the prison's perimeter walls (fig. 1.2). Each cell consisted of a small eight-by-twelve-foot living space, which prisoners occupied during the day, except for an hour or two during which they exercised in individual exercise yards, located behind each cell. As his description makes clear, Haviland planned the prison so that watchmen could easily monitor the cellblock passages and the grounds.

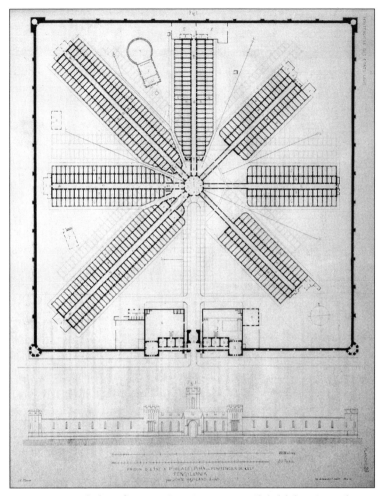

Fig. 1.2. Ground plan of Eastern State Penitentiary, Philadelphia, Pennsylvania. From F. A. Demetz and G. A. Blouet, *Rapports . . . sur les Penitenciers des Etats-Unis.* Paris: Imprimerie Royale, 1837, plate 23 opposite p. 64. Courtesy of The Library Company of Philadelphia.

Although guards could not literally see into all of the cells from the central tower, the architect hoped to craft a design that expressed a sense of omnipresent, totalizing surveillance that would imply authority of the commonwealth and its proxies—prison officials—to control the actions of inmates.

In the plan of Eastern State, Haviland and his patrons believed they had discovered an ideal instrument for the exercise of penal discipline, especially suited for the solitary system. The design was meant to ensure that inmates would constantly feel subject to the scrutiny of their captors. Prison officials also hoped that the foreboding appearance of the prison, including the prominence of the central tower, would keep prisoners from challenging the guards' authority. The building commission of Eastern State, for example, insisted that "the exterior of a solitary prison should exhibit as much as possible great strength and convey to the mind a cheerless blank indicative of the misery that awaits the unhappy being who enters within its walls."[3] But shortly after the penitentiary opened in 1829, prison officials realized that the building did not provide for totalizing discipline to the degree that its architect and his supporters anticipated. The sheer size of the prison and the lack of provisions for surveillance over individual cells limited the extent to which prisoners believed they were perpetually subject to the keeper's gaze. Despite Haviland's efforts to isolate inmates from one another, prisoners used the plan's limitations to enable communication between their solitary cells. Shortly after the prison opened, administrators hired additional sentinels to occupy the subsidiary towers along the prison's perimeter walls as well as roving guards to patrol the cellblock corridors and the exercise yards. Later in the nineteenth century, construction of several of the cellblocks as two-story units required that inmates housed in second-story cells exercise together in yards located between the radial arms. Surveillance from the central watchtower by a single guard thus proved insufficient to convey a sense of omnipresent discipline that Haviland and his supporters had hoped for, as prisoners communed in the yards and thus broke the rules of solitary confinement. By the 1840s roaming watchmen had become a fixture in the prison, suggesting that prison officials had recognized the inadequacies of architectural means of surveillance and had come to rely on other, nonarchitectural strategies to assert their authority.

Even though Eastern State's opening predates the Victorian period, the history of the penitentiary provides a convenient starting point from which to investigate surveillance in Victorian American architecture. It allows us to explore a kind of environment—the prison landscape—with which surveillance is most readily linked through a pioneering example of penal architecture. To be more specific, the early history of Eastern State prompts consideration of how concerns about surveillance informed design of prisons in nineteenth- and early-twentieth-century America even as prison officials came to rely on other strategies to discipline prisoners and maintain control of the prison environment. Haviland and his supporters believed strongly in the need to incorporate provisions for surveillance into penal architecture—something that motivated prison design well into the Victorian period and beyond. Yet as much as the history of Eastern State reveals an abiding faith in surveillance as an instrument for the exercise of prison discipline, it also invites us to consider prison officials' knowledge that architectural forms of surveillance alone were themselves not sufficient as a means of control. Prison officials and penal reformers consistently worried about the limitations of built forms of surveillance, particularly given that keepers could not oversee all of the inmates simultaneously. But if surveillance at Eastern State and other nineteenth-century American prisons remained limited in practice, architects and their patrons continued to design prisons around it, prompting questions about the ideology of surveillance in a context of punitive discipline.

Exploring the design and history of American prisons built during the nineteenth and early twentieth centuries shows the ways that architects and their patrons planned institutions of confinement around surveillance and exposes the reasoning behind their choices. The design of these prisons reveals the faith that penal reformers had in the disciplinary potential of surveillance. Although architects and prison reformers upheld a belief in surveillance as realized in countless prisons built during the Victorian period, provisions for surveillance in these prisons were never comprehensive in intention or actuality. Investigating prison buildings and discourse around them shows that the ideology of surveillance driving prison design resulted in prison arrangements where surveillance proved more symbolic than actual. To understand surveillance in a context of discipline thus entails focusing on the degree to which gazes in prisons worked less as a means of regulating prisoner behavior in practice and more as a means of reminding those inside and outside of the prison of the possibility of a disciplined landscape.

Architecture of Surveillance in Nineteenth-Century American Prisons

The importance of Eastern State Penitentiary to prison architecture in Victorian America has to be understood against the backdrop of a longer history of prison design and penology. Historians have often lauded Eastern State for its originality, despite the fact that it clearly draws on features from earlier prisons and other institutions of confinement (namely asylums) in England and other parts of Europe.[4] The Philadelphia penitentiary's importance lies in the way that its architect brought together ideas from these earlier designs and merged them with the goals of his patrons to create a prison that suited the needs for punishment by solitary confinement. Stylistically the prison incorporates medieval features—notably embattlements, pointed arch windows in the entrance gate, and buttresses along the walls—making it an early example of the Gothic revival in American architecture (fig. 1.3).[5] Haviland also drew on planning principles behind institutional structures in Western Europe. The outside-cell configuration that Haviland adopted for the cellblocks, in which rows of cells are

Fig. 1.3. View of Fairmount Avenue entrance from the southeast, Eastern State Penitentiary, Philadelphia, Pennsylvania. Courtesy of the Library of Congress, Prints and Photographs Division (Historic American Building Survey collection), HABS no. PA-1729-2.

positioned on either side of a central aisle, may have derived from the Hospice of San Michele, an institution of confinement for delinquent youths that was built in Rome in 1704 for Pope Clement XI. The plan of Eastern State, with its centralized tower and radiating cellblocks, also may be based on the design of a well-known eighteenth-century prison, the Maison de Force in Ghent, Belgium, designed by Jean Jacques Philipe Vilain in 1771. Although organized around the principle of inside- versus outside-cell construction, the Ghent house of correction had a central rotunda off of which radiated eight cellblocks, between which were located yards for prisoners to exercise. Even if Haviland did not copy these particular designs, he would have known of them through his knowledge of contemporary English prison design. Trained in London prior to his immigration to Philadelphia in 1816, Haviland knew much about prisons and other institutions built by the English architect William Blackburn. Blackburn typically employed radial plans of organization in his prisons, outside-cell construction in cellblocks, and medieval stylistic elements.[6]

 Haviland's knowledge of earlier institutional buildings was coupled with his abiding interest in penal reform movements in England and America during the late eighteenth and early nineteenth centuries. The architect professed an appreciation of the ideas of John Howard, an English penal reformer, who lobbied for institutionalization as a means of punishment during the late eighteenth century. Howard advocated solitary confinement of inmates to hard labor, believing this would force prisoners to repent as well as learn a trade.[7] Howard's scathing review of the state of English prisons, published in his 1777 book, *State of the Prisons in England and Wales,* greatly influenced Haviland. From Howard, Haviland learned of the idea of solitary confinement as a means of discipline, which he incorporated into the solitary system at Eastern State. Given his English training, Haviland was also familiar with Jeremy Bentham's design for the panopticon, a scheme for any institution in which "a number of persons are meant to be kept under inspection." Bentham conceived his centralized design for the panopticon around the principle of perpetual, anonymous surveillance as its chief disciplinary mechanism.[8] Bentham himself was influenced by Howard, and his plans for the panopticon must be understood in part as an attempt to devise an architectural model in keeping with Howard's ideas. As Bentham explained in his description, the panopticon worked to remind inmates of their lot through the exercise of anonymous and unremitting surveillance (or the potential of it).[9] Although Haviland's radial plan for Eastern State Penitentiary bears little similarity to Bentham's panoptic layout with a row of cells surrounding and facing a central watchtower, Haviland's choice to include a central rotunda from which emanated the threat of perpetual and hidden surveillance reveals a debt to Bentham. As Haviland's description of Eastern State quoted earlier suggests, he intended the centralized watchtower to function as the chief means of control, something that the panoptic scheme also realized, if in a very different material form. Finally, the Philadelphia Prison Society's ideas on solitary confinement as a means of reform greatly shaped Haviland's thinking. Their ideas led the architect to design solitary cells in a way which isolated prisoners from guards and from one another as much as possible. In bringing these ideas together in his plan for Eastern State, Haviland created a building that echoed ideas in broader circulation but overall represented something entirely novel in its arrangement, particularly in terms of how it incorporated surveillance into the plan itself as a chief feature of the prison's disciplinary program.

Haviland received the commission for Eastern State at a critical moment in the history of penology that also helps explain its realization. Although the principle of punishing criminals by means of imprisonment is now accepted as normative, this was not the dominant mode of discipline prior to the late eighteenth and early nineteenth centuries. During the eighteenth century in Europe and the American colonies, physical punishment served as the chief means of correction. As Foucault and others have discussed, punishment prior to this time involved reproducing the horrors of the crime on the body of the guilty person, usually to the degree that the punishment echoed the severity of the crime. Such eye-for-an-eye punishment involved a further component: that of spectacle. Exercise of discipline took place in front of the populace, which enforcement officials argued reinforced the guilt of the condemned. Holding such a spectacle was hoped to dissuade others from committing future crimes because they bore witness to the consequences. The state punished criminals on the gallows, in the pillory, with brandings or whippings, with a fine, or with execution, which was usually reserved for murder cases. Incarceration meanwhile served largely as a means of temporarily housing (and thus segregating from the mainstream population) those awaiting trial or retribution, not itself constituting a means of punishment. Buildings used to house criminals thus hardly compared with the penitentiaries of the next century, structurally or operationally.[10]

By the late eighteenth century, corporal punishment waned as the preferred method of disciplining criminals in favor of incarceration. The reasons for the shift are complex but relate to the spread of Enlightenment ideas regarding the cruelty and ineffectiveness of corporal punishment as well as the recognition of human liberties and equal rights in circulation around the circumstances of the late-eighteenth-century political revolutions in Western Europe. Reformers lobbied for the replacement of corporal retributions with what they saw as a more humane solution of incarceration. Their thinking involved recognition that in democratic societies based on the idea of one's inherent liberties, deprivation of freedom served as a powerful form of punishment. In the United States stirrings for a penal system focused on incarceration originated immediately after the Revolution. Although in many ways the history of penal reform in America followed that of Europe, anti-British sentiment also played a part in the pace of reforms on the western side of the Atlantic. American reformers associated the older forms of punishment with methods in England and claimed that their methods were ultimately opposed to the older British ones, even if, ironically, many advocates looked to Howard and other British reformers for ideas.[11]

As mentioned earlier, the Philadelphia Prison Society initiated a major charge for penal reform during the Federal period that led to the construction of Eastern State. Since the organization of the society in May 1787, its members advocated for what they deemed to be a more humane mode of punishment by incarceration. Its members were undoubtedly familiar with Howard's ideas, circulating widely in America by 1790, and drew on them while pushing for the building and organization of prisons specifically around solitary confinement. First winning piecemeal reforms in the existing Walnut

Street Jail during the 1790s, the society continued to lobby for their most important goal: to secure funding for state institutions of confinement based on the solitary system. Their efforts paid off during the second decade of the nineteenth century, when the Pennsylvania legislature designated funds for the erection of two penitentiaries, one in the western part of the commonwealth and the other in the east.[12] The Philadelphia Prison Society was one of several reform societies that coalesced during the Federal period that advocated solitary confinement as a means of discipline. Their influence may be seen in a number of larger penitentiaries built in the wake of Eastern State around solitary confinement, including prisons in Maryland, Massachusetts, Maine, New Jersey, Virginia, and Rhode Island.[13]

Prisons built under the impact of penal reform during the nineteenth century incorporated provisions for surveillance into their design, although the specific schemes devised by architects, builders, and their patrons varied. Eastern State exemplifies a radial scheme of organization—a scheme adopted occasionally in prisons in the United States but more commonly in facilities abroad during the nineteenth century.[14] As defined by Norman Johnston, radial schemes include "any arrangement of cell buildings that converge on a center."[15] In the case of Eastern State, the central point was the multistory watchtower, from which seven one-story cellblocks extended, resulting in a scheme that resembled a pinwheel. Cell designs and layout options in other radial prisons varied considerably; there could be two wings or many, and the specific configuration often related to whether or not the cells were intended for solitary confinement, as they were at Eastern State. Because of requirements of solitary confinement at Eastern State, administrative functions were minimal. Administrators were housed away from the cellblocks near the entrance along the fortress wall. In other radial prisons, blocks extended directly from the administrative center. An example of this may be seen at the New Jersey State Prison at Trenton, also designed by Haviland, built between 1833 and 1836. Laid out as a half-wheel-and-spoke plan, the five original cellblocks of this prison radiated from a centralized structure that housed all the prison's functions outside of the cells, including the cooking areas, the warden's quarters, and the observatory (fig. 1.4).[16]

Eastern State's counterpart in western Pennsylvania, the first Western State Penitentiary, represented an early-nineteenth-century example of a second layout option for Victorian-era prisons, which I call quasi-panoptic.[17] Western State was completed in 1826 after a design by the American architect William Strickland. With its cells arranged in a circular fashion around a center, it recalls Bentham's panoptic scheme though with some significant changes (fig. 1.5). Whereas Bentham intended his panopticon to be multistory, Strickland's

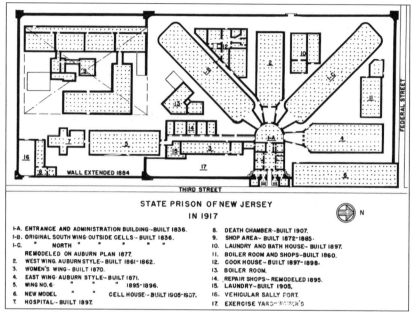

Fig. 1.4. Ground plan of New Jersey State Prison at Trenton in 1917. The prison, which opened in 1836, was designed by John Haviland as a half-radial plan. This plan shows how later cellblocks were added along the lines of the Auburn model. From *Handbook of Correctional Institution Design and Construction* (Washington, DC: United States Bureau of Prisons, 1949), 37.

plan provided only for a single-story cellblock.[18] Further, unlike Bentham's scheme in which all of the cells faced the watchtower, the round cellblock at Western State comprised two rows of single-story cells, intended for solitary confinement, positioned back-to-back. Finally, the central watchtower never appears to have been built. Even if the tower had been completed, it likely would have proven inadequate as a means of conveying a sense of omnipresent surveillance. It would have stood quite far from the rear row of cells, making literal gazes into them challenging if not impossible. It also likely would have proven inadequate to monitor the interior cells, which were divided by a series of high walls that would have limited surveillance from a central vantage point. Likely in anticipation of this, Strickland planned for the construction of additional watchtowers along the monumental octagonal stone wall enclosing the prison grounds. The wall surrounding the prison was to be unbroken save for a massive entrance gate/administration building that housed the Warden's residence and prison offices and several subsidiary watchtowers. Probably because of the design's shortcomings, few prisons were built along the model of Western State or any derivation of the panoptic scheme.[19] Still the panoptic idea was

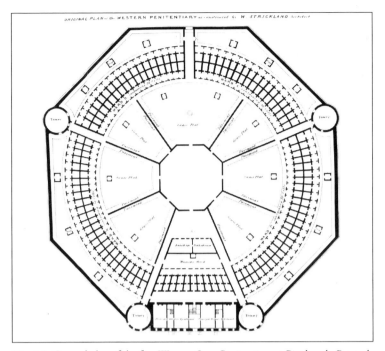

Fig. 1.5. Ground plan of the first Western State Penitentiary at Pittsburgh, Pennsylvania, designed by William Strickland, opened in 1826. From William Crawford, *Report of William Crawford, esq., On the Penitentiaries of the United States, Addressed to His Majesty's Principal Secretary of State for the Home Department* (London, 1835), plan #4, appendix p. 15. Courtesy of The Historical Society of Pennsylvania (HSP).

not entirely lost, as the construction of four circular, quasi-panoptic cellblocks at the Illinois State Prison at Stateville between 1916 and 1924 suggests.[20]

Roughly contemporary with Western State, the New York State Penitentiary at Auburn, New York, pioneered a third popular layout that dwarfed the radial and quasi-panoptic schemes in extent and influence in the United States prior to World War I.[21] Opened first in 1817, the prison had a plan from 1835 published as part of a report on U.S. penitentiaries for the British government that suggests its early arrangement (fig. 1.6). What immediately distinguishes the prison layout from those of its counterparts in Pennsylvania is the small amount of space devoted to cellblocks relative to the large amount devoted to shops and other spaces. This relates to the disciplinary regimen employed at Auburn, eventually dubbed the Auburn system, which revolved around congregate work for prisoners during the day and solitary confinement at night. Sleeping cells were thus compact, while congregate spaces made up most of the prison. The main cellblock, constructed in 1825, was five stories in height. As originally planned, Auburn also possessed a sizable number of workshops and other communal spaces for prisoners, who assembled for work and recreation during the daytime. Workshops were perpetually subject to surveillance. Crawford's ground plan shows a narrow passage running along the perimeter of the work areas, measuring three feet wide, through which guards and visitors to the prison could surreptitiously watch workers laboring in the shops.[22] The congregate mode of imprisonment depended on surveillance for its success, especially to maintain silence in the workshops. In addition to architectural features built into the workshops, a prominent guardhouse towered over the prison. Roving guards also regularly patrolled the cellblocks at night along the outside corridors. Watchtowers added over the course of the nineteenth century along the perimeter helped enforce the rule of silence among prisoners on the grounds.[23] Subsequent prisons built along the Auburn model varied in

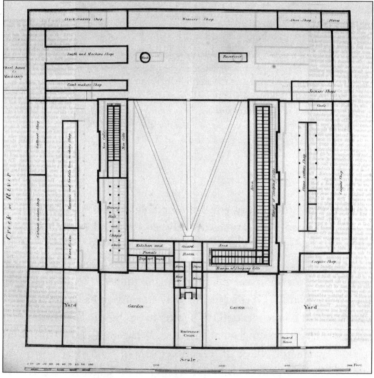

Fig. 1.6. Ground plan of the New York State Prison at Auburn, as it appeared in 1834. From William Crawford, *Report of William Crawford, esq., On the Penitentiaries of the United States, Addressed to His Majesty's Principal Secretary of State for the Home Department* (London, 1835), plan #6, appendix p. 23. Courtesy of The Historical Society of Pennsylvania (HSP).

terms of plan, but typically they had one or more multistory rectangular cellblocks, sometimes joined or interspersed with communal spaces under rigorous surveillance.

American prisons built in the wake of these early-nineteenth-century prisons more or less derived from their examples. The choice of plan often resulted from the system of discipline in place there. In institutions built in Pennsylvania or in nearby regions, such as New Jersey, prison complexes tended to be organized around solitary confinement and thus followed the radial plan. Meanwhile, in prisons outside of the mid-Atlantic region, the Auburn, or congregate, model of penal discipline resulted in more variable configurations. Despite their differences prisons built in the U.S. through World War I share many features, in large part because of their relation to the penal reform movement. Prominent surrounding walls exist in most cases, serving to demarcate the prison space and also provide a formidable barrier against escape. Entering the grounds typically required moving past a monumental boundary, the entrance gate, which acted as a sort of mediating zone between the prison and the outside world. Two principal kinds of spaces existed inside the walls: spaces for prisoners and spaces for prison employees. Although the kinds of areas occupied by prisoners depended on the disciplinary strategy in question, prisoner spaces generally included cells, exercise areas, and spaces where inmates convened for labor or recreation. These areas were clearly bounded. Walls, bars, or other impenetrable barriers restricted inmates from moving beyond spaces allotted to them. Areas used principally by the warden and guards were less defined, for they, as free citizens, retained the right to move throughout the prison. Still employees largely moved through a select set of spaces forbidden to prisoners that included offices in the administration building and guard towers.

Despite individual variations surveillance held an important place in American prisons built during the nineteenth and early twentieth centuries. Most prisons contained prominent watchtowers to facilitate surveillance of guards over inmates. The placement of these towers varied. Watchtowers could be located at the center of the complex, on the outside wall, or, most often, both. Architects and builders incorporated less obvious, but nonetheless pervasive, accommodations for surveillance elsewhere in the prison landscape. Long, open hallways in the cellblocks offered guards a means of accessing and thus monitoring prisoners' cells. At Eastern State peepholes in the corridor walls originally allowed guards to gaze into the solitary cells unbeknownst to the inmates.[24] At Auburn the walls separating cells from one another extended beyond the plane of the cell bars, so that prisoners would be unable to see when the guard approached their cells (fig. 1.7).[25] Surveillance in these prisons was intended to be aural as well as visual. Some prisons had complex acoustical

Fig. 1.7. Mid-twentieth-century interior view of cellblock in old south wing at the New York State Prison at Auburn, showing multistory cellblocks. Note how the walls between each cell project outward beyond the cell entrance—which was intended to limit prisoners' knowledge of the guards' approach and limit conversation with neighboring inmates. From *Handbook of Correctional Institution Design and Construction* (Washington, DC: United States Bureau of Prisons, 1949), 9.

networks designed for the guard inside the tower to be able to hear the noises inside the cells. At Eastern State the cells were tall and vaulted, which Haviland planned to reduce the ability of prisoners to hear into neighboring cells as well as direct sounds toward the centrally-positioned keeper.[26] At Auburn similar provisions helped the sentinel to "hear a whisper from a distant cell, in the upper story."[27] As William Crawford described in his 1835 report to the British government, the recessed placement of the cell doors several feet back from the cell wall made "any conversation on the part of the prisoners impossible without being overheard by a watchman in the gallery."[28]

Above all surveillance figured into nineteenth-century prison design in the positioning of the prisoner and guard spaces relative to one another. Spaces for the warden and his agents dominated—physically as well as symbolically— over spaces occupied by inmates. In prisons designed around solitary confinement, surveillance extended over the cells by means of a centralized observation tower buttressed by subsidiary observation towers along the exterior wall.

In congregate prisons such as Auburn, the predominant gaze emanated from observation mechanisms built into the fabric of communal areas where prisoners worked and recreated and in guard towers strategically placed along the prison's perimeter.[29] Regardless of the particular system at work, the relationship of guard to prisoner space, tied directly to the gaze of the former over the latter, underlies the design of the model early-nineteenth-century prisons, which influenced prison design well into the twentieth century.

The prominence of surveillance in prison design during this period expressed the belief among prison reformers that penal discipline should be totalizing and comprehensive. As Robin Evans has discussed, the idea of perpetual monitoring of inmates—a defining feature of English prisons on which American penal reformers drew for inspiration—was part of a comprehensive program geared toward achieving total control over inmates' actions.[30] Classifying inmates by severity of offense, separating them from one another, instituting labor programs, and using surveillance worked to help transform prisoners into moral, obedient, and productive citizens.[31] In his pioneering study of penitentiaries and related institutions in the United States, David J. Rothman showed how these prisons were intended to circumscribe inmates' experience, keep them in line, and thus lead them down the path of reform:

> The promise of institutionalization depended upon the isolation of the prisoner and the establishment of a disciplined routine. Convinced that deviancy was primarily the result of the corruptions pervading the community, and that organizations like the family and the church were not counterbalancing them, they [prison reformers] believed that a setting which removed the offender from all temptations and substituted a steady and regular regimen would reform him. . . .
>
> As a result of this thinking, prison architecture and arrangements became the central concern of reformers of the period. Unlike their predecessors, they turned all their attention inward. . . . The layout of cells, the methods of labor, and the manner of eating and sleeping within the penitentiary were the crucial issues.[32]

As Rothman explained, segregating prisoners and policing their movements via surveillance was a key aspect in a comprehensive program geared toward their reformation.

For Rothman the construction of these large-scale prisons and other reformative institutions during the early to mid–nineteenth century related to the rapidly changing social order in nineteenth-century America.[33] Like attempts to combat the urban expansion that Americans faced during the nineteenth century, the proliferation of surveillance-oriented prisons was meant to contest the chaotic and rapidly changing economic, social, and cultural circumstances in American society in several ways. These institutions offered a means of preventing crime, by isolating wrongdoers from mainstream society. In addition reformative institutions sought to cure offenders and correct deviant behavior through rigorous disciplinary measures. Finally, as reformatories of vice, these kinds of institutions offered a utopian form of social organization, in which all movements and actions across time and space were strictly regulated. Thus, although the prison landscape was spatially and socially distinct from other aspects of American society, its careful classification, distribution, and regulation of bodies in space suggested a paradigm for society-at-large organized around discipline.[34] Although Rothman's model of American exceptionalism may now seem problematic and somewhat dated, his points about the desire for order in prisons providing a paradigmatic template for cultural order remain persuasive, and they help explain the interest in surveillance in this context.

Regardless of how surveillance was built into particular designs, it lay at the core of the penal mission to correct, train, and reform prisoners. Haviland vehemently articulated his goals, noting in his 1824 description of Eastern State's plan that it was "of the first importance in a building of this nature that it should be conveniently and securely watched."[35] Supporters of the Auburn system saw its strategies of surveillance, however much they differed from those of the Pennsylvania system, as key to its mission as well. In 1826 Gershom Powers, a Boston-based prison reformer, stressed the importance of surveillance in the Auburn facility: "It cannot be too often or too forcibly repeated, that the ease and success of prison discipline depends, vastly, on the construction of its buildings and yards. After separation of convicts, by solitary cells, *facility of inspection* is almost every thing." Powers liked the simplicity of the New York penitentiary's plan with the open interior yard because it could "be surveyed at a glance." In addition the shops had "no bye-ways and corners to screen the prisoners from the view of the keepers."[36] Echoing these sentiments, Charles Bulfinch, in recommending designs for a prison in Washington, DC, in 1827, praised modern prisons for providing for rigorous inspection as a fail-safe means of discipline: "One watchman on each side can notice every movement, and hear every word uttered by each prisoner. . . . The security against combination or escape is complete, for if one should even break from his cell, he would be still enclosed in the surrounding passage."[37] The goal of the architects and reformers was unequivocal: architecture could aid discipline by instilling a sense of omnipresent surveillance through the grounds.

The Limits of Surveillance in Prisons

Judging from the abundant provisions for surveillance in the plans of the institutions and from statements about them offered by their architects and supporters, it is tempting to assume that these surveillance measures actively helped wardens and guards discipline inmates. Moreover, the fact that the layout schemes outlined above remained dominant through the early twentieth century suggests that the modes of surveillance built into the prisons' plans succeeded, or prison administrators and reformers would have developed other schemes. However, changes in the buildings over time and in the documentary record show that architectural provisions for surveillance often proved inadequate, requiring that additional measures be put in place—some architectural, some otherwise. Efforts to justify and improve disciplinary measures in these institutions during the nineteenth century suggest awareness about the limits of architectural forms of surveillance as instruments of discipline and signal the need to revise prevailing ideas about architecture and surveillance to account for this.

In *Discipline and Punish,* Foucault explored prisons and the ideas of late-eighteenth- and early-nineteenth-century prison reformers as foundations in developing the disciplinary mechanism that informed modern institutional design.[38] Foucault linked rather different-looking prisons together through the panopticon, which he posited as the "architectural programme" lying behind the design of most prisons built in Europe and America.[39] By segregating inmates and subjecting them to continuous and anonymous surveillance, prisons derived from the panopticon made them perpetually visible and thus knowable to their keepers. With surveillance working continuously and silently, it induced in the inmate a feeling of "conscious and permanent visibility" that ensured the "automatic functioning of power" in which those under the gaze became complicit in their subjugation. For Foucault the relationship between keeper and inmate in the panopticon, and prisons deriving from it, was bound together, creating an ideal disciplinary apparatus in which power functioned relationally rather than being imposed by the guards on the prisoners. The anonymity of the panopticon's keeper (or keepers) also defined the panoptic mechanism, as anyone (or no one) could be in the tower and it would still function to discipline.

Foucault indicates that surveillance in these prisons was omnipresent and totalizing in its intent as well as its exercise. Although Foucault acknowledged its failures in prisons and other institutions of confinement, he felt that such failures resulted from the ways that builders incorporated surveillance into these "complete and austere institutions." Any breakdown served merely to spur reassertions of similar, if more rigorously enforced, disciplinary measures to ensure even more seamless operating of the disciplinary mechanism. Foucault viewed failures as part of the system, meant to justify the perpetual search for more complete disciplinary measures, thereby creating a continuous cycle in which surveillance repeatedly reaffirms itself as the primary means of control. Within this cyclical pattern, resistance was futile; according to Foucault, inmates were as bound up in the mechanism of power as their keepers and, by means of their own subjugation, perpetuated the maintenance of discipline, even if unbeknownst to them. Foucault found it equally bleak outside of the prison context. The omnipresent disciplinary gaze functioning in prisons penetrated modern culture at every turn, creating what Foucault characterized as modern surveillance society.

Foucault's account rests on several underlying, but deeply problematic, assumptions. First, he characterized the prison itself as the most complete of the disciplinary institutions that, however different in particulars, ultimately derived from the prison. Second, he characterized surveillance as an omnipresent and ultimately singular force, the disciplinary gaze, which pervaded disciplinary settings in a similar fashion across a broad span of time, the modern period, varying little according to the context in which it worked. Finally, he believed those under surveillance were powerless against it, since it aimed at their ultimate subjugation. In other words, they had no capacity to resist it. Yet examining nineteenth-century prisons and other buildings organized around surveillance challenges these assumptions, and thus Foucault's argument. For one thing the variety of forms surveillance took in different building types in a wide range of settings make it impossible to speak of a singular ideology of surveillance, as later chapters in this book will show. Even in a context of punitive discipline, what lies behind surveillance in the penal landscape is more complicated than Foucault suggested. The obvious anxiety on the part of prison reformers and officials evinces that they foresaw that architecture could not provide for the fail-safe discipline necessary to maintain order in the penal landscape.

As much as prison administrators in nineteenth-century America depended on architectural means of surveillance, they also regularly expressed concern that measures might not be foolproof. Eastern State Penitentiary underwent a series of modifications throughout its history, many of which were related to expansion across the nineteenth century, but others were related to flaws in Haviland's design that became obvious after it opened. One point of contention involved the centralized tower, which Haviland intended to be the hub of surveillance and thus a chief instrument of discipline in the penitentiary. From the outset, prison administrators found fault with the watchtower. A major criticism stemmed from the fact that the platform around the centralized rotunda did not provide adequate views of exercise yards, particularly those located toward the end of the cellblocks. Because of these concerns, within months of the prison's opening, officials hired additional guards to patrol the exterior walls while the prisoners were exercising.[40] In addition officials worried that the mammoth size of the prison made it difficult for prisoners to believe that a centrally placed guard could monitor all of the cellblock corridors emanating from the tower comprehensively. Rev. Louis Dwight, for instance, offered that it would "take a guard for every five feet of wall to prevent any conversation between the prisoners during their exercise."[41] By the end of the nineteenth century, wardens installed mirrors in the central tower on the first floor to allow the guard to see down all corridors at once.[42] Wardens also found Haviland's plan lacking in terms of preventing communication between prisoners, who, as noted above, talked to one another during periods of exercise. The problem became so acute that prison officials ultimately staggered periods of exercise so that no two neighboring prisoners were in their yards at the same time.[43]

During the course of the nineteenth century, further renovations at Eastern State reveal continued skepticism about the ability of Haviland's design to provide for comprehensive discipline via surveillance. The construction of the fourth, fifth, sixth, and seventh cellblocks as two-story units because of a growing inmate population dramatically changed the security provisions in Haviland's original plan. Exercise now took place communally for prisoners in the second-story cells in the grassy areas between the cellblocks, which required roaming guards to try to keep them from communicating. To prevent the prisoners from conversing, a major goal of the solitary system, prisoners had to wear hoods from time to time during their incarceration if they left their cells, as a warden's journal from 1855 noted.[44] Within two years of the penitentiary's opening, the practicality of having openings in the cells accessible from the hallways led to a reconfiguration of the entrances there that also made surveillance more challenging. Initially one entered from the rear of the cells through the exercise yards, but this was changed to entry by way of the cellblock corridors shortly after the prison opened. Although Haviland's original plan provided for feeding trays in the main hallways and peepholes in the hallway walls to allow keepers to monitor the inmates' activities, officials did not originally have to worry much about patrolling the cellblock halls, since prisoners could not communicate with one another or escape via that path. The new arrangement meant patrols had to increase to convey to prisoners that they were under watch. Further, day-to-day operations of the prison practically necessitated prisoners spending more time outside of their cells than originally anticipated. Bathing, gardening to grow food for the prisoners to eat, working, and the holding of congregate religious services required that prisoners commune, and additional surveillance helped ensure minimal communication during these periods. However complete and functional Haviland claimed his plan for the prison to be, it ultimately proved inadequate given all of these changes. Officials modified surveillance measures in hopes of maintaining their disciplinary authority.

Yet even with these additional measures, surveillance proved inadequate as a means of sustaining the solitary form of penal discipline at Eastern State. A report produced by Thomas McElwee, appointed by the Pennsylvania legislature to investigate the conditions of the prison in 1834, described conditions there unfavorably. McElwee castigated Warden Samuel R. Wood and other prison officials for deviating from the agenda of the Pennsylvania system of discipline, which relied on solitary confinement under rigorous supervision. The report accused the warden of letting prisoners outside of their cells far more than necessary, sometimes to wait on his table or maintain the conditions of the prison. Both of these infractions invited prisoners to socialize, something inimical to the separate system of discipline. Further, officials imposed punishments on the prisoners that solitary confinement was intended to prevent. These punishments included forcing prisoners to wear iron gags and to take shower baths in which water was poured from high above and placing them in straitjackets or in tranquilizing chairs for long periods of time. The ultimate result of the charges was minimal. The board that ruled on the accusations mandated that such practices be corrected, mainly through keeping prisoners apart from one another more rigorously and keeping better watch over the inmates. But the fact that such charges were brought at all suggests that built forms of surveillance were proving inadequate as a means of discipline there and that officials had resorted to other changes as part of their disciplinary regimen.[45]

Likewise the early history of Western State Penitentiary suggests surveillance built into the original plan proved insufficient. Shortly after the prison's opening in July 1826, the warden reported problems that would lead to a complete remodeling of the building during the 1830s. The warden perceived that the design failed to provide for thorough surveillance, despite the pains that Strickland and his supporters had gone through to ensure it. In 1830 the warden expressed continuing concerns about the limited range of surveillance there. He complained that the cooking facilities between his dwelling on the external wall and the interior prison yard prevented him and the guards from inspecting the facility from their apartments. More significant, the warden found that the facility did not convey the sense of omnipresent surveillance he felt was necessary to keep prisoners in line:

The cells being arranged in a circular form, only a part can be seen at one view, and when several convicts are unlocked for the purpose of labour or exercise, and are distributed along the line in front of their cells, some of them are necessarily a part of the time out of the view of the overseer. . . . A well constructed prison is free from recesses and covert places; but this prison abounds in those evils. The construction and arrangement of the cells are such as to afford the convicts every facility to evil communications. . . . And while the keeper is inspecting one section or division of cells, the remaining three-fourths of the prison is wholly without inspection.

Even more critically, the layout violated one of the chief principles of the panopticon (as Bentham had defined it), which was stealthy visual monitoring of the entire prison: "The apartments are so arranged that the keeper cannot inspect the convicts without being himself inspected."[46] At Western State surveillance from a central point—at the center of the yard—was open and available for all prisoners to see, rather than concealed as it would have been in a faithful panoptic design. The prisoners thus knew when the warden and guards watched them, and they could, in moments when they were free of the gaze, cavort with other prisoners or otherwise resist the disciplinary surveillance imposed on them. Despite efforts that Strickland had taken to guarantee a sense of complete, perpetual supervision, his design failed to provide the thorough, discreet surveillance that the warden believed would maintain disciplinary order. The warden's fears were apparently justified. By January 1828, a few years after the prison's opening, prisoners had successfully mounted six escapes.[47] Three years later Western State underwent a rebuilding more along the lines of its Philadelphia counterpart.[48]

Prisons designed around the Auburn system of discipline similarly show problems with built-in provisions for surveillance. Wardens of these facilities deemed surveillance to be absolutely necessary to ensure that inmates did not communicate during the periods they were outside of their cells, such as in the workshops where they assembled each day. In the original plan of the State Penitentiary at Auburn, designers positioned workshops on the perimeter of the prison so that prisoners could be monitored from a two thousand-foot-long, three-foot-wide enclosed passageway along the prison's exterior walls. Through peepholes from this passageway, guards could monitor prisoners without their knowledge, creating a kind of panoptic situation whereby prisoners felt they were under surveillance even if it was only intermittently exercised.[49] Even with such elaborate architectural provisions, officials instituted additional means of surveillance shortly after the prison was built. As reformer Gershom Powers explained, additional guards watched prisoners from inside the shops on elevated stools, providing a form of embodied surveillance on top of the surreptitious disembodied modes exercised from the secret passageways. This likely resulted from the large number of inmates in the shop. Prison administrators feared that communication between prisoners was likely and thought additional surveillance would help prevent it.[50] At night, when the convicts slept in their individual cells, patrolling watchmen kept perpetual watch over the cellblocks. Additional safeguards—such as having the roving guards check in at the guard station in the administration building at set times—were instituted to watch the guards and prevent loafing.[51]

Undoubtedly many of the additional safeguards implemented in these prisons were put in place because the original designers failed to consider the realities of prison life as well as the fact that prisons had to grow as demands for space to house inmates grew. At Eastern State and Auburn, for example, prisons officials made many of the changes in the interests of religious and work activities, both of which required prisoners to leave their cells far more than was anticipated originally. Ministering to prisoners—a key part of reform programs at both institutions—led to changes in weekday routine for prisoners as well as surveillance practices. Moreover, as prisons expanded, builders worked with prison officials to devise new arrangements to convey to prisoners that they were still subject to watch, often by adding additional watchtowers. Still it is clear that from the start prison officials knew that built forms of surveillance were themselves inadequate to enforce discipline. No matter how hard architects worked to build features into their plans, anxieties about points where surveillance might cease to discipline those under its scope led prison reformers and administrators to ponder, and eventually undertake, revisions and changes.

Realizing the myriad ways that architects incorporated these features into prison buildings challenges any claims of consistency about surveillance and discipline in this context. The fact that the Pennsylvania and Auburn systems had different strategies of discipline necessitated different degrees and types of surveillance, and efforts to combat challenges to their disciplinary strategies thus evolved differently. Further, given all of the changes made in prisons in response to actions challenging (or potentially challenging) authority there suggests that the ideology of surveillance itself was constantly evolving, responding to changed circumstances as well as potential fears about challenges to it. Fears about breakdowns in disciplinary surveillance have been minimized in Foucault's and others' discussions of the disciplinary gaze's all-encompassing potential, but clearly these concerns informed decisions about surveillance and its exercise almost continually. Prisoners at Western State managed to escape, whereas prisoners at Eastern State took advantages of opportunities to communicate with one another in strict violation of the disciplinary regime in place there. At Western State the result was the remodeling of the prison, while at Eastern State and Auburn Prisons the wardens saw to the introduction of supplementary surveillance measures, some built and others not. Thus however much prison officials hailed surveillance as a disciplinary strategy, they clearly recognized its limits, particularly in terms of how architecture could facilitate it.

Surveillance and Discipline

Concerns about the limits of surveillance did not prevent prison architects and their patrons from incorporating it into buildings. Indeed those responsible for building prisons in the Victorian period and beyond continually sought ways to improve discipline as they modified existing penal structures and built new facilities replete with architectural means of surveillance in them. The reliance on architectural forms of surveillance signals that even if measures were not foolproof in a practical sense, they proved at least somewhat functional or architects and reformers would have developed other alternatives. This suggests a lingering belief in the disciplinary potential of the gaze, even if prison officials knew that architectural forms of surveillance were fallible. Architectural means of surveillance ultimately served those inside and outside the prison as a symbol of disciplinary authority, even if practically they proved a limited means to instill discipline among inmates and over the prison landscape.

Despite the problems at Auburn, Eastern State, and other early-nineteenth-century prisons, the plans developed by prison reformers in New York and Pennsylvania remained dominant throughout the Victorian period.[52] As Johnston and others have demonstrated, the Auburn system dwarfed that of Pennsylvania in nineteenth-century America, even affecting prisons originally designed along the model of solitary confinement. At the State Prison at Trenton, New Jersey, for example, Strickland's original half-radial plan was modified over the course of the nineteenth and early twentieth centuries, with cellblocks (noted in the plan as nos. 4, 5, and 6) built along the lines of the Auburn model (fig. 1.4).[53] A 1949 handbook on prison design issued by the U.S. Bureau of Prisons maintained that a "fortress mentality" dominated during the Victorian period in the United States. Any innovations typically lay with measures to enhance security, which the bureau complained resulted in accrual of "unnecessary expenses," since most cells had been designed for maximum security needs, despite the fact most prisoners were not a threat. They contended that many Victorian prisons were made with bars "more than twice as strong, as those used in zoos to restrain lions or giant Kodiak bears." Bureau of Prisons officials felt that these efforts wore on the warden and guards as much as they did on the convicts and also they had resulted in outrageous expenditures.[54] In his 1930 book, *Prisons and Prison Building,* the architect Alfred Hopkins criticized this trend in prison design:

> All this to retain men the majority of whom were quite content to work all day long out in the open and to return peacefully at night to sleep quietly behind a triple row of tool-proof steel without thought of either killing the guard or breaking jail . . . the design of every prison was based upon the theory that it must everywhere detain the worst possible prisoner. To build an entire institution on the basis of its worst possible inmate is nonsense.[55]

Hopkins's criticisms and those of the Bureau of Prisons stemmed largely from financial considerations, but such statements also reveal the dominant mindset behind prison design in Victorian America. Concerns about creating secure penal bastions to forestall any resistance to discipline and prevent unwanted escape partly drove the perpetuation of prisons designed after the model institutions in New York and Pennsylvania.

A noticeable break in prison design came during the early twentieth century, when a new alternative became popular. The telephone layout first appeared in the United States in the State Prison at Stillwater, Minnesota, designed around 1909 by Clarence Johnston, then the state architect (fig. 1.8). Following European precedents, notably Wormwood-Scrubs Prison in London (1874–91) and

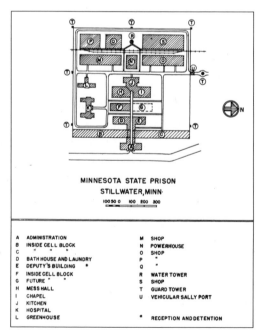

MINNESOTA STATE PRISON
STILLWATER, MINN·
100 50 0   100   200   300

A	ADMINISTRATION	M	SHOP
B	INSIDE CELL BLOCK	N	POWERHOUSE
C	" " "	O	SHOP
D	BATH HOUSE AND LAUNDRY	P	"
E	DEPUTY'S BUILDING *	Q	"
F	INSIDE CELL BLOCK	R	WATER TOWER
G	FUTURE " "	S	SHOP
H	MESS HALL	T	GUARD TOWER
I	CHAPEL	U	VEHICULAR SALLY PORT
J	KITCHEN		
K	HOSPITAL		
L	GREENHOUSE	*	RECEPTION AND DETENTION

Fig. 1.8. Ground plan of Minnesota Prison at Stillwater, designed by C. H. Johnson and opened in 1914, as it appeared in 1949. The prison was the earliest American manifestation of the telephone-pole layout, in which buildings housing different functions extended parallel to one another off a central, covered corridor. From *Handbook of Correctional Institution Design and Construction* (Washington, DC: United States Bureau of Prisons, 1949), 61.

the Seine Departmental Prison at Fresnes-les-Rungis on the outskirts of Paris (1894–98), the plan for the prison at Stillwater shows an organization in which buildings housing different functions extend outward in a parallel manner off of a central, covered walkway. As Norman Johnston suggests, the scheme at Stillwater was transitional in many ways. The long, main cellblocks (originally A and B) toward the bottom of the telephone pole are inside cellblocks modeled on those at Auburn and its successors. The fact the administration building anchors the telephone pole recalls radial plans in that it occupies a kind of nerve center off of which other elements—such as the cellblocks—radiate, albeit not as centrally as they would in a radial plan. The architect of Stillwater also followed earlier precedents by incorporating prominent watchtowers into the plan. As an early–twentieth century photograph suggests, watchtowers stood along the perimeter walls, numbering seven in all (fig. 1.9). Movements to the shops were clearly strategically planned in this scheme around the towers, where alleys were clearly located in view of the guard towers to ensure close watch over prisoner movements. Thus the prison preserves many aspects of Victorian American prison design, including the emphasis on surveillance as a means of discipline.

Surveillance was important to telephone-pole-layout prisons such as the new Minnesota State Prison, though it did not practically solve all disciplinary problems here. The 1949 Bureau of Prisons manual criticized the excessively long corridors of the large prison blocks for undermining surveillance. The

Fig. 1.9. Undated (likely early-twentieth-century) aerial photograph of the Minnesota State Prison at Stillwater. Note the prominent watchtowers along the perimeter wall. From *Handbook of Correctional Institution Design and Construction* (Washington, DC: United States Bureau of Prisons, 1949), 61.

bureau also noted that some buildings, notably the hospital, were oddly disconnected from the main telephone pole layout, which inhibited close monitoring of these spaces from a practical standpoint. Yet despite this, surveillance built into the fabric of the prison remained important symbolically. Hopkins claimed that the layout seen in "telegraph-plan" prisons such as that at Stillwater proved even more successful in conveying the impression of perpetual visual control than earlier plans:

> [The telephone-pole layout] lends itself to even a better means of supervision. The end of every building opening full width upon the connecting corridor is of glass so that from the corridor . . . every building may be seen down its entire length and across its entire width. Remembering that a fly upon the windowpane may blot out a cow upon a hillside, all columns are omitted. The buildings, long and narrow, are unobstructed and from the inspection corridor a clearer view may be had and maintained over the entire institution than is possible by any other arrangement.[56]

Hopkins's assessment of the virtues of the layout emphasizes the omnipresent possibility of surveillance afforded by the telephone scheme. As with earlier plans, what mattered here was the sense that prison buildings conveyed of a perpetual gaze, not whether it actually worked as an instrument of discipline.

The layout of the Minnesota State Prison, its provisions for surveillance, and even the style of the facility worked together to indicate the potential of a disciplined institution. Stylistically the building departed from earlier precedents, such as Eastern State and Auburn, in putting aside associations with medieval architecture in favor of a streamlined modernism. Smooth concrete walls surround three sides of the prison, the fourth being formed by two long cellblocks built of yellow, glazed brick. Capped originally with a red tile roof, the building espouses an aesthetic of efficiency and order while at the same time showing restraint and a sense of strength that fit with the ideas of a regulated, bare-bones disciplinary program. As noted above, provisions for surveillance here suggested that views could be had of all areas of the grounds (if not always convincingly to prisoners). Finally, in contrast to the haphazard manner that often characterized prison architecture, the plan for a structure that was carefully ordered, carefully contained, and organized as an entity implied order, suggesting in physical form the same discipline that officials hope would characterize day-to-day operations at the prison. Thus regardless of how well the prison did or did not work, the design conveyed disciplinary order through its built fabric, offering to the prisoners, the guards, and visitors an impression of a neatly ordered and disciplined penal landscape, one in which surveillance played a critical role, if intermittently and symbolically.

Aspects of the telephone-pole layout also hint at other frameworks through which we might understand the importance given to surveillance in prison designs as well in other aspects of Victorian American architecture. Several novel elements in the facility at Stillwater, particularly the segregation of prison functions in different buildings off the central corridor, relate to the design of other environments in late-nineteenth- and early-twentieth-century America, including some discussed later in this book. Some of these features suggest how interwoven ideas about prison building were with Victorian American culture at large as well as indicates other motivations lying behind the interest in surveillance in the prison landscape.

A striking feature at the Minnesota State Prison involves the degree of specialization in the plan, complicating the division between guard and prisoner spaces seen earlier. Functions previously housed in a central administrative structure are pulled out in the Stillwater facility as separate structures, or otherwise distinguished and demarcated. While many of these spaces, such as hospitals, laundries, and chapels, had been part of earlier prisons, they often were added haphazardly as afterthoughts, whereas at Stillwater the plan accommodated all functions right from the start. Beyond this, specialization is manifest with the different cellblocks, which were used for different categories of prisoners, separated by sex and severity of offense. Such specialization seen here recalls that apparent elsewhere in the Victorian American landscape, perhaps most strongly in industrial facilities, where specialization became increasingly common, especially after the Civil War. The plan for the prison at Stillwater compares rather strikingly with the plan for a model factory by F. A. Scheffer discussed in chapter 2 (fig. 2.25), which has a central administrative hub from which radiate the various shops.[57] Specialization in the industrial landscape resulted from a complex set of factors. Industrial reformers justified it in the name of efficiency. Given that Stillwater, like many prisons, operated as a workspace as well as a prison, as the abundant spaces noted as shops in the plan suggest, provisions for order and discipline evident in the organization and the numerous watchtowers undoubtedly revolved around concerns about efficiency as much as punitive discipline. Thus perhaps it is not surprising that concerns about efficiency motivated the interest in surveillance in Stillwater as it did in workspaces from the same period.

The specialization seen in the Minnesota State Prison also suggests concerns about hierarchies among individuals who moved throughout the prison grounds. The prison landscape is a hierarchical one, as most of the plans discussed in this chapter show. Areas frequented by figures in authority—that is, the spaces occupied by wardens, guards, and their proxies—are at the highest and usually center-most points in the structure: the administrative buildings and the watchtowers. Surveillance obviously played a critical part in maintaining these hierarchies. At Stillwater, Johnston emphasized these hierarchies to a greater degree than previously had been done, through the way he conceived the plan. Indeed the telephone-pole layout allowed for different cellblocks in which different kinds of prisoners were categorized. For Hopkins a primary benefit of the telephone-pole layout was that it allowed for different classes of prisoners, subject to different forms of discipline, to be categorized and classified.[58] Provisions for surveillance at the Minnesota State Prison and others designed after its example thus varied according to the space under the gaze and its kind of occupant. As Hopkins explained, congregate areas, such as recreation facilities, required greater security than cellblocks for minimum security inmates, especially at night.[59] Moreover, surveillance from the central corridor sought to preserve hierarchies, which were necessary to maintain order in the penal landscape.

Perhaps most surprisingly, surveillance served as a marker of order at Stillwater by conveying to onlookers inside and outside of the prison that the prison was a disciplined landscape. In extolling the virtues of prisons derived from the telephone pole plan (including several of his own structures), Hopkins made explicit the important role of prison design: "The value of decent design in prison architecture, as a beneficent influence on the prisoner himself, must be patent to everyone interested in observing any evidence whatever of artistic appreciation by those either in jail or out of it."[60] Hopkins maintained that an efficient, hierarchical prison plan, replete with surveillance measures, improved the morale of inmates and prison workers. Beyond this it extended to those outside the prison walls, who, regardless of their acquaintance with the prison or its occupants, would see a well-designed prison as a symbol of society's beneficence. An ordered prison offered inmates the promise of reformation while it assured those who supported it that society provided for its delinquent class. A well-ordered prison mirrored a well-ordered society. Although the prison landscape was literally and figuratively separate from society at large, the promotion of the prison as a regulated, ordered landscape reinforced a sense of cultural order to those outside the prison, affirming these institutions as proper vehicles of punishment in a democratic society. The public's appreciation of a well-designed prison allowed for the maintenance of the disciplinary system. In this way, then, surveillance measures in prisons became markers of cultural order and cultural unity—something that confirmed Americans' confidence in their justice system and American society more broadly.

Thus surveillance served multiple functions, even in the penal setting where discipline was its primary agenda. Subsequent chapters explore these functions in greater detail, by focusing on settings where other concerns—

namely, about efficiency, hierarchy, and fellowship—became primary goals behind the imposition of surveillance. The next chapter takes up another disciplinary environment: the modern workspace. Like prison officials, owners and managers relied on surveillance as a strategy of control, but with a twist. Surveillance in this context functioned less as a tool of punishment than as a tool of production. This can clearly be seen through the way in which provisions for surveillance were incorporated into buildings as part of the efficiency movement of the late nineteenth and early twentieth centuries.

Chapter 2

EFFICIENCY

How to make the most of everything, and how to reduce to the utmost the inevitable waste which takes place wherever a number of workmen are employed, should be the first object of every one to whom is entrusted the supervision of a factory or workshop.

—Frederic Smith, *Workshop Management: A Manual for Masters and Men, Comprising a Few Practical Remarks on the Economic Conduct of Workshops* (1879)

*D*uring the winter of 1901, postal inspectors at the post office in Colorado Springs, Colorado, began mailing test letters, stuffed full of cash, in an attempt to lure suspected thieving postal clerks into action. Mail had been disappearing at this post office for months, leading inspectors to commence a lengthy investigation there. In January four inspectors took up an extended, furtive watch of the clerks from a small room located on the second story, which they designated as the lookout. Through four small holes the size of a lead pencil drilled in the floor, inspectors assessed all aspects of the post office's operations. Some of the comments in their lengthy final report related to evidence of theft on the part of several clerks. On 27 January inspectors watched Clerk Bowers open a test letter and ponder taking six dollars inside it. On 6 February, they saw Bowers take a letter, depart for a few minutes to the swing room (the break room), and then return a few minutes later empty-handed. But most of the inspectors' observations had nothing to do with mail theft, relating instead to the lack of work discipline that pervaded the workroom. They caught Bowers sleeping during his shift. Another worker, Clerk Edwards, wrote letters during working hours, and Clerk McLain admitted unauthorized persons into the mailing room. They severely criticized Clerk Moldin, for he was guilty of "consuming considerable time reading post cards from 12:00 м. (noon) to 1:30 p.m., and did not make proper effort to distribute all mail before the closing of mail for Denver, Colorado, at 1:00 p.m." Other infractions by the clerks included leaving the office unlocked, stealing magazines, and not working at an efficient pace. Inspectors used evidence gleaned from the lookout to recommend firing several clerks, demoting others, and reorganizing the post office along more efficient lines.[1]

The inspectors' lookout in Colorado Springs resembled observation mechanisms that had been built in other post office workrooms throughout the United States since the mid-1880s. Although clerks were unaware of the makeshift lookout used in the investigations at the Colorado Springs post office, most lookouts built during the late nineteenth and early twentieth centuries were permanent and prominent features in post office workspaces, usually occupying space on a half story or mezzanine floor. Post Office Department officials believed that the high visibility of lookouts contributed to their deterrent effect. An inspector at the main post office in New York City alluded to their potential to prevent misdoings in his 1893 description of the new lookout there: "From the new gallery the work of the city department clerks can be seen at all times. And men from this office will be on duty in that gallery at all times. I believe it will tend to prevent dishonesty," he wrote, praising its conspicuous placement above the workroom floor.[2] From lookouts inspectors hoped to command views of workrooms and the clerks working therein.

The case of post office lookouts cannot be studied in isolation, for surveillance was pervasive in the landscape of work during the late nineteenth and early twentieth centuries. Owners and managers of other American workplaces, such as factories and office settings, developed a variety of forms of built-in surveillance during the Victorian period to monitor the activities of their workers. Raised platforms, corner offices, and open workroom plans facilitated the gazes of supervisors over workers, which management hailed as essential for workplace efficiency. An advice writer for *System: The Magazine of Business* in 1906 explained the importance of visual supervision in the American workplace: "His two eyes are still the manager's most useful mediums for keeping in touch with the details of his business. And they will be so long as the human brain receives impressions more quickly through the eyes than through tables of figures or reports of written words."[3] Growing industrialization during the late nineteenth and early twentieth centuries gave rise to an immense prescriptive literature directed at business owners and managers that heralded surveillance as a chief strategy of workplace management. As Smith's quote at the beginning of the chapter suggests, running a successful workplace depended on those in power monitoring the actions of those who labored under their supervision.

This chapter examines architectural forms of surveillance in Victorian American workplaces, considering how supervisors, owners, and managers enlisted such features in the service of efficiency and for what reasons. Understanding surveillance in work settings requires wresting the concept of work discipline away from that of discipline as punishment, the operative system of control in prisons discussed in the previous chapter. By work discipline, I refer to a mode of discipline that sought to regulate the labor of workers for its commodity value as an element of production. Ultimately the rise of surveillance in the modern workplace revolved around the issue of productive labor. As capitalist modes of production superseded craft-based manufacturing in the nineteenth-century United States, entrepreneurs attempted to seize power and control from workers over the quantity and quality of their work.[4] Through increased mechanization and division of labor, the workers' investment in the product they produced declined, and managers feared that this reduced labor itself to a mere commodity. The challenge for management laid in extracting maximum labor from workers. For capitalists to profit, they needed to translate labor power (the potential of labor) into actual labor.[5] Labor, as opposed to labor power, resulted from a negotiation between management and workers, since the latter retained the right to refuse to work as much as management sought to induce them to exceed their inclinations.

From the perspective of management, behind the implementation of surveillance measures of concern here was the transaction between them and their employees, which revolved around the issue of control.[6] By control I refer to the definition offered by the historian Richard Edwards as the desire of management to procure the maximum level of work from labor. The more control that management believed they achieved through securing productive labor from workers, the more efficient they hoped their businesses could become. During the late nineteenth and early twentieth centuries, the disciplining of labor occupied the attention of numerous reformers who attempted to minimize the discrepancy between labor and labor-power, what they dubbed the labor problem, mainly through developing modern managerial strategies. One of these reformers was Frederick Winslow Taylor. At the end of the nineteenth century, Taylor identified failings with capitalist modes of production to operate efficiently, which he attributed to insufficient management. Taylor recognized that mechanization and division of labor had not in themselves maximized production, largely because they did not ensure that labor power was translated into actual labor. He strove to find ways in which management could seize control over work processes, measures that included personnel management, increased supervision through functional foremanship, and setting the pace of the workers' tasks based on carefully measured time studies.[7] Increased surveillance supplied owners, managers, and reformers such as Taylor another strategy by which they attempted to gain an upper hand in the workplace.

In the Victorian-era workplace, surveillance worked as a means of discipline, but in ways that contrasted tellingly with the disciplinary gaze discussed in the previous chapter. Both modes of surveillance, that of discipline as punishment and that of work discipline, aimed to manipulate the body of those under the gaze to achieve control. In prisons, visual supervision over inmates sought to place physical limits on movement of bodies in space, restraining prisoners' liberty as a form of punishment. As the last chapter showed, surveillance served as one of many strategies by which this was accomplished, and often built-in mechanisms to facilitate the disciplinary gaze served more of a symbolic role than a functional one. Although the gaze in the workplace also aimed to regulate the body, it worked differently in this context and with a very different intent. Owners and managers relied on built-in surveillance features as a primary means by which they regulated the behavior of workers and their workplaces. Gazes from supervisory spaces helped bring method, order, and uniformity to the tasks that workers performed, a process of regulation that stressed a temporal component as much as a spatial one. The gaze of efficiency in the workplace thus was meant to control physical movement as well as to manipulate the pace of workers' specific actions; observations of workers provided managers data by which they judged efficiency. Moreover, surveillance in the workplace strove to transform the behavior of workers in order to manage their labor for its productive value. Regulating the body functioned as a principal strategy to accumulate capital on which industrial capitalism thrived.[8]

Many advocates of workplace surveillance argued that its success in this context depended on its visual prominence. This contrasted with surveillance in prisons, which succeeded to the extent it was relatively concealed. As a result the ways in which entrepreneurs and builders incorporated spaces for visual supervision into workspaces differed. Surveillance in the workplace was very much an embodied gaze, linked directly and prominently to the figure in charge. In some work settings, managers or supervisors occupied strategically placed spaces that gave them comprehensive views of their employees while also serving as visual reminders to workers of their omnipresence. In other work settings, the open design of the workspace facilitated surveillance of employees while also impressing on them that their visibility made them always subject to the eye of management. In still other work environments, such as post offices, those responsible for inspection remained hidden, so that workers were unaware when they were actually being watched. In these cases prominent built-in visual supervisory mechanisms assumed a managerial role themselves, acting as signifiers of management's perpetual presence even if such spaces were not continuously occupied. Whether or not such built spaces revealed the person exercising the gaze or not, surveillance in the Victorian-era workplace was linked to its visual prominence. Owners and managers seized on the organization of the workplace around conspicuous forms of built-in surveillance as a tool to regulate the behavior of workers in hopes of increasing efficiency.

Surveillance in the Post Office Department

Postal lookouts provide a convenient starting point into examining surveillance in the Victorian-era workplace, because the Post Office Department viewed them as a primary component of their efficiency efforts during the late nineteenth and early twentieth centuries. As a result of a growing industrial economy, the department found itself under pressure to accommodate increasing volumes of mail. In registered matter alone, the number of pieces traveling annually through the mail rose from 275,000 in 1866 to 15 billion in 1892, an increase of approximately 5,300 percent.[9] In addition the department faced challenges in terms of an ever-expanding workforce. In part this related to the expansion of mail delivery—first in cities, then in rural areas by the turn of the century with the institution of rural free delivery—which meant hiring carriers to bring mail to individual homes and businesses. In response to these developments, the department implemented a series of programs designed to increase efficiency. Some programs attempted to establish minimum standards for post offices and postal employees in order to keep the service consistent throughout the country, whereas others focused on increasing efficiency through mechanization. Sorting and delivery methods also received scrutiny by growing numbers of postal bureaucrats, who sought to increase efficiency through standardizing procedures.[10]

The construction of more uniform and efficient post office buildings represented another important component of the department's efforts as the federal government's building program expanded to meet the needs of industrial America. Although small post offices (typically designated as fourth class) generally filled space in rented buildings or homes well into the twentieth century, the department asked Congress for annual appropriations between the 1870s and 1910s to build new federal buildings in large cities throughout the country to house postal facilities. Once appropriated, funds went to the Office of the Supervising Architect of the Treasury Department, who saw to the design and construction of federal facilities.[11] Often these buildings served

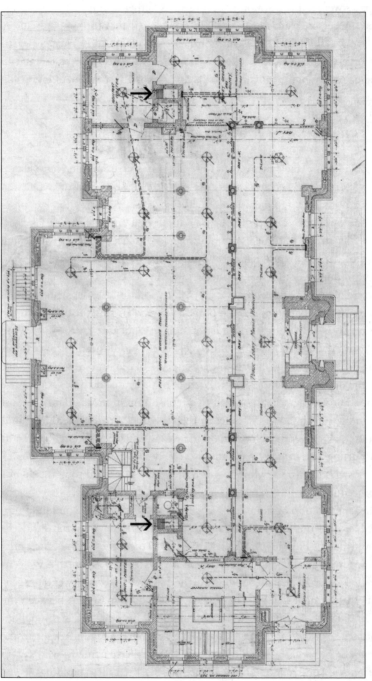

Fig. 2.1. First-floor plan of the Wilmington, Delaware, Post Office and Courthouse, 1891 (Drawing #5A), showing the location of the post office working room—which occupies most of the first floor—relative to the lobby area. The ladders indicate the location of the lookouts on both ends of the long side of the workroom. From Wilmington, Delaware, Post Office and Courthouse Records, National Archives at College Park, Maryland (Cartographic Records).

dual purposes, containing federal courtrooms or other federal offices as well as postal facilities.[12] Whether multipurpose or designated for use only by the Post Office Department, spaces in federal buildings allocated for postal uses remained relatively consistent between 1880 and 1920. In most cases postal work areas were concentrated on the first floor, whereas service areas, such as locker rooms, lunchrooms, and restrooms, and federal offices occupied spaces in the basement and upper stories.

The post office and courthouse built in Wilmington, Delaware, completed in March 1897, no longer stands, but demonstrated state-of-the-art post office construction at the time it was built. The structure's original configuration can be gleaned through the extensive collection of plans surviving in the National Archives produced between 1891 and 1896. The postal area on the first story was divided into two principal spaces: a large working room and a public lobby, which were separated from one another by a postal screen, pierced at several points by service bays (fig. 2.1).[13] The workroom behind the lobby contained a large open space, with offices for the postmaster, assistant postmaster, and other managerial personnel lining its perimeter. Service areas for the post office, meanwhile, filled space in the basement, while federal courtrooms and other federal offices took up room in the upper stories.

Lookouts were standard features in postal facilities in larger cities such as Wilmington during the late nineteenth and early twentieth centuries. When the federal building in Wilmington was completed in March of 1897, two lookouts accommodated inspectors as they monitored activities in the first floor workroom. One lookout was located near the postmaster's office, while the other stood on the opposite side of the room near the office of the assistant postmaster.[14] These original lookouts at Wilmington were each one room in size, and utilized space on a mezzanine floor above the vaults (fig. 2.2). Small windows pierced in the walls of the lookouts provided inspectors with views of the workroom floor. The fairly elaborate lookouts at Wilmington differed from the makeshift lookout at Colorado Springs described earlier, which seems to have originated as an impromptu measure adopted out of urgency in order to detect mail thieves. Increasingly after the mid-1890s, the Post Office Department replaced such temporary supervisory spaces with permanent, designed lookouts, which ranged in size from one-room units (such as those at Wilmington) to large-scale galleries surrounding post office workspaces.

As with postal workspaces in general, lookouts rapidly became standardized during the 1890s. By 1900 three types had been developed that would dominate in post office architecture during the late nineteenth and early twentieth centuries: the turret type, the hanging gallery type, and the floor type.[15] In terms of scale, the most modest type of lookout was the turret type. Varying

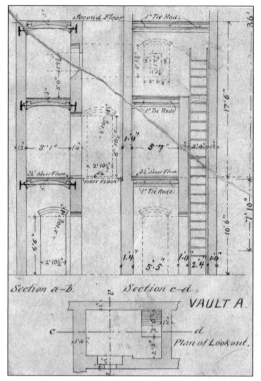

Fig. 2.2. Detail of plan and sections of lookout over Vault A, a turret-type lookout, showing ladder accessing it. From first floor plan of the courthouse and post office in Wilmington, Delaware, 1891 (Drawing #3a). From Wilmington, Delaware, Post Office and Courthouse Records, National Archives at College Park, Maryland (Cartographic Records).

in size but rarely larger than twelve by twelve feet, turret-type lookouts usually occupied space in a half story or mezzanine floor above vaults or offices. The post office in New Castle, Pennsylvania, designed in 1904, contained this type of lookout. A plan of the mezzanine floor shows two turret-type lookouts located on opposite sides of the workroom (fig. 2.3).[16] Each lookout included louvered vents at the inspectors' eye level; when opened, the vents facilitated views of the postal workroom and workers within it with minimal risk of detection (fig. 2.4). Inspectors reached these lookouts via ladders, one originating in the basement and the other on the opposite side of a locked door next to the postmaster's office. Turret-type lookouts were pervasive in post offices built throughout the late nineteenth and early twentieth centuries. New Castle's lookout scheme was somewhat unusual in its size and that one of the lookouts provided for observation of the swing room and water closets was located on the mezzanine level. Surveillance of service spaces was common, but architects usually placed these spaces in the basement or in the second story, which required a separate lookout of a different type, the floor-type lookout.

Another option for lookouts, the hanging-type, or suspended-type, gallery, dwarfed turret-type lookouts in size and typically provided visual surveillance

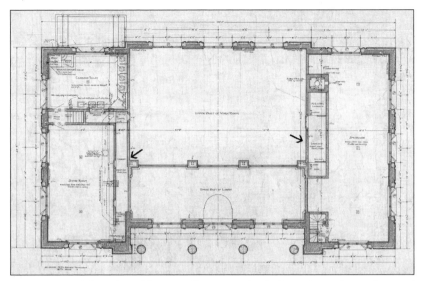

Fig. 2.3. Second-floor plan of the post office in New Castle, Pennsylvania, November 1904 (Drawing #5), showing location of the elevated inspectors' lookouts above on either side of the workroom. Note that the leftmost lookout provides for observation of the workroom below, as well as of the swing (break) room and carriers' toilets. From New Castle, Pennsylvania, Post Office Records, National Archives at College Park, Maryland (Cartographic Records).

Fig. 2.4. Photograph of the interior of the working room at the post office in New Castle, Pennsylvania, July 16, 1906. The louvered vent above the door (leading to the postmaster's office, according to the first-floor plan) signals the location of the lookout. From New Castle, Pennsylvania, Post Office Records, National Archives at College Park, Maryland (Still Picture Unit).

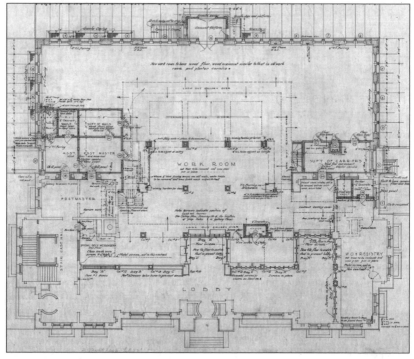

Fig. 2.5. First-floor plan of remodeled Wilmington, Delaware, Post Office and Courthouse, April 1911 (Drawing #3 extension). The addition extended off the back of the original 1896 structure, significantly enlarging the original workroom. The gallery is shown as a continuous passageway (indicated by dotted lines) that surrounds the workroom. Louvered vents provided inspectors views of the workroom from both sides of the lookout. From Wilmington, Delaware, Post Office and Courthouse Records, National Archives at College Park, Maryland (Cartographic Records).

of larger workspaces. Rare before 1900 except in very large post offices of the first class, hanging-type galleries became widespread in post offices of all sizes during the first two decades of the twentieth century.[17] The Post Office Department often saw to the installation of lookout galleries when older post offices were expanded, but they were also built in new post offices as well.[18] Like turret-type lookouts, these galleries generally were situated on a half story or mezzanine floor. However, they were much larger, forming lengthy enclosed catwalk systems that in many cases surrounded the postal work area. The Wilmington Post Office received a hanging gallery during a remodeling around 1910, at which point it replaced an original twin-turret scheme (fig. 2.5). The gallery consisted of a continuous passageway, roughly eight feet wide, which spanned the entire workroom.[19] Suspended from the joists above, this gallery contained louvered vents at eye level, similar to those in the turret-type lookouts at New

Fig. 2.6. Interior view of working room at the post office and courthouse in Wilmington, Delaware, ca. 1911. The hanging-type lookout here is shown suspended from the ceiling and over the workroom floor. Note the peepholes in the floor of the lookout as well as the louvered vent visible through the scaffolding in the left center of the image. From Wilmington, Delaware, Post Office and Courthouse Records, National Archives at College Park, Maryland (Still Picture Unit).

Castle, but also had peepholes, each roughly four inches in diameter, at regular intervals on the gallery's floor (fig. 2.6).

The third lookout type, the floor type, was generally built in spaces in post offices where ceiling clearance did not permit room for other kinds of lookouts, such as basements or half-story spaces. Rarely were floor-type lookouts installed alone in a post office; rather, such lookouts typically provided for surveillance of spaces not supervised by lookouts of the other two types, such as lavatories and swing rooms. Floor-type lookouts varied in plan more than the other two types. They could be one-room in size or extend along a continuous passageway. Although these lookouts were built on the same floor as the spaces they observed, steps provided inspectors using them access to the slightly raised floor inside to give them an elevated view. A floor-type lookout was built in the basement of the post office in Wilmington during the 1910 renovation to provide for supervision of the service areas there. A basement plan shows the floor-type lookout consisting of a narrow corridor, arranged in a U-shape

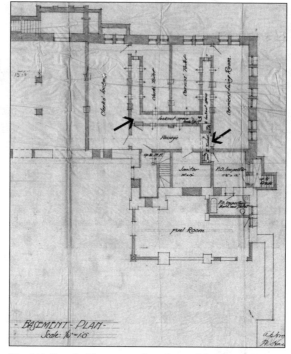

Fig. 2.7. Detail of basement plan of remodeled post office and courthouse in Wilmington, Delaware, 1911. As indicated on the plan, this floor-type lookout provided for observation of the carriers' swing room, the carriers' toilet, the clerks' toilet, and the clerks' lockers (as well as the passages connecting these spaces). To access the lookout, the inspector had to pass through a tunnel that opened into the lookout space. From Wilmington, Delaware, Post Office and Courthouse Records, National Archives at College Park, Maryland (Cartographic Records).

(fig. 2.7).[20] From this space, inspectors could observe the locker room, men's toilet facilities, the swing room, and the passageway connecting these spaces.[21] Inspectors usually reached floor-type lookouts through locked doors that entered directly into them. However, at Wilmington inspectors accessed the lookout via a tunnel that extended from the inspectors' office underground for several feet before opening into the lookout.

Architects in the Treasury Department, responsible for designing spaces for use by the Post Office Department in federal buildings, employed these three types of lookouts relative to the size of the post office in which they were built. In the smallest post offices (especially those of the third class), one lookout might have been sufficient, whereas in larger post offices, hanging galleries spanned large open workrooms. Floor-type lookouts, meanwhile, provided

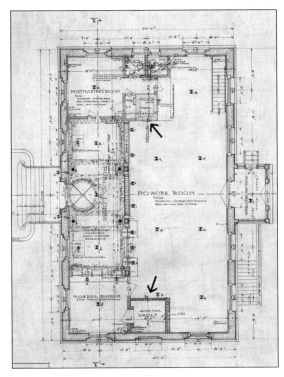

Fig. 2.8. First-floor plan of post office in Milford, Delaware, 1908 (Drawing #3). Here two turret-type lookouts are located on opposite sides of the workroom floor, one over the vault (bottom center) and the other next to the stack near the postmaster's office (labeled "LO" on the plan). From Milford, Delaware, Post Office Records, National Archives at College Park, Maryland (Cartographic Records).

views of basement or upper-story service areas. Lookout types remained consistent from the late nineteenth through the early twentieth century. Variations involved means of access to and between lookout spaces. The post office built around 1907 in Milford, Delaware, appears at first unexceptional in its plan, which incorporates a twin-turret scheme of lookouts (fig. 2.8).[22] But whereas inspectors typically gained access to turret-type lookouts from the ground floor or basement, they could enter one of the lookouts at Milford only from the attic above (fig. 2.9). To reach this second lookout, an inspector would have climbed the ladder from the basement, passed the lookout over the postmaster's office to the attic, walked across the floor to another ladder, and descended to a second lookout over the vault.[23] Other variations occurred when architects renovated lookout systems when constructing additions. During a remodeling of the post office in Danville, Virginia, in 1911, an odd L-shaped workspace led architects to design a mixed turret- and hanging-type gallery (fig. 2.10).[24] These cases show that although there may have been standardization among the types of lookouts, they never were quite the same.

Lookouts became widespread in postal buildings by the 1890s, when the Post Office Department instituted efficiency efforts that continued well into the twentieth century. Postmaster General William F. Vilas (1885–1888) was

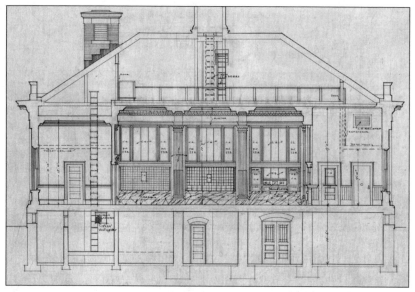

Fig. 2.9. Longitudinal section of post office in Milford, Delaware, 1908 (Drawing #6). The route that inspectors would have to take to access the lookouts (note the lookout register above the vault on the right-hand side of the drawing) would have involved climbing a series of ladders between the basement and the attic. From Milford, Delaware, Post Office Records, National Archives at College Park, Maryland (Cartographic Records).

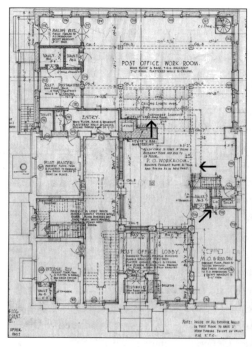

Fig. 2.10. First-floor plan of remodeled post office and courthouse in Danville, Virginia, ca. 1909 (Drawing #102). The L-shaped lookout in this post office represents an unusual combination turret-/suspended-type gallery. From Danville, Virginia, Post Office Records, National Archives at College Park, Maryland (Cartographic Records).

instrumental in bringing modern business principles to the running of the department and laying a path continued by his successors. Vilas was a lawyer by training, but among his clients in his Wisconsin-based practice were lumber companies in northern Wisconsin and the Chicago and Western Railroad. Working with these clients and serving on the board of directors of other companies, Vilas gleaned knowledge of modern business practices, which he brought to the department during his tenure as postmaster general.[25] In 1887 Vilas laid out a plan for reorganizing post offices along more efficient lines. Based on the findings of a commission he appointed to study the department's efficiency, Vilas's plan involved grading and grouping post offices, setting work standards and compensation rates for employees, and working with architects in the Treasury Department to develop standardized plans for post offices. Vilas lamented that post offices often shared space in federal buildings with other government entities, such as customs houses and courthouses. Even in freestanding post offices, Vilas contended that architects in the Treasury Department rarely if ever made an effort to design spaces around postal needs.[26] He deemed this unacceptable, believing that the design of postal quarters bore directly on efficiency. Vilas argued that well-organized facilities had potential to improve the morale of workers and provide control over their behavior:

> The conviction has become strong in my mind, from the observation and experience enjoyed in this place, that the Government should build its postoffices separately and solely for postal uses; that they should be constructed wholly by this [Post Office] Department, and with requisite precautions of law to secure economy, suitability, and harmony of design. . . .
>   . . . With the aid of the Supervising Architect of the Treasury, or otherwise, and subject to proper approval, a design for a post-office should be so devised that, with modification in size only, similar buildings may be built in different cities without limit of number.[27]

Appropriations increased for the construction of post offices during and after Vilas's tenure. Although a single template design was not developed, post office architecture became increasingly standardized.

During his tenure as postmaster general between 1889 and 1893, John Wanamaker continued Vilas's efforts to professionalize operations of the department, instituting countless measures to "make the mails go faster, more safely, and more frequently."[28] The founder and president of Wanamakers of Philadelphia, which he opened in 1876, Wanamaker pioneered the concept of the modern department store. Wanamaker brought his experiences in business to his tenure as postmaster general, trying to adopt modern business principles involving transportation, sales, and marketing to postal needs. Wanamaker viewed business as a science. He studied various methods in use, weighing what they could mean for the department:

> Many of the newer and more useful discoveries in applied science might be utilized and fashioned into a quicker and more satisfactory service than the present agencies, which are now plainly proving themselves too slow. He [the Postmaster General] would secure transit for mail on faster schedules; provide quicker collections and distributions in cities and towns by pneumatic tubes or other improved and more rapid couriers than now exist; push forward American mails as the forerunner of extension of American commerce; lift the entire service into a larger usefulness for the people and a larger increase for itself.[29]

Just as he had brought innovations into the acquisition, marketing, and sales of goods in his department stores, Wanamaker incorporated varied and wide-ranging reforms into the daily workings of the postal service. Measures he instituted included rural free delivery, carrying mail by pneumatic tubes in urban areas, the use of mailboxes, grading of post offices and clerks, and a dramatic increase in the size and scope of the inspection force in post offices.[30]

Wanamaker also aspired to reform postal facilities, recognizing that well-designed spaces might help to control and regulate the mail service. He agreed with Vilas that lavish expenditures on large federal buildings were wasteful, advocating instead structures constructed solely for postal purposes.[31] Critical of post offices that sported "towers and turrets," Wanamaker recommended the construction of simpler buildings in accord with American ideals of "utility and taste." Motivated in part by his frustrations over a new eight-story federal building then under construction in Washington, DC, Wanamaker proposed that all new post offices be constructed as free-standing, one-story buildings. He felt this would secure "abundant light from the roof and good air" which had potential to "quicken every movement of the mails." If a post office had to share a building with other federal offices, Wanamaker insisted that these offices occupy upper floors while the post office would be housed on the ground story. He argued that visual supervision would be enhanced by keeping postal functions on a single floor.[32] Like Vilas, Wanamaker viewed buildings as more than mere containers for production. For both men the buildings themselves bore directly on efficiency and, if they were designed properly, could provide better control over postal workers and operations. In his previous experience in retail sales, Wanamaker expressed an interest in building design for its value in a productive context. Wanamaker's interest in design, largely as a means of advertising, but also for supervision, extended throughout his life and his continued leadership of his department stores.[33]

To improve efficiency of the postal service, Wanamaker lobbied for increased supervision of workers, partly by increasing the size and scope of the Inspection Service. Although the department occasionally had hired personnel to investigate mail depredations prior to the Civil War, a formal collection of special agents was appointed for the first time in the late 1870s.[34] The agents' main charge was to reduce mail theft by ferreting out thieving employees. But as Postmaster General David M. Key (1877–1880) explained in 1878, their duties included "investigating irregularities, securing safety to the mails, and increasing the efficiency of all branches of the postal service."[35] From a modest fifty-four in 1879, the number of inspectors grew to more than one hundred by the early 1890s and continued to increase through World War I.[36] Wanamaker played an instrumental role in this expansion. Fretting that the few times the department came in contact with the more than fifty-nine thousand post offices scattered throughout the country were related to some kind of complaint, he asked that inspectors regularly visit all post offices to measure efficiency. Wanamaker redefined and expanded inspectors' responsibilities beyond mail depredations. Besides being "thief catchers," they were in charge of supervising and instructing employees about proper and efficient methods.[37] After Wanamaker's tenure inspectors increasingly worked in this supervisory capacity.

Wanamaker's desire for close supervision derived from his business background. He believed that daily rounds of his business improved morale and stimulated his thinking about improvements he could make. According to his biographer, Wanamaker's presence reverberated throughout his stores; there workers felt constantly "under the eye of the taskmaster."[38] An anecdote from this biography reveals Wanamaker's dependence on visual supervision as part of his management approach:

> Wanamaker took a distinguished visitor to one of these conferences [staff meetings]. When they returned to the private office, the visitor asked: "How do you do it? You covered so many things, and your criticisms were all about to-day's conditions and to-morrow's problems. You must have wonderfully able scouts."
>
> "Here are my scouts," answered Wanamaker, putting two fingers over his eyes, "and here are their able aids," pointing to his feet. "I do have people shopping in the other stores, of course, all the time, but I depend upon myself for my knowledge of my own stores. Do you suppose I sit at this desk all day long? No, I am out on the floor."[39]

His biographer explained that Wanamaker believed in being out on the floor to supervise—but this was harder to do once he assumed his role as Postmaster General. Recognizing that the size of the Post Office Department prevented him from personally overseeing all post offices, Wanamaker appointed inspectors to serve as his proxies. Based on inspectors' observations, reforms were instituted that included adopting new methods of paperwork, changing personnel schedules and salaries, and establishing other measures relating to the speed and accuracy of mail operations.

Postmaster General W. S. Bissell (1893–1895), Wanamaker's successor, also believed that close supervision enhanced efficiency, but he sought to go beyond Wanamaker in extending the supervisory capacity of the department. He and his staff called for more frequent inspections of post offices in order to learn about the "practical workings of the service."[40] The department's continued preoccupation with supervision and efficiency is evident in the implementation of a program during Bissell's tenure that sought to weed out dishonest, inefficient letter carriers. Under the spotter system, the department hired special agents, or spotters, to follow carriers on their routes, partly to ascertain their speed and accuracy.[41] Spotters' reports served as the basis of evaluation for carriers' continued employment and also contained critical information about mail routes and post offices. Commenting on the program prior to its dissolution in 1896, the first assistant postmaster general defended it by arguing that spotters collected information that could not be gathered any other way: "The improved efficiency of the service in the offices investigated must be credited to [the spotter system]. At every office the discipline of the force and efficiency of the service have been much improved, the work more equally distributed among the letter carriers, and at many offices extensions made and facilities increased without additional cost."[42] Through the spotter system, the department linked surveillance with their broader efficiency program. On the basis of spotters' reports, the department fired and promoted carriers, redrew postal routes, and remodeled and built post offices, all of which officials claimed improved the postal service's efficiency.

After the Post Office Department abandoned the spotter system, inspectors assumed many of the spotters' duties (though in a much less stealthy manner). As part of their annual inspections of post offices during the early twentieth century, inspectors attempted to determine the best business methods in use. On being appointed postmaster general, Albert Burleson (1913–1921) ordered an extensive series of inspections, during which inspectors assessed the interior arrangement of post offices to determine their efficiency. Burleson felt inspectors had unique skills: "[Inspectors are] experts in postal affairs and thoroughly familiar with the requirements of post offices . . . their services could be utilized advantageously both in the selection of sites and in the interior arrangement and equipment of post offices."[43] After studying operations of a series of post offices, inspectors forwarded recommendations and criticisms to the department, who implemented changes through revising policy or, if necessary, by working in conjunction with Treasury Department architects to make any necessary design modifications.[44] With his obsession for standardization and efficiency, Burleson carried the idea of close supervision further than Vilas, Wanamaker, or Bissell had envisioned, expanding inspectors' duties to make them postal experts, an unofficial title they bore through the mid–twentieth century.[45]

Lookouts aided inspectors in their newfound role as arbiters of efficiency. Case files of inspections by the Philadelphia Division of the Inspection Service between 1896 and 1909 show the varied uses to which inspectors put lookouts. Investigations at the main post office in Philadelphia in the last decade of the nineteenth century reveal how inspectors used lookouts to discover thieving mail clerks. On 12 July 1897, Inspector Holden apprehended a letter carrier, George Kelly, for stealing mail matter: "At the hour mentioned, Kelly was seen by me from my position in the 'lookout' over-head, to approach this table, and after seating himself, slyly take a handful of letters from one of the pigeon-holes and place them in his outside coat pocket."[46] With the help of the assistant superintendent at the post office, who was assisting him in the lookout, Holden arrested Kelly, who was tried, found guilty, and sent to Eastern State Penitentiary to serve a one-year sentence for larceny. Two years later Holden arrested a second clerk at the Philadelphia office, based on his observations from the lookout, a clerk he described as particularly sneaky. Holden justified the utility of lookouts in this case file, arguing that they provided a means to catch thieves that were so sly that their actions escaped everyone's notice.[47] In a separate investigation a few years later, Holden expressed frustration about large amounts of missing mail at the post office branch in West Philadelphia (Station B). Holden worked at Station B for months before catching the culprit, which he felt took so long because he had to rely on mailing test letters alone: "The detection of Honesdale took months of patient, painstaking work that might have been done in weeks or days, had this station been provided with a suitable lookout from which might have been observed the sections of clerks and carriers employed therein. . . . I know of no place where the work [depredation investigations] has been so difficult or taken so much time."[48] Holden urged the chief inspector to see to the construction of a lookout at Station B. Despite the arrest of Honesdale, continuing reports of missing mail meant that Holden had to spend more time at the post office in the coming months.

Although inspectors such as Holden as well as postal bureaucrats supported construction of lookouts to catch depredators, they valued lookouts for a variety of reasons beyond this. The department believed that the visual prominence of lookouts helped assure worker compliance with efficiency standards.

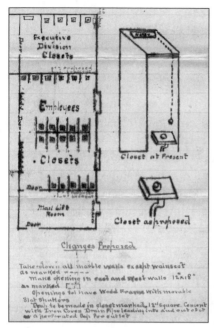

Fig. 2.11. Detail of Inspector Warren Edgarton's recommendations on changes to the basement lavatories at the post office and courthouse in Pittsburgh, 1892. Sketch appended to letter from Edgarton to the Chief Postal Inspector, March 22, 1892, Pittsburgh, Pennsylvania, Records of the Public Buildings Service, National Archives at College Park, Maryland (Textual Records).

Inspector Warren P. Edgarton, a senior inspector with the Philadelphia Division of the Inspection Service, urged the construction of a lookout that would provide observation of the restrooms and locker rooms in the post office in Pittsburgh as a preventative measure. Edgarton pleaded with the chief inspector in 1892 to construct a suitable lookout in the basement of the Pittsburgh office specifically to prevent "the plundering and destruction of the people's mail." In addition to recommending the lookout, Edgarton also requested that the marble walls around the toilets be removed so as to make clerks' actions more easily detectable (fig. 2.11).[49] For Edgarton part of the value of lookouts lay in the deterrent potential. Through their conspicuous placement, they expressed the omnipresent gaze of the inspectors to postal workers.[50] Like built-in surveillance in prisons, lookouts took on symbolic significance as indications of managerial authority even if actual use of them was only intermittent.

In contrast to facilities for inspection in prisons, however, lookouts also provided their users with concrete data that the Post Office Department relied on to help improve efficiency at individual post offices and in the postal service more broadly. Case files suggest how essential inspectors' observations from lookouts were, serving as a chief means by which reforms instituted in the name of efficiency were made. In May of 1892 Inspector Edgarton visited the post office in Paterson, New Jersey, in response to the postmaster's request to hire additional personnel. Edgarton surveyed the clerks in stealth from 6:30 A.M. to

8:30 P.M. He concluded that despite the diligence and enthusiasm of the clerks there, they were overworked. Edgarton recommended that more clerks be hired immediately.[51] A similar watch was conducted in 1901 at the post office in Allegheny, Pennsylvania, where inspectors conducted an extensive investigation, a good part of which was done from a lookout. Based on their watch, they rearranged the duties of clerks, assigned some to other areas, and reorganized the flow of work.[52] These cases and others suggest ways in which lookouts helped inspectors observe personnel and operations, resulting in changes that affected post office workspaces and the workers laboring within them.

Lookouts helped inspectors assess the interior design and arrangement of post offices as well. During his inspection of the Pittsburgh Post Office in 1892, Inspector Edgarton made recommendations about the lookout in the main workroom, a turret-type lookout, from which he conducted his investigation. Located toward the back of the room, Edgarton appreciated its visual prominence for its deterrent effect but lamented that its placement prevented the flow of mail between sorting stations. In his report, he suggested tearing the tower obstruction down and erecting a more efficient hanging gallery lookout in its place, which would have radically changed the interior arrangement of the post office (fig. 2.12).[53] While the department rejected Edgarton's design suggestions, they took his concerns seriously, seeing to the erection of a hanging-type gallery in the Pittsburgh Post Office a few years later. This inspection and others

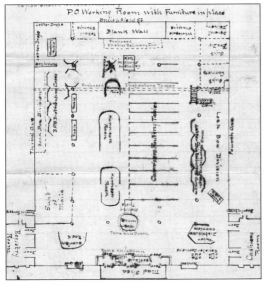

Fig. 2.12. Inspector Warren Edgarton's proposed changes to the working room at the post office and courthouse in Pittsburgh, 1892. He proposed to tear down the older tower-type lookout, erecting in its place a suspended-type lookout gallery. Sketch appended to letter from Edgarton to the Chief Postal Inspector, March 22, 1892, Pittsburgh, Pennsylvania, Records of the Public Buildings Service, National Archives at College Park, Maryland (Textual Records).

show the pivotal role that inspectors and the lookouts played in affecting working conditions in post offices as well as their physical layout.

Postal lookouts represent an exceptional case study in the sense that such elaborate forms of surveillance, by means of lookouts and inspection forces, were not possible or even appropriate in most work settings of the period. The scale of the postal service, its coordination of thousands of branch offices, and the administration which the size of operations necessitated made standardization and close supervision a means by which the department attempted to support and sustain this complex bureaucracy. But visual supervision facilitated through architecture was not limited to post offices or large bureaucratic organizations. Owners and managers of other kinds of workspaces incorporated less complete, but no less pervasive, forms of surveillance into buildings during this time that they hoped would help increase efficiency.

Surveillance in the Landscape of Work

Scholars have lately enhanced understanding of industrial history of the Victorian period in the United States by looking at the layout and design of factory buildings. Their work has shown that design of buildings was part and parcel of the efficiency movement in this context, not simply a byproduct of it.[54] While these scholars have acknowledged that surveillance concerns were tied to the design of workspaces in this period, a more in-depth look at how spaces for supervision were built into factories is necessary to better understanding of surveillance in a context of efficiency. Plans and historic photographs of late-nineteenth- and early-twentieth-century industrial workspaces in archival records and prescriptive literature reveal myriad ways that buildings were designed to allow managers to watch workers. The particular form surveillance took in work settings depended on a variety of factors, including the size of the space to be supervised, the business strategy of the owner(s)/manager(s), and the kind of work in question.

Locating the offices or desks of owners, foremen, and supervisors on raised platforms above the workroom floor represented one popular strategy for visual surveillance. In textile mills supervisors in charge of getting the work done as efficiently as possible watched workers from their physical positions on elevated platforms. Although the origin of raised platforms in textile mills is unclear, one mill superintendent, describing the practice in 1879, suggested that raised platforms had become common by the mid–nineteenth century.[55] A later example of this arrangement appeared in the first- and second-floor plans of an ideal mill illustrated in a prescriptive manual for engineers from 1906 (figs. 2.13 and 2.14).[56] This ten thousand–spindle cotton mill contained a main, rectangular

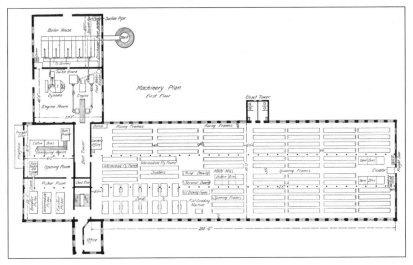

Fig. 2.13. First-floor plan of a two-story cotton mill, ca. 1900, showing overseer's office as an elevated space at one end of the workroom. From *Yarns, Cloth Rooms, Mill Engineering, Reeling and Baling, Winding*, International Library of Technology, vol. 78 (Scranton, PA: International Textbook Co., 1921), 26.

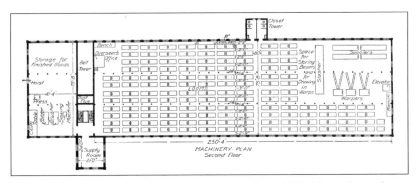

Fig. 2.14. Second-floor plan of a two-story cotton mill, ca. 1900. The workroom layout echoes that of the first-floor plan, including the placement of the overseer's office at one end. From *Yarns, Cloth Rooms, Mill Engineering, Reeling and Baling, Winding*, International Library of Technology, vol. 78 (Scranton, PA: International Textbook Co., 1921), 27.

work area measuring roughly 250 feet long and 75 feet wide. On each floor an overseer's office stood at one end of the room, elevated slightly above the workroom floor as the steps providing access to it suggest. From the overseer's vantage point, he would have commanded a view of the workspace as well as the main entrance, which implied that he could also monitor workers' comings and goings. The raised platform proved to be a workable solution in small

Fig. 2.15. Raised superintendent's platform at the C. A. Dunham Co. metalworks, Canada, ca. 1915. From "Piloting a Shop from the 'Bridge,'" *Factory* 14 (Apr. 1915): 244.

factories as well as office settings.[57] The layout of a Canadian metalworks that made use of a raised platform for supervision drew praise from writers of *Factory* magazine in 1915 (fig. 2.15). The article described how the superintendent of the C. A. Dunham plant was able to oversee the main floor of his works and the storage space on the gallery above him from his desk, which was located on a platform occupying a mezzanine level (fig. 2.16).[58] By the end of the Victorian period, the elevated office option had become so pervasive in industrial architecture that a trade catalog published by Austin Standard Factory Buildings Company in 1919 showed one of its designs, the Austin no. 2 standard, having a raised platform at one end of the building (fig. 2.17).[59]

A more common, if less ambitious, surveillance strategy involved partitioning off offices for supervisors at eye level. Although views from these spaces may not have been as comprehensive as from elevated platforms, these built-in supervisory features cost much less to construct. They gave owners and managers some ability to monitor the work area while also serving as a reminder to workers of the ubiquitous presence (and importance) of management. This solution also proved attractive in that multiple offices could be enclosed in different areas of the workspace, which provided more pervasive views than a single raised platform would have done. Although partitioned offices pervaded all kinds of workspaces during the Victorian period, such areas were especially common in large textile mills as well as machine shops and metalworks, as fire insurance plans of the Ernest Hexamer and Sons Company from the late nineteenth century suggest.[60] An 1889 survey's floor plan of the Powhatan Mills located near

Fig. 2.16. View from raised superintendent's platform at the C. A. Dunham Co. metalworks, Canada, ca. 1915. From "Piloting a Shop from the 'Bridge,'" *Factory* 14 (Apr. 1915): 244.

Fig. 2.17. Interior of "Austin No. 2 Standard" factory building, showing the elevated supervisory area at the far end. From *Austin Standard Factory-Buildings* (Cleveland, OH: The Austin Company), 1919. Courtesy of Hagley Museum and Library.

Baltimore, Maryland, shows a typical configuration of a factory that incorporated partitioned offices to aid visual supervision (fig. 2.18).[61] In this mill originally built in 1809, an addition made during the last quarter of the nineteenth century accommodated supervisors' offices on each of the four floors. Windows punched in the walls of the older section of the mill offered supervisors views of the spinning, weaving, and carding rooms from their offices.

Although the partitioned office represented a pervasive option for visual surveillance in the manufacturing landscape, the placement of these offices varied. Location of offices often involved factors other than visual supervision, such as fire prevention, the nature of the work in question, the desire to segregate

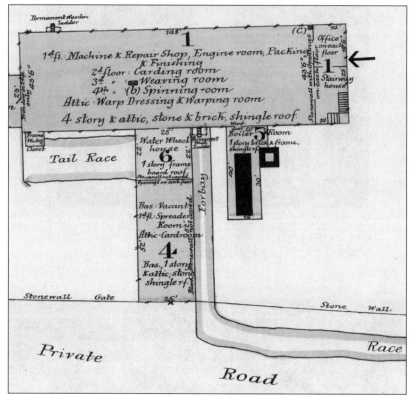

Fig. 2.18. First-floor plan of the Powhatan Cotton Mill owned by Powhatan Manufacturing Company, Powhatan, 2nd District, Baltimore County, Maryland. Note the supervisors' offices located on each floor of the machine shop in this plan (as indicated by arrow). Openings in the partition walls between the offices and the shops enabled managers and foremen to visually supervise employees on the workroom floor. From *Hexamer General Surveys,* vol. 23 (Philadelphia: E. Hexamer and Sons, 1889), plate 2235. Courtesy of the Map Collection, Free Library of Philadelphia.

particular work functions, and convenient access for visitors.[62] It also depended on the size of the supervisory force and whether administrators and clerical personnel shared space in offices with foremen and line supervisors or if they occupied offices removed from the factory floor. But the extent of desired supervision also played a significant role in the location of these offices. In most cases offices stood in the part of the workroom that offered the most comprehensive view of the workspace and were visible to the most workers: the corner. At Powhatan Mills the corner location of the supervisors' offices provided expansive views of workspaces as well as the stairs, which would have allowed supervisors to see workers entering, leaving, and moving through the workspace.[63]

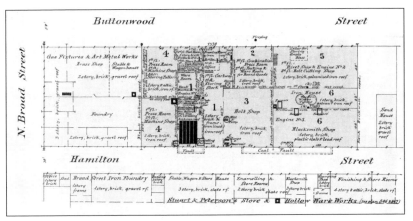

Fig. 2.19. Ground plan of Hoopes and Townsend's Bolt, Nut, and Rivet Works, Philadelphia, Pennsylvania (1883). Note the absence of supervisors' offices within the body of the plant. From *Hexamer General Surveys*, vol. 19 (Philadelphia: E. Hexamer and Sons, 1884), plates 1756–57. Courtesy of the Map Collection, Free Library of Philadelphia.

Large manufacturing operations adopted partitioned supervisory offices as a surveillance measure frequently, since these offices could be built throughout work areas with relative ease and minimal expense. Many factories grew in a piecemeal fashion during the second half of the nineteenth century, evolving from small shops into huge complexes employing hundreds of people. In most cases owners did not have the luxury or capital to build a large structure from scratch—and thus they added mechanisms for visual supervision over time. An example of this may be seen in the development of the Hoopes and Townsend Bolt, Nut, and Rivet Works in Philadelphia. When E. Hexamer and Sons surveyed the plant for fire insurance purposes in 1883, the company employed 525 people who worked in a series of shops spread out along North Broad Street (fig. 2.19). In 1883 the only office space in the company occupied a section of building no. 1. There were no other obvious spaces for supervision elsewhere in the complex. Significant changes were evident by the time of another Hexamer survey in 1894 (fig. 2.20). By this date the company employed more than 900 workers and had built additional workshops to the south of the original complex. The site plan showed foremen's offices located in most of the new one-story shops as well as added into older shops. As the works grew, so did the need for order and supervision. Partitioned supervisory spaces helped the company try to meet this need.[64]

Another way in which architecture facilitated surveillance related to the growth of open workspace layouts. Enclosing all or most of the work area in

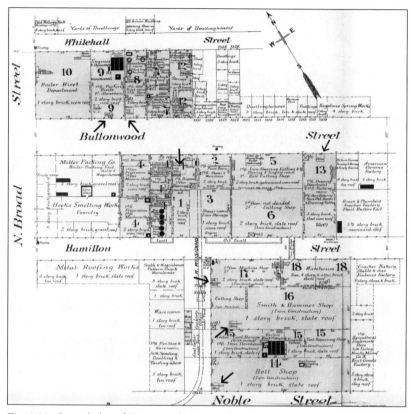

Fig. 2.20. Ground plan of Hoopes and Townsend's Bolt, Nut, and Rivet Works, Philadelphia, Pennsylvania (1894). Note the proliferation of supervisors' offices throughout the works. From *Hexamer General Surveys,* vol. 29 (Philadelphia: E. Hexamer and Sons, 1895), plates 2796–97. Courtesy of the Map Collection, Free Library of Philadelphia.

a large, unpartitioned workroom became a popular option in all kinds of industrial and white-collar workspaces during the late nineteenth and early twentieth centuries.[65] Open workrooms were not new. As early as the late eighteenth century, owners had designed textile mills in New England free of spatial divisions for accommodating equipment and large numbers of workers. In the late nineteenth and early twentieth centuries, all kinds of workspaces were built using open workrooms, as builders utilized advances in building technology and materials to enclose larger open spaces and accommodate a growing workforce. Large, unobstructed workrooms proved useful because of their adaptability to changes in work flow, but business owners and managers also appreciated that these arrangements allowed for unobstructed views of workspaces. One industrial engineer went so far as to extol the open workroom arrangement strictly for its surveillance potential.[66] Open workrooms also induced in workers a sense that their actions were perpetually subject to management, very much like the open shop layout of the workshops at congregate prisons such as Auburn. The use of glazed partitions to divide spaces also related to surveillance. Although entrepreneurs and managers appreciated glazed partitions for multiple reasons, including the fact they allowed light to penetrate the interiors of workspaces, such partitions also permitted managers to more readily supervise their employees.

Machine shops, which by their nature required large spaces for assembly, represented one industrial venue in which open workrooms became standard by the early twentieth century. The Essington, Pennsylvania, plant of the Westinghouse Electric Corporation erected many of its multiple shops as open workrooms. A photograph of the no. 1 machine shop during its construction in 1918 revealed that a large expanse of uninterrupted space characterized the interior (fig. 2.21).[67] In this machine shop, used for the assembly of turbines,

Fig. 2.21. Interior view of no. 1 machine shop, Essington, Pennsylvania, plant of Westinghouse Company, near Philadelphia, Pennsylvania, ca. 1918, showing the large expanse of open space that helped facilitate surveillance. This view was likely taken from a traveling crane that carried materials from one part of the space to another. From Westinghouse Electric Corp., Photographic Collection, photograph #12743. Courtesy of Hagley Museum and Library.

Fig. 2.22. View of operators at work at the blade shop at the Essington, Pennsylvania, plant of the Westinghouse Company near Philadelphia, Pennsylvania (undated), showing how the open workroom arrangement helped facilitate surveillance of workers at stations located throughout the plant. From Westinghouse Electric Corp., Photographic Collection, photograph #28791. Courtesy of Hagley Museum and Library.

surveillance in the form of elevated platforms or corner offices would have proven rather limited, giving supervisors views of single machines and perhaps a worker or two out of the many that worked in the large shop. Instead the open character of the work area facilitated the gazes of managers as they walked through the shop. The orderly arrangement and distribution of machines and workers within these open workspaces also aided supervision. In the blade shop at the Westinghouse plant, the different departments were organized around batches of machines neatly arranged in rows.[68] Managers would have appreciated the benefits of this arrangement in terms of visual supervision, since foremen could gaze down endless rows of workstations and notice if anything (or anyone) was out of place. This was not lost on workers, who realized misbehavior would be easily ascertained (fig. 2.22).

Owners and managers of white-collar workplaces also lauded the surveillance potential of the open workroom layout during the early twentieth century. Echoing texts by industrial engineers, a burgeoning literature on office management during the first two decades of the twentieth century explored the possibilities of open office planning. Surveillance was among the reasons office planners extolled this arrangement. A photograph of stenographers at

Fig. 2.23. View of stenographers at work at National Cash Register Company in Dayton, Ohio, ca. 1907, under the supervision of their supervisor in the foreground. From "The Battlefields of Business," *System: The Magazine of Business* 12 (July 1907): 53. Courtesy of Business, Science and Industry Department, Free Library of Philadelphia.

the National Cash Register Company from *System* magazine in 1907 depicts them sitting side by side in neat rows facing their supervisor, who watched them from her desk at the front of the room (fig. 2.23).[69] Although placing the supervisor's desk at the head of the room was generally accepted, advice writers debated the orientation of the employees under the gaze. Angel Kwolek-Folland described how the manager at Greenfield Tap and Die Corporation in the early twentieth century believed that efficiency of the company's typing department improved by 20 percent once he turned the desks of the typists away from the supervisor. The manager liked the scheme because it prevented the typists being able to ascertain when they were under watch, leading them to assume that surveillance was always present. This shows the pervasiveness of Bentham's thinking about the potential of continuous but anonymous surveillance over a century later.[70]

Entrepreneurs often used these various forms of architectural surveillance concurrently. One example appeared in a 1905 advertisement for the Columbia Phonograph Co. showing a portion of Sears offices (fig. 2.24). Although the open configuration of the room and the orderly rows of desks aided supervision, the manager's position on a raised platform enabled him to have a view

Fig. 2.24. Advertisement for Columbia Phonograph Co., showing supervisor's position relative to his employees. From *System* 8 (Oct. 1905), n.p. Courtesy of Business, Science and Industry Department, Free Library of Philadelphia.

of all of the workers under his charge.[71] Each company's particular solution was but one manifestation of a shared concern among employers and their management proxies: how to get more work out of workers to satisfy an ever-expanding market and best their competition.

Surveillance and Efficiency

As Lindy Biggs has shown, American entrepreneurs during the late nineteenth and early twentieth centuries realized the important place that workplace design held in the manufacturing process. What Biggs termed the "rational factory" was an ideal promulgated by factory owners, managers, and industrial engineers beginning in the late nineteenth century and continuing into the twentieth. Although influential, the rational factory ideal spoke less of conditions in actual factories than of the struggles owners and managers faced as they attempted to come to terms with new social conditions of production that had emerged after the Civil War.[72] Still it is in this context of architects and engineers in a struggle with new conditions of production that we can account for the interest in designing surveillance measures in workplaces during the

Victorian period and beyond. Like new ideas for factory layouts promulgated in trade literature, books, and other printed sources, surveillance efforts in these plans as well as in buildings constructed after them represent telling indicators of entrepreneurs' desire to regulate labor in pursuit of efficiency.

Prescriptive literature on factory design reveals the significance that architects, builders, and their patrons placed on surveillance measures as part of their quest for efficiency. Advice literature on factories proliferated in the early twentieth century, appearing as full-length books devoted to factory management, articles in trade literature, and also in magazines such as *Factory*. Though this literature grew in quantity and influence during the first two decades of the twentieth century, writers began earnestly exploring ways to enhance efficiency through design much earlier. Indeed many of the architectural strategies for visual supervision discussed above were manifest in factories built during the 1870s and 1880s and thus served industrial reform writers as evidence of successful examples. The explosion of prescriptive literature between 1900 and 1920 evinced less a new trend than a codification of reforms that had been ongoing during the second half of the nineteenth century.[73]

Most industrial engineers believed that changes to the design of industrial workspaces could solve problems associated with production inefficiency.[74] In 1917 Moritz Kahn highlighted the place of architecture in production, echoing the views of many of his contemporaries: "It is a primary necessity, in the consideration of any new scheme for a manufacturing plant, to recognize the established fact that the cost of production is materially affected by its general design and layout. . . . There is probably no part of a modern industrial works, machinery and equipment included, towards the improvement of which a little extra care and investment will bring such enhanced returns as the buildings themselves."[75] If a majority of writers on factory design agreed on architecture's importance, they differed in planning the arrangement of workspaces. Some argued that all departments within a company should be housed under one roof whereas others preferred a shop arrangement comprising multiple buildings. Another point of disagreement revolved around whether single-story or multistory buildings were more efficient. Kahn preferred a multistory scheme, in part because it facilitates expansion and "simplifies the general supervision of the work," but he recognized that it depended on the nature of the business in question.[76] Other writers supported construction of one-story buildings, and still others pointed out benefits and drawbacks of each.[77]

Visual supervision was at the forefront of these writers' concerns about single-story or multistory industrial buildings. In his *Treatise on the Design and Construction of Mill Buildings and Other Industrial Plants* of 1911, Henry Grattan Tyrrell explained that many argued for the one-story arrangement because it facilitated surveillance by the foreman and also reminded workers they were perpetually subject to his scrutiny:

> It is claimed by some shop superintendents that when workmen are all on one floor that is unobstructed by partitions, and when they are at all times under the eye of the superintendent or foreman, there is less tendency to loafing and idleness among the employees. It is also claimed by these advocates of one-story buildings that the foreman's office should be so located that every operator on the floor will be directly in view and his presence can at all times be seen from the office.[78]

Tyrrell questioned the degree to which this was true, since the large size of many workspaces made it difficult for foremen to judge if work was being done properly, particularly from a single office. For large workspaces he advocated the construction of multistory buildings in order to reduce the chance of nonsurveillance (or the impression of it), as foremen could more effectively supervise a smaller area on each floor. Another prominent industrial reformer, Hugo Diemer, lauded one-story buildings for accommodating visual supervision. His preference for one-story buildings related to his overall factory design philosophy, which centered on surveillance:

> It is important that as great floor space as possible should be visible at all times. Hence, all angles, "L's," "E's" and "H's" should be avoided in favor of the plain, long, rectangle. The same consideration of visibility and the avoidance of unnecessary walking or elevator riding, argues for the single-floored structure as against multi-floored buildings. Even the single gallery is best avoided, as it forms a more or less isolated area not readily visible, and increases walking and trucking. "Avoidance of unproductive travel" demands a minimum of passage ways, which passages should always be under the close supervision of watchmen who must note all wandering clerks and workmen, and who must be so informed as to the employees and their duties, that they may be able to observe and report illegitimate or aimless wandering.[79]

For Diemer the layout of factory workspaces bore directly on efficiency. He supported the use of the one-story, open workroom, since it permitted all workers to be kept under watch and conveyed that impression to them. Diemer believed that offices and other kinds of partitioned spaces should be kept to a minimum, confined to areas where gases, smoke, and noise required segregation.[80] Diemer also paid attention to service areas, such as locker rooms, washrooms, and water closets. He wanted these spaces to be constantly under the gaze in order to keep workers from loitering in these areas and in passageways, stairs, and elevators leading to and from them.[81]

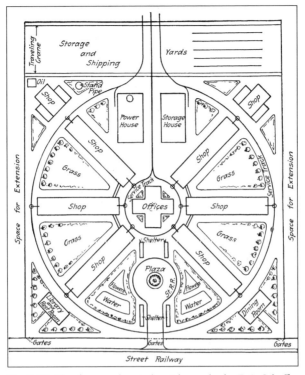

Fig. 2.25. Plan for a modern industrial complex by F. A. Scheffer. The plan is laid out radially, the benefits of which are explained by Henry Grattan Tyrrell largely in terms of the efficiency of the centrally located offices. From Tyrrell, *A Treatise on the Design and Construction of Mill Buildings and Other Industrial Plants* (Chicago: Myron C. Clark Publishing Co., 1911), 3.

Though less comprehensively than Diemer, many industrial engineers explored ways that space in factories could be organized around surveillance. Herbert Simpson pondered various locations for foremen's desks and offices in relation to the area they supervised, examining advantages and disadvantages of locating offices in the main workroom, on raised platforms, or in separate buildings.[82] J. Slater Lewis, a mill engineer, advocated raised platforms.[83] Oscar Perrigo was less specific about the placement of the foreman's office, stressing only that it needed to be prominently located.[84] F. A. Scheffer offered another solution for an industrial complex in Pennsylvania (fig. 2.25). In addition to having foremen's offices located in individual shops, he planned the buildings in a radial layout. The main office occupied the space at the center, a deliberate move that ensured that management could keep "in close touch" with the various shops. As noted previously, Scheffer's design recalled that of Victorian

American prisons, suggesting a degree of exchange and influence between building plans in two different contexts for quite different purposes.[85]

Reformers also recommended more subtle means of surveillance in factory designs. Edward Stradley appreciated the plan of one industrial complex because of the way it controlled pedestrian traffic. He praised the provision for a single entrance, which allowed managers stationed at the gate to monitor workers' movements in and out of the factory. Further, Stradley extolled the designers of the complex for organizing its departments around a centralized supply room in order to minimize movement through the factory, and this kept workmen constantly under the eye of the foreman in charge of their department.[86] The placement of service areas, especially toilets, in relation to the main workspace also received extensive attention in prescriptive literature on factory design. Henry Hess warned readers of the danger of placing service areas in out-of-the-way dark spaces, seeing this as an invitation for workers to "loaf and smoke."[87] Sanitary engineers also weighed in on this debate. The D. A. Ebinger Sanitary Manufacturing Company advocated placing toilets on a raised platform above the workroom floor (fig. 2.26). Such a plan allowed management to monitor

Fig. 2.26. Advertisement for the D. A. Ebinger Sanitary Mfg. Company, Columbus, Ohio. This ad suggests an inversion of sorts, with the employees' toilets on the raised platform (rather than the supervisor). From *Factory* 14 (January 1915): 40.

this space, a curious reversal of the usual relationship where management occupied an elevated position.[88] The Standard Sanitary Manufacturing Company advertised open arrangements for lavatories and washrooms, in part because it facilitated hygiene but also because such arrangements prevented workers from lingering in stalls and around sinks (figs. 2.27 and 2.28).[89] Illustrations from a 1913 trade catalog showed toilet stalls without doors and sinks clustered about at the center of the room, both of which would have inhibited any sense of privacy for workers. Lighting of the manufacturing plant also related to surveillance, for as Arthur Anderson explained, artificial lighting provided for "easier supervision of the men."[90]

Toward the end of the Victorian period, entrepreneurs and planners of white-collar settings began to take up ideas explored in the manufacturing sector, considering how office planning might aid efficiency. Many industrial engineers considered the arrangement of white-collar areas of factories, giving office reformers some precedents to follow. An author of a 1919 manual on office management recommended an open office plan, where clerks, managers, and the president worked together in one room. If this was impossible, the writer argued that supervision should still be provided: "Whoever else must be allowed private offices, the office manager himself should generally

Fig. 2.27. View of modern sinks, without walls dividing them to facilitate ease of supervision and prevent loitering. From *Factory Sanitation* (Pittsburgh: Standard Sanitary Manufacturing Co., 1913), xx. Courtesy of the University of Michigan Library.

Fig. 2.28. View of modern restroom stalls, showing them without doors—which facilitated supervision and prevented loitering during breaks. From *Factory Sanitation* (Pittsburgh: Standard Sanitary Manufacturing Co., 1913), xii. Courtesy of the University of Michigan Library.

be out in the open, located where he can exercise general supervision of those who are under him. It is, of course, possible to achieve the same object in an office set off by clear glass partitions which shut out noise without shutting off vision."[91] The writer of this manual also insisted on using flat desks as opposed to the more traditional high-backed roll-top ones. These modern desks forced clerks to keep their work areas neater, since there were no pigeonholes in which to hide work materials. Further, their low height permitted a supervisor "an unobstructed view of the men under his supervision."[92]

Most reformers contended that efforts toward integrating surveillance into the landscape of work extended management's control over labor, which they insisted was necessary given the large size of many late-nineteenth- and early-twentieth-century workplaces. Some reformers claimed that better means of visual supervision benefited workers by enhancing camaraderie between them and management. Such arguments represented a defensive strategy and can be explained as a preemptive response aimed at forestalling worker resistance to such efforts. A 1904 article on the Armour and Company meatpacking firm illustrates this. The author discusses how the president, Philip Armour, ran his administrative offices from an elevated platform over the workroom. The article maintains that Armour's employees—all ten thousand of them—believed the owner to be fair and just, and thus they worked harder than they otherwise would have if the owner was not watching them.[93]

Desire on the part of owners and managers for increased provisions for supervision—architectural and otherwise—stemmed from a pervasive anxiety about labor. Prescriptive literature on factory design abounded with complaints that workers would loaf without supervision if given the opportunity. J. Slater Lewis wrote that unless managers made themselves visible first thing in the morning, workers would linger in the locker room: "It is really astonishing what a length of time it takes a man to pull off his coat and get to work when it is known that the Foreman is not about!"[94] This kind of dawdling related to one of management's chief concerns of the late nineteenth and early twentieth centuries, known as "soldiering," in which workers gave the impression of working diligently even when they were not. Concerns about soldiering informed Frederick Winslow Taylor's philosophy of scientific management, which he developed through working as an industrial engineer in the 1890s and early 1900s. Taylor suggested that there were two kinds of soldiering. The first involved what he claimed was an inherent inclination of workers to slow down when they see others slacking off. The second, what Taylor called systematic soldiering, was a deliberate and organized form of resistance, done out of an effort for what workers thought was the preservation of their interests.[95] Taylor's and the others' distrust of workers stemming from this profoundly negative attitude led to extensive use of architectural forms of surveillance that they hoped would prevent and solve such problems.

Distrust of labor and a desire for control on the part of entrepreneurs were certainly not new to this period. Architectural provisions for supervision had been in place in large work settings, such as textile mills, since at least the early nineteenth century.[96] Yet large textile mill complexes (and large workplaces in general) were an anomaly in the American landscape of work during the antebellum era.[97] The physical size of mills as well as their level of output, number of employees, and extensive use of mechanized equipment distinguished these workspaces from the majority of work settings outside of the home, which for the most part were small shops employing a few workers.[98] Face-to-face interaction characterized the employer-employee relationship in most workspaces during the eighteenth and first half of the nineteenth centuries. To some extent this reduced management's distrust of their workers. The small size of these businesses allowed the entrepreneurs to believe they could see, and thereby know, everything that was going on.[99] Through constant contact with his employees, an owner retained a sense of command over all aspects of the business, minimizing concerns about their labor force. This system seemed functional for entrepreneurs as long as staff and output remained modest.

During the Victorian period, however, particularly after the Civil War, owners and managers struggled to maintain a sense of control, as workplaces expanded and workforces swelled in the face of a rapidly growing market and increased competition.[100] Typical manufacturing businesses, previously small and craft-based, grew dramatically during the last three decades of the nineteenth century in terms of number of workers and their physical size. Such growth may be attributed partly to the opening of markets by means of more expansive transportation networks, but it also related to changes made in response to increased demand. Although mechanization had occurred in some manufacturing settings earlier in the nineteenth century, machines became widely adopted in all kinds of manufacturing settings after 1850. Mechanization reduced dependence on the craft aspect of labor and decreased the level of skill required to perform a task. New methods of materials handling, such as assembly lines and traveling crane systems, also resulted in the reorganization of many workplaces by subdividing labor and breaking up the shop system, which had previously served as the dominant form of workplace organization. Like mechanization, new working conditions alienated workers from production, as their effort contributed to only a small part of a much-larger process.[101] For the most part, owners and managers welcomed these changes. Such innovations reduced their dependence on skilled workers and increased production levels—but they also created new problems in the domain of management, which entrepreneurs struggled to address.

Workers' efforts to organize themselves into unions compounded the anxiety that many business owners and managers felt about all these changes.[102] Strikes that garnered national attention—such as the Pullman Strike of 1894 by the American Railway Union (ARU)—led businessmen to fear the potential of organized labor movements to challenge their authority and resist their demands for greater efficiency.[103] Similar movements toward union organization occurred in the Post Office Department, which led to anxiety among postal officials. Letter carriers first organized as the National Association of Letter Carriers (NALC) in 1889. Ultimately the NALC challenged the legality of the spotter system in the mid-1890s, and it continued to fight against other measures the workers felt curbed their rights.[104] By the early twentieth century, labor unions in manufacturing and white-collar industries had petitioned for shorter workdays and workweeks, as well as other benefits that led employers increasingly to feel threatened by the power of the workforce. Richard Edwards has suggested that entrepreneurs during the Victorian period experienced a crisis of control in the wake of labor unions and other changes, ultimately resulting in measures designed to combat and minimize the growing power of labor.[105]

Beginning in the 1870s and 1880s and continuing into the next century, owners and managers struggled to combat these and other problems by instituting a variety of new management systems, which business historians have labeled "systematic management."[106] Joseph Litterer coined the term to refer to early practitioners of management engineering who worked in the decades after the civil war. Such systematizers, as Litterer called them, spurred the efforts of better-known engineers that followed, such as Taylor, whose influence mainly held sway during the early twentieth century. According to Litterer, advocates of systematic management examined internal workings of their businesses to find more efficient means of operation, but they lacked the rigor and pursuit of the "one best way" pursued by Taylor and his early-twentieth-century followers.[107] In books, pamphlets, and industry trade journals published between 1875 and 1900, systematizers explored subjects such as personnel policies, delegation of duties, responsibilities of a manager and/or foreman, and management practices and human relations.[108] Despite a diversity of opinions, Litterer argued that late-nineteenth-century reformers all shared a pursuit of controlling the workplace more efficiently.[109] For most the problem centered on lack of system, as John Tregoning suggested in 1891:

> There is no doubt that the subject of Factory Organization has been sadly neglected in past years. . . . The first and foremost want of many of our large factories is not work, but a thorough revision of the machinery that manages and directs the whole concerns. It is not a want of brains, it is not the difficulty of working out a vast and complicated scheme, it is not a matter of involving the company in a large outlay of money,—it is simply a question of *method,* the application of a few simple rules, and a respect for the time-honored principle that Order is the First Law of the Universe, and the nearer our approach to it the more harmonious will our arrangements work.[110]

Tregoning's position echoed that of most systematizers writing before 1900. Although they advised business owners on aspects of management and production control, none offered a comprehensive approach. Instead they urged owners and managers to think about how they could be more efficient and institute more systematic procedures.

After 1900 reformers presented more comprehensive approaches to management, first in publications on factories and later in tracts addressing other business settings. The first two decades of the twentieth century saw an explosion of prescriptive literature on business management, representing a culmination of efforts that ran throughout the Victorian period. Writers continued to publish in trade journals, but they also wrote lengthy books and contributed to management journals such as *System* and *Factory,* which had been founded in 1900 and 1907, respectively, to provide a forum for this kind of discourse. Like their systematizing predecessors, early-twentieth-century reformers generated a plethora of ideas to ensure worker output and combat any potential problems. Many advocated visual supervision, facilitated through the design of buildings, as a strategy. The prominent role of surveillance in management discourse may seem to contradict recent interpretations of the period that have examined the waning of power among foremen during this time. Some historians have argued that foremen lost power in the era of scientific management to personnel departments, who took on duties such as hiring and firing, setting wages, and fixing production rates.[111] Yet if the overall scope of the foremen's duties diminished, foremen retained the power to oversee the execution of the work, which became more critical during the heyday of industrialization. All of these efficiency strategies, from surveillance to new accounting methods to work measurement devices, formed part of a much-expanded effort to systematize management, far exceeding anything that had existed previously.

Frederick Winslow Taylor's well-known and influential ideas on scientific management reflected an extreme response to anxieties about labor. In his 1911 book, *Principles of Scientific Management,* Taylor argues that maximizing production depended on the degree to which entrepreneurs controlled labor.[112] Taylor proposed a strategy by which this could be done through subdividing tasks, setting a pace for workers to perform said tasks, tracking worker performance, and enforcing the pace of work through an extensive system of supervision. Taylor characterized his works as scientific. Rather than base the ideal pace on past performance, he derived the rate from studying what tasks a so-called first-class man could perform under ideal conditions, thereby eliminating any potential for keeping numbers down through soldiering. Another key to Taylor's management philosophy resided in separating task planning from execution.[113] By creating a planning department responsible for hiring and firing, production control, and payment of wages, Taylor freed foremen from these tasks so that they could devote their full attention to "teaching, leading, and instructing" workers on the shop floor. Taylor recommended further subdivisions within the planning and executing departments. No longer would there be a single foreman or manager. Rather, each worker answered to at least four separate functional foremen: the speed boss, the repair boss, the inspector, and the gang boss, all of whom supervised different aspects of production and thus different components of workers' behavior.[114] The planning department had similar divisions within it, so that in essence, all positions in the workplace were subdivided as much as possible. Everyone had more than one supervisor, and in theory the managerial system held everything in check.

Another form of management developed during this period—welfare capitalism—also represented a response to the managerial anxiety about labor.[115] With origins in paternalism, welfare efforts of the early twentieth century claimed to have the goal of improving conditions for workers. Sometimes an owner of a company provided housing or low-cost loans to his employees. In other cases companies built libraries, social clubs, and restaurants or arranged for sporting events, picnics, or other leisure-time activities for their workers. Some reformers of the period considered providing modern washrooms and water closets as welfare activities. Although these efforts may have arisen because of progressive reformers who protested management's poor treatment of workers, they ultimately became another means through which owners and managers sought to manipulate employees' actions in hopes of improving production. Most entrepreneurs discussed welfare activities in terms of how they improved the workers' lot by providing lunchrooms, restrooms, or recreational facilities for their workers, but they undoubtedly also had their own interests in mind. Advocates of such programs believed that by surrounding employees with pleasant surroundings and productive ways to spend their free time, they could shape them into better workers. As William Littmann has discussed, many spaces built out of the impulses of welfare capitalism were under the same rigorous visual supervision as other workspaces. Littmann cited an example at the Deering plant of International Harvester, in which matrons assigned to supervise the women's restroom were specifically charged with preventing loafing on the part of employees there.[116]

By the end of the Victorian period, managerial philosophies varied as much as the spatial means of surveillance in these workplaces did. In addition to Taylor's scientific management, cost accounting developed as a means of pinpointing sources of excess expense (such as labor, production, or overhead). Personnel departments also represented an important trend in management after World War I. These departments attempted to regulate hiring and firing practices, to develop job descriptions, to measure and evaluate performance, and also to implement and enforce rules and guidelines in the workplace, matters which, if they were addressed at all, previously fell to foremen and production managers. Personnel managers developed all kinds of record-keeping systems that monitored job performance.[117] Mechanical counters, which were affixed to the machine at which the worker labored, came into widespread use by the 1920s and 1930s as a means of measuring output. The methods pioneered in factory settings during the Victorian period set the stage for further developments later in the twentieth century as well as the spread of techniques into white-collar environments.

Surveillance played a role in most of these systems of management, though to varying degrees. Often the choice of which method to adopt depended on the nature of the work in question, the size of the business, and the philosophy of those in charge. In the case of the C. A. Dunham metalworks, personal supervision from an elevated platform served as the primary means of work discipline (figs. 2.15 and 2.16). At larger companies, such as General Electric in Schenectady, New York, owners instituted welfare programs along with a more elaborate and hierarchical supervisory structure and cost-accounting programs.[118] Philip Armour preferred personal and direct visual supervision at Armour and Company. Other owners and managers, many of whom wrote about their philosophies in *System* magazine, favored having as much tracked on paper as possible. The extent and types of management methods that employers adopted often depended on the nature of the work conducted. For example, in machine shops such as those at Westinghouse, visual supervision alone would have proved ineffective, since the size of the equipment and manufactured goods limited views of workers. At the Ford Factory, meanwhile, the assembly line itself set the pace of tasks and needed little visual control, if any at all, to be effective. Technology itself, the assembly line, became a form of work discipline.[119] If visual supervision was less important than other means of work discipline at Westinghouse or Ford, it was nonetheless a factor in most, if not all, cases. As one reformer indicated, surveillance, while not always sufficient to achieve control in itself, was essential regardless of the workplace in question.[120]

The idea of a managerial gaze and its all-seeing potential also functioned as a potent metaphor throughout managerial literature of the period. Postal inspectors, for example, were described in the early 1890s as functioning as the eyes and ears of the Post Office Department and noted for, through their diligent efforts, seeing and correcting irregularities in the mail service.[121] Philip Armour's gaze from his elevated platform at the Armour Company was both literal and figurative. From it, one author wrote, he "could look over, and some have thought even into, the heads of the three hundred clerks and managers about him."[122] Articles in *System* and *Factory* repeatedly advised readers to be "on the watch" for potential problems and to broaden their "range of vision."[123] Advertisements in these periodicals showed the extent to which metaphors of seeing penetrated managerial discourse during these years. A 1916 advertisement for Cyclone Fence Company from *Factory* promoted the use of a chain-link fence rather than a watchman for security, depicting eyes between the links of the fence (fig. 2.29). The accompanying narrative was littered with the language of surveillance, noting the fence would provide one with security as good as "a million eyes."[124] An advertisement for a hot-water meter from 1905,

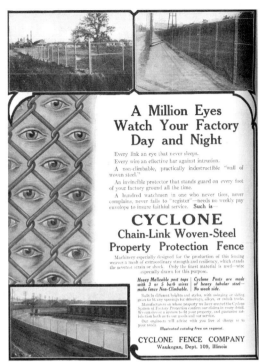

Fig. 2.29. Advertisement for Cyclone Fence Company, Waukegan, Illinois. From *Factory* 17 (May 1916): 438.

meanwhile, described the benefit of having such a device as a watchdog on the coal pile to guard against waste and promote economy (fig. 2.30).[125] One of the most suggestive advertisements came from a 1920 volume of *System* (fig. 2.31). The graphic artist depicted a clerk working at a calculating machine, while two additional images of his head float over him as if to monitor his work. The narrative explained how using these calculating machines gave management "an extra set of eyes," since it checked the work of the clerks.[126] In all three advertisements, inanimate objects became endowed with attributes of surveillance and function themselves as instruments of managerial control. Images such as these testify to how potent the ideology of surveillance had become in the workplace by the early twentieth century, which has continued to influence the landscape of work up to the present.

Despite all of the efforts to institute elaborate systems of visual supervision in Victorian-era workplaces, owners, managers, and reformers remained skeptical that surveillance could ensure efficiency. Like prison officials they seemed to recognize that even the most elaborate means of planning—architectural and otherwise—could not in itself maximize efficiency. In part some of the anxiety of entrepreneurs and engineers related to problems with the methods they developed. Employers abandoned visual supervision as a managerial strategy

Fig. 2.30. Advertisement for Worthington Hot Water Meter, Henry R. Worthington, Harrison, New Jersey. From *System* 8 (July 1905): n.p. Courtesy of Business, Science and Industry Department, Free Library of Philadelphia.

Fig. 2.31. Advertisement for Monroe Calculating Machine. From *System* 37 (Mar. 1920): 579. Courtesy of Business, Science and Industry Department, Free Library of Philadelphia.

in some cases because they recognized that the spaces they developed did not provide comprehensive views of workspaces. The sheer size of some workplace establishments prevented overseers from seeing everything. Even with open workrooms and glazed partitions to create an open landscape, owners and managers could view only part of the room at a time and thus could not convey the impression to workers of uninterrupted surveillance. Some reformers warned of this possibility. One writer even prescribed a maximum area that should be allotted to any one supervisor to watch.[127] By the 1920s personnel departments and cost-accounting systems became the chief means of monitoring employee performance at the expense of architectural spaces designed for managers to watch workers.[128] The popularity of the assembly line after World War I also reduced the need for management to supervise visually the execution of the work. Inspection at various points in the line assured quality, and there was no need for supervisors to push the quantity of output since it was fixed by the line itself. Any absence or slow down resulted in the line's shutdown, automatically notifying management of a problem.[129] Even though the Post Office Department continued after World War I to advocate construction of lookouts in post offices, it also adopted more systematic recording strategies to increase efficiency and track performance.[130] In post offices and elsewhere, architectural arrangements designed to facilitate supervision continued to be built, but these increasingly worked in conjunction with other efficiency measures.

Although employers still built spaces for surveillance in workplaces to enforce work discipline, they increasingly realized that the gaze's visibility invited resistance. Spaces occupied by supervisors were often placed conspicuously in view of workers to enhance their deterrent effect—but this had consequences that became more apparent over time. For example, when the Post Office Department saw to the installation of the first lookouts, postal inspectors found that clerks sought spaces in post offices, such as restrooms and locker rooms, where they could hide from surveillance. Inspectors countered by recommending the installation of lookout mechanisms in these areas, such as Inspector Edgarton did in Pittsburgh.[131] But soon they realized that clerks found other forms of resistance, developing mail-sorting techniques that made them look industrious, even if they were slacking off on the job or stealing mail.[132] Employers lamented similar resistance efforts in other kinds of workspaces. Numerous articles in *System* and *Factory* as well as in Taylor's writings suggested management's anxiety about the fact that even under the strictest visual supervision, workers seized opportunities to slow down the pace forced on them by managers.[133] Reformers described common ways in which workers countered surveillance: making frequent trips to the bathroom or drinking fountain, carrying tools or equipment between one end of the shop and the other, and pretending to be working when they were not. Over time owners and managers accepted that the same architectural strategies that they had developed to facilitate visual supervision, such as the use of glazed partitions and open workrooms, not only made their gazes possible, but also those of the workers toward management. As much as employers gazed on workers, workers could better see management and thus know when they were or were not being watched.

Even in cases where employers remained committed to visual supervision as a strategy of work discipline, fears of resistance undermined their confidence in surveillance as a managerial strategy. In these settings, employee resistance resulted in a reduction in production efficiency, which owners, managers, and reformers stressed was unacceptable in an increasingly competitive market. But they also foresaw a more serious ramification: the potential that resistance had to undermine the management-labor hierarchy. Writers warned that sustained resistance on the part of the workers could disrupt the chain of command necessary to maintain efficiency over the long term. This suggests another aspect of surveillance essential to understanding the ideology behind its imposition in workplaces as well as in other modern settings beyond its potential as a means of work discipline: the threat resistant actions posed to hierarchies between surveillants and those under their gaze.

The next chapter focuses on another sort of workspace—the Victorian American middle-class house—in order to explore this aspect of surveillance in depth. If fears about the potential of resistance to surveillance informed attitudes of employers in workspaces and prisons, it is strongly evident in discourse about the gaze in the private sphere as well. In middle-class houses and prescriptive discourse about them, architects and advice writers cautioned their audiences about potential consequences of resistance on the part of their hired household help. From this evidence it becomes clear that more was at stake than concerns about efficiency or discipline. Rather, fears of resistance to surveillance motivated middle-class Americans to worry about its potential to destabilize and invert hierarchies between employer and employee.

Chapter 3

HIERARCHY

[Domestic service has become] a sort of domestic wrangle and struggle between the employers, who secretly confessed their weakness, but endeavored openly to assume the air and bearing of authority, and the employed, who knew their power and insisted on their privileges.

—Catharine Esther Beecher and Harriet Beecher Stowe, *The American Woman's Home* (1869)

At present there seems to be an antagonism between mistress and maid—the mistress looks upon the maid as some curious sort of animal, entirely different from herself, for whom she must be constantly on the watch; and the maid regards the mistress as an enemy, of whom she is to take every possible advantage.

—Frank R. and Marian Stockton, *The Home: Where it Should Be and What to Put in It* (1873)

$\mathcal{I}$n a chapter of an 1853 book, *Trials and Confessions of an American House-keeper*, the heroine, Mrs. Jane Smith, reflects on one of the most trying days in her experience of keeping house. It begins when her husband tells her at breakfast that he has planned to invite a friend to dine that afternoon. Mrs. Smith immediately grasps her pivotal role in this event. Although Mr. Smith has arranged for delivery of the turkey and other foodstuffs, Mrs. Smith holds ultimate responsibility for the preparations. As her husband has impressed on her by stating that he sees this event as a chance to show off his young wife to "best advantage," Mrs. Smith knows that her own domestic virtue is at stake. Maintaining her authority as mistress of the house, on which her and her family's respectability depends, means dinner must go off without a hitch.

Immediately after her husband has left for work, Mrs. Smith hastens to the kitchen to make arrangements, albeit with some trepidation. Although her newly hired cook has proven to be skilled in the culinary arts, clean and neat in self-presentation, and generally good tempered, Mrs. Smith frets that Kitty is frequently "too literary in her inclinations." Mrs. Smith often has entered the kitchen to find her young servant engrossed in a book, magazine, or newspaper "when it was but reasonable . . . to expect that she would be working." From the moment that Mrs. Smith first visits the kitchen that day, she fears things will not go smoothly. On her initial entrance, she watches her cook hastily trying to conceal a book under her apron. Despite feeling put out by Kitty's blatant disregard for her morning tasks, Mrs. Smith proceeds to communicate her instructions. She stresses to her domestic that for the rest of the day things must be done promptly and in the best manner. Several hours later Mrs. Smith returns to the kitchen to find that little has been done towards preparing the meal. When asked about the delay, Kitty apologizes to her mistress and immediately begins "bustling about to put things to rights." After giving Kitty instructions about baking dessert, Mrs. Smith retires upstairs to prepare her toilet and attend to the children, despite lingering concerns about potential mischief below stairs.

Approximately an hour before the guests arrive, Mrs. Smith smells something burning. As she descends the service stairs from her chamber above, she grows anxious as a resounding silence greets her ears. Standing at the bottom of the stairs, unbeknownst to her cook, Mrs. Smith peers into the kitchen. There she sees Kitty seated next to the stove, completely engrossed in a book and oblivious to the fact that the dinner hour is fast approaching. The moment when Mrs. Smith discovers Kitty's transgression is pictured in an engraving by William Croome that accompanies the story (fig. 3.1). Mrs. Smith's outstretched arms and stunned expression suggest her astonishment with her cook's actions. Kitty's degree of engagement is conveyed by her wide-eyed focus on her book, which implies that what she is reading is rather scandalous. Signs of indolence surround the young cook. A mop and dishrag lay idle, a kettle of water has boiled over on the stove, smoke billows from the oven where the lemon puddings are cooking, and a cat is consuming a fresh turkey. The narrative concludes with Mrs. Smith's efforts to put together a modest meal for her dinner guests. As they eat, Mrs. Smith tries to hide her mortification and embarrassment, knowing that she has not lived up to expectations in her role as manager of the domestic sphere.[1]

Fig. 3.1. William Croome, "Showing Why the Dinner Was Late." Illustration from T. S. Arthur, *Trials and Confessions of an American Housekeeper* (Philadelphia: Lippincott, Grambo and Co., 1854), 20. Accompanying chapter 2, "Something About Cooks," this image shows the climax of the story, when the mistress, Mrs. Smith, discovers her cook reading to the complete neglect of her household duties. Water billows from the pot on the stove while the cat feasts on a turkey. Courtesy of the University of Delaware Library, Newark, Delaware.

This account from a mid–nineteenth-century confessional by T. S. Arthur offers tantalizing insights into surveillance in a domestic context from a middle-class perspective.[2] From the vignette, one sees that Mrs. Smith relies on visual oversight of servant spaces as she attempts to assert her domestic authority. More significant, the account invites us to examine resistance and consider its potential to influence relationships between servants and the employers for whom they toiled. Kitty's repeated transgressions pose a challenge (whether intentionally or not) to the authority behind her mistress's gaze. Mrs. Smith's anxiety stems as much from the possibility of resistance as it does from actual events. Her concern about Kitty's "interest in reading" drives her preoccupation with happenings in the service zone to the extent she worries about consequences of not watching it closely enough. Whether real or imagined, resistance served as a key point around which mistress and servant in the middle-class Victorian American house asserted and challenged their social and spatial relationships to one another. Concerns about resistance suffused domestic advice literature in the Victorian period, suggesting how middle-class Americans envisioned surveillance as a strategy to thwart challenges to household hierarchies.

This chapter examines the ideology of surveillance in a domestic context, focusing on a pervasive belief in Victorian American culture that visual supervision could help safeguard boundaries between servants and those they served.[3] Mistresses closely monitored the principal spaces where their domestics lived and worked—namely the kitchen and associated workspaces, servants' living quarters, and passages connecting these spaces. This regularly brought middle-class women into the service zone, an area designed to be separate from genteel rooms of the house but positioned proximate enough so mistresses could easily keep an eye on it. Through traversing intermediate spaces dividing the service zone from the rest of the house, mistresses believed they could exercise surveillance, assert their authority, and thus regulate the time and behavior of their servants. As their husbands and others often reminded them, this offered them a means of affirming their place as managers of the domestic sphere. But mistresses worried that their servants would challenge these gazes of authority to disastrous consequences. This potential for resistance contributed to a pervasive anxiety on the part of middle-class women. They feared servants' rebellious behavior held potential to upset the boundaries between servant and served that surveillance sought to enforce, leading them to more rigorous attempts to monitor servants' actions by surveillance and other means. Concerns about resistance thus influenced surveillance in the Victorian house and shaped relationships between household occupants.

By resistance I refer to actions by someone under surveillance that explicitly or implicitly challenge expectations or prescriptions implied within the gaze. Although resistance implies opposition, resistance for resistance's sake may not necessarily be the motivating factor behind a particular behavior. Rather, I use the term *resistance* to describe actions by the person under surveillance that the gaze, by its implied or actual presence, purports to disallow. I focus on behaviors that others have called everyday forms of resistance—informal, covert acts intended to secure immediate gains for the resistor. Such everyday acts differ from more political, collective, and overt forms of resistance meant to overthrow a practice or institution to secure permanent change.[4] Whether Kitty's reading represents a purposeful attack aimed at undermining her mistress's authority, then, is beside the point under this definition. The servant's rebellious behavior constitutes an act of everyday resistance because it allows her a moment of freedom in an otherwise unrelenting schedule that her mistress's gaze seeks to enforce. Anthropologists and social scientists have lately shown that everyday forms of resistance may ultimately have little impact in terms of upsetting entrenched systems of domination, but this does not make the concept of everyday resistance any less important.[5] Regardless of the impact of such resistance on the power structure of a given household or the mistress-servant relationship more broadly, fears of its potential drove those in power to reinforce hierarchies in attempt to preserve their authority. Again, the example of Kitty and Mrs. Smith is revealing. Mrs. Smith worries about Kitty's behavior even though it hardly threatens the practice of domestic service in her household or in general.

Resistance influences surveillance in prisons, workplaces, and other settings, such as the home. Inherent in any gaze is a relationship between two parties: a viewing subject (surveillant) and a gazed-on object (the person under surveillance). The fact that surveillance involves two parties predetermines the possibility for resistance, which influences the actions of those under the gaze as well as of those who exercise it. If surveillance is always dyadic, the forms and degrees of resistance vary, from merely returning the gaze to outright attempts to challenge it. In prisons, discussed earlier, multiple restrictions placed on inmates by various strategies of confinement limited their options to resist surveillance. As Foucault explained, the spatial layout and design of many modern prisons restricted prisoners' knowledge of when they were being watched. This led them to internalize the gaze and more or less police themselves—a situation which curbed the possibility of rebellious acts even if it did not quell worries on the part of prison officials about resistance.[6] In modern workplaces, discussed in the previous chapter, surveillance operated in a much less stealthy manner than in prisons. Owners and managers seized on the potential of a highly conspicuous embodied gaze to enhance work discipline. But as owners and managers came to realize, prominent supervisory spaces potentially invited resistance, since workers could ascertain when they were or were not being watched. This allowed them to assert a modicum of control over their labor and to counter entrepreneurs' ambitious goals for surveillance.

Like late-nineteenth- and early-twentieth-century post offices and factories, Victorian houses served as workspaces of a sort, but anxieties about surveillance were magnified in this setting. If both servants and their mistresses helped bring order to the domestic realm, their tasks and the way they viewed them differed. Mistresses managed the household; they performed little physical work themselves, leaving this to their hired help. The fact that mistresses supervised tasks rather than undertook them functioned as a constant reminder to servants of the divisions that separated them from their mistresses. Further, the motivations for middle-class women and their domestics to conduct household work also diverged. If mistresses worried about housework out of concern for their families' comfort and reputation, servants performed domestic tasks first and foremost because their employers paid them. The fact that domestics often lived with the families they served further exacerbated tensions between mistress and maid, since the lines between work and leisure were constantly blurred.

Servants' perpetual confinement to domestic drudgery contrasted strongly with what they perceived as their mistresses' apparent freedom from it and spawned animosity on the part of domestics. One Victorian servant described her feelings about her mistress's unrelenting demands on her time: "I hadn't any place that I could be alone a minute. . . . It's hard to give up your whole life to somebody else's orders, and always feel as if you was looked at over a wall like."[7] Such antipathy obviously represented a potential threat to domestic tranquility.

Builders and owners of middle-class houses believed properly designed, well-organized dwellings would limit servants' abilities to resist the authority of their employers. As hiring live-in domestic servants became common during the early nineteenth century, spatial divisions that had long undergirded the relationship between servant and served spaces became more strongly articulated. The labor pool increasingly consisted of those from the working-class or immigrant ranks whose ethnic, racial, and religious backgrounds differed from their employers. Such differences served to strengthen the middle-class desire to segregate these "strangers in the home," a label frequently applied to domestics. Boundaries between family and service spaces in the form of hallways and butler's pantries became more common during the Victorian period, as did the construction of service stairs. Although live-in service waned during the first decades of the twentieth century in favor of day work or live-out service and as the composition of the potential pool of servants broadened, most homeowners continued to preserve such buffers in their home. For all that builders sought to spatially manifest and thus reinforce social divisions, such efforts ironically had the effect of encouraging resistance. Segregation of servants' quarters offered domestics an arena where they could be, however momentarily, free from supervision. Although certainly the organization of other kinds of environments invited resistance as well, such as the workplaces discussed earlier, Victorian houses did so in an obvious way that makes them an ideal space through which to hone in on this aspect of surveillance.

I focus in this chapter on the middle-class anxiety about resistance and how this affected middle-class women's understanding of surveillance in this setting. By no means does this negate the value of discussing resistance to surveillance from the point of view of servants or any party under the gaze. But as my chief concern lies with exploring the ideology of surveillance in the Victorian period, questions regarding practice, while important, largely fall outside the scope of the current discussion. Part of the reason for this lies in the nature of historical evidence. The lack of surviving documentation makes getting at servants' voices difficult, if not impossible, since many Victorian American servants were illiterate.[8] Prescriptive literature survives in abundance, however. Through it one can get a very clear sense of middle-class women's anxiety about servants that in itself provides a partial, though certainly incomplete, index of everyday life from a middle-class perspective. Because this chapter centers on fears about resistance, I make little distinction between actual acts of servant resistance and imagined acts recounted in domestic advice literature. Acts of servant resistance undoubtedly raised mistresses' fears about their ability to maintain their authority in the household, and indeed incidents are detailed in numerous accounts. But fictional accounts of what might happen—in advice literature as well as in novels such as Arthur's discussed above—also prompted middle-class women to enlist surveillance as part of their strategy of household management.

Ultimately advice writers fretted that servants' rebellious actions could destabilize already tenuous hierarchies separating servant from served. In the Victorian period, the mistress-servant relationship was fraught with tensions revolving around class, race, ethnicity, and gender. During the late nineteenth and early twentieth centuries, servants came from the working-class ranks, typically from different backgrounds than their employers. These cultural differences had potential to create conflicts in the household. Mistresses were certainly unaccustomed to different linguistic, religious, and cultural manners of their servants, many of whom were foreign-born.[9] Advice writers frequently singled out Irish servants for their vernacular language and practicing Catholicism, just as they criticized domestics from mainland Europe for speaking in a foreign-tongue and having foreign manners. But if these differences troubled advice writers, the lack of education, refinement, and gentility they perceived in hired help worried them even more. Often authors deplored their servants' dress, which they faulted for being improper, risqué, or flashy. In other cases writers condemned servants for the ease with which they entertained suitors, shirked difficult tasks, exhibited poor table habits, and displayed poor standards of personal hygiene.[10] All of these deficiencies fed into stereotypes in advice writings—that domestics were crude, unrefined, and inherently lazy—which compounded mistresses' suspicions of servants. Middle-class women came to believe through reading advice literature that imprudent actions of their servants could impinge on the respectability of their genteel households and threaten their domestic virtue. They hoped surveillance could help them curtail such resistance, and they relied on the design of their homes as a means of preserving their physical and social dominance in the household hierarchy.

The Zonal Organization
of Victorian American Houses

As Gwendolyn Wright and Clifford Clark have discussed, middle-class American houses built during the late nineteenth and early twentieth centuries tended to be organized into zones based around their principal occupants: servants and members of the family. Servant spaces occupied the least desirable zones in the spatial hierarchy, despite their importance to the functioning of the household. These spaces were clustered together in the back parts of houses, basements, attics, and service wings. This stratified organization of Victorian houses mirrored the gazes of mistresses over their hired help. It also shaped the ways in which mistresses attempted to exercise surveillance as they tried to affirm their role as household managers.

Architectural pattern books impart useful evidence for thinking about surveillance in late-nineteenth- and early-twentieth-century American houses. As architectural and social historians have pointed out, these books offered prescriptive designs for houses rather than illustrations of fully realized dwellings.[11] Even in cases where books describe already-built houses, they show plans as architects or builders believed they should operate, not as their owners actually lived in them, and therefore provide only abstractions of everyday experience.[12] Although pattern books are prescriptive rather than descriptive, they still constitute useful forms of evidence for scholars interested in Victorian domestic life.[13] As my interest lies in the principles behind organization and layout of domestic spaces, pattern books are helpful in conveying in distilled form a sort of domestic code that directly or indirectly informed the design of Victorian houses of all types and scale.[14] Yet the variety in these books is overwhelming. As architectural historians studying nineteenth-century domestic buildings have long recognized, there is no such thing as a typical Victorian dwelling plan in terms of number or types of rooms and their configuration.[15] Besides the proliferation of kinds of rooms and diversity of formal arrangements, the nomenclature of household spaces differs dramatically across individual plans, books, and various authors. One house might contain a hall, drawing room, and library on the first floor, whereas another will have a parlor only (seemingly incorporating the public social functions in one space). In some cases linguistic assignments appear to relate to social status. Rather than search for literal formal patterns, the typical house plan may be extracted from the myriad of designs if one thinks about patterns in terms of room function.[16] The driving principle during the Victorian period lay with organizing clusters of similar kinds of rooms arranged in hierarchical zones, in which rooms used for similar functions tended to be grouped together and separated from other groups of rooms, usually by an intermediate space or architectural feature such as a door, wall, or staircase.[17]

One of the most influential pattern books published early in the Victorian period in America, *The Architecture of Country Houses,* written by the landscape architect and tastemaker Andrew Jackson Downing in 1850, illustrates this zonal organization well.[18] The designs for houses of all sizes in Downing's pattern book exhibit a zonal layout underlying the arrangement of domestic spaces that echoed and framed how surveillance worked there. While plans for cottages in Downing's book—intended for families without servants—reveal a zonal pattern of organization, it is in designs for more genteel houses where hierarchical planning is most pronounced. In his scheme for a northern farmhouse, Downing sharply distinguished spaces occupied by the farmer, his family, and their guests from those occupied by servants and farm laborers (fig. 3.2).[19] The farmhouse comprises three distinct sections, denoted on the exterior by intersecting rooflines. The main block of the house stands two-and-one-half stories in height. Contained within this block on the first floor

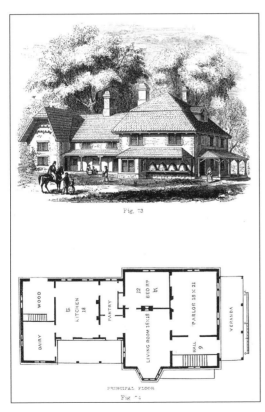

Fig. 3.2. Schematic view and principal floor plan of a "Northern Farm House." This plan illustrates the hierarchies that underlie houses in Downing's book of all scales and sizes. The first-floor plan shows how spaces occupied principally by the family and their guests lie towards the front of the house, while service areas—used mainly by servants and farm hands—occupy space toward the rear. Note how the pantry separates the kitchen from the main section of the house and how a service stair at the rear provides separate access for non-family members to the upper floors. From A. J. Downing, *The Architecture of Country Houses* (New York: D. Appleton and Co., 1850). Courtesy of the University of Delaware Library, Newark, Delaware.

are a living room (which would have also likely doubled as a dining space), a parlor, an entrance hall, and a master bedroom. Four chambers of varying sizes occupy space on the second floor of the main section, as the second floor plan shows (fig. 3.3) A staircase next to the twelve-by-fifteen-foot room on the second-floor plan leads to a third-floor garret. A two-part ell, standing one-and-one-half stories in height, extends off the main block of the dwelling. The most substantial section of this ell, which contained space for the kitchen and pantry, directly abuts the back of the main section. The area behind the kitchen houses a storage area for wood, a dairy, and a secondary staircase leading to sleeping spaces in the half story above.

Downing distinguished public and private spaces in his model farmhouse through the horizontal and vertical distribution of rooms as well as through the employment of spatial buffers. Placing the kitchen in an ell articulated a hierarchical front-to-back organization of domestic space. The front-to-back distribution of served-to-servant zones on the first floor was repeated on the second floor. Downing positioned unheated sleeping spaces for laborers immediately above the kitchen on the second story at the point furthest back in the house. These sleeping spaces differed markedly from those used by family

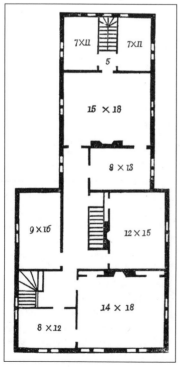

Fig. 3.3. Second-floor plan of a "Northern Farm House." This chamber-floor plan consists solely of sleeping spaces. Hierarchical organization informed Downing's scheme here as on the first floor. Spaces toward the front were intended for family members, while the two small rooms at the rear—accessed via a service stair—were for use by farm workmen. The stair adjacent to the 12 x 15 room provides access to the garret. From A. J. Downing, *The Architecture of Country Houses* (New York: D. Appleton and Co., 1850). Courtesy of the University of Delaware Library, Newark, Delaware.

members, evident by their small size, lack of a heat source, marginal placement, and, above all, by means of access. Laborers reached their sleeping spaces by ascending a secondary staircase located at the back of the house. Moreover, Downing emphasized distinctions between different categories of rooms in the farmhouse by inserting spatial buffers between marginalized servant spaces and more genteel parts of the house. On the first floor, a pantry separated the kitchen from the family zone, whereas on the second floor, a small foyer between the family bedrooms and those of laborers acted as a mediating space dividing servant from served areas.

Downing's designs for elite homes—country houses or villas—revealed an even greater degree of zonal articulation. Downing defined a villa as a "country house of a person of competence or wealth sufficient to build and maintain it with some taste and elegance. . . . A villa is a country house of larger accommodation, requiring the care of at least three or more servants."[20] In a scheme prepared for Downing's book by Gervase Wheeler, Wheeler relegated all spaces associated with servants—including their work areas, bedrooms, and passages

Fig. 3.4. Schematic view of a "Large Country House" as designed by Gervase Wheeler. Wheeler's villa appears much larger than Downing's cottage and farmhouse plans, yet the hierarchical design—front to back—remains consistent. In this view, the kitchen offices are located at the rear, behind the carriage porch, in the two-story section (as opposed to the main block of the house which stands two and one-half stories). From A. J. Downing, *The Architecture of Country Houses* (New York: D. Appleton and Co., 1850). Courtesy of the University of Delaware Library, Newark, Delaware.

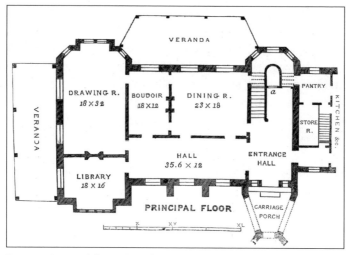

Fig. 3.5. Principal floor plan of a "Large Country House" as designed by Gervase Wheeler. This part of the plan illustrates the main section of the house—the spaces occupied by the family and their guests. The kitchen offices abut this section to the right. Note how Wheeler uses the stairhalls to buffer the connection between the kitchen and other parts of the house. From A. J. Downing, *The Architecture of Country Houses* (New York: D. Appleton and Co., 1850). Courtesy of the University of Delaware Library, Newark, Delaware.

between them—to a side ell (figs. 3.4, 3.5, and 3.6). Workspaces such as the kitchen, laundry, larder, scullery, pantries, and servants' hall occupied space on the first floor, whereas bedrooms for servants were located immediately above (fig. 3.7).[21] A service stair connected the two areas, minimizing the need for servants to leave the service zone en route to their quarters. Another interesting feature of Wheeler's plan lies in the attention he gave to servants' movements when they were required to leave the service zone as part of their household duties. A small hallway led from the kitchen into the main hall so that servants could answer the door without traversing other household spaces. This hallway would have allowed them to move silently and invisibly from the rear service area into a minimal portion of the family zone to which their movements were limited otherwise.

In later Victorian pattern books, the zonal organization seen in *The Architecture of Country Houses* became more prominent. With increasing frequency, buffer spaces separated rooms occupied by servants from those reserved for the family and their guests. Design no. 23 in A. J. Bicknell's 1881 pattern book, *Cottage and Villa Architecture,* showed myriad refinements that magnified the degree of separation of servant and served spaces seen in earlier plans by

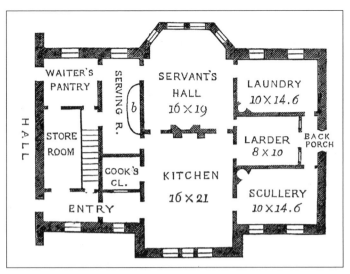

Fig. 3.6. Plan of kitchen offices occupying the side ell of a "Large Country House" as designed by Gervase Wheeler. The kitchen and servant hall are removed from the main portion of the house by buffer rooms and halls, thus keeping the "sights, smells and sounds" of the kitchen isolated. Downing praised Wheeler's attention to the kitchen offices, which he felt was "least appreciated" in U.S. house design (as opposed to English design). From A. J. Downing, *The Architecture of Country Houses* (New York: D. Appleton and Co., 1850). Courtesy of the University of Delaware Library, Newark, Delaware.

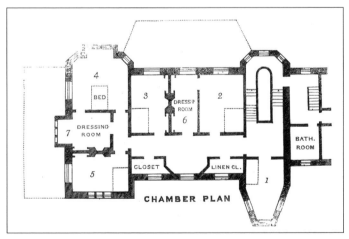

Fig. 3.7. Chamber-floor plan of the main part of a "Large Country House" as designed by Gervase Wheeler. The servant spaces are not pictured but located off to the far right—directly over the service ell—separated from the family areas by the bathroom and service stairhall. From A. J. Downing, *The Architecture of Country Houses* (New York: D. Appleton and Co., 1850). Courtesy of the University of Delaware Library, Newark, Delaware.

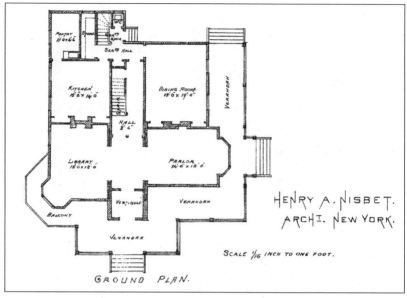

Fig. 3.8. Ground plan of Design #23 by Henry A. Nisbet. The plan illustrates common ways in which pattern book authors isolated service spaces from those frequented by family members. The service area—containing the kitchen and pantry—is positioned at the back, connected to the main portion of the house only via a service hall/butler's pantry positioned at the rear. A service stair provides separate access for servants to the upper floors, thus allowing them to move stealthily through the house without intruding upon polite family spaces. From A. J. Bicknell, *Bicknell's Cottage and Villa Architecture* (New York: William T. Comstock, 1881), plate 37.

Downing, Wheeler, and their contemporaries (figs. 3.8 and 3.9).[22] The architect confined means of direct access from servant spaces to more formal rooms. Access to privileged household spaces could be gained only from the principal hall running down the center of the house. Although the kitchen abutted this hall, direct access could not be had between the two rooms; rather, servants accessed the kitchen from a separate service hall. Placed perpendicular to the main hall, the service hall served multiple functions beyond dividing the two zones from one another. It provided passage between the kitchen and dining room, thus keeping the dinner route separate from polite spaces of the house. The service hall also housed a secondary stair set aside for servants' use. This secondary staircase led directly to a foyer above, off of which was an unheated servant's bedroom. Another door off this foyer opened onto the landing of the main stair, so that the foyer acted as a spatial buffer between servant and family zones comparable to the role played by the service hall immediately below. In this plan the designer confined servants' movements between the kitchen and their chambers, a strategy seen in many late-nineteenth-century designs for

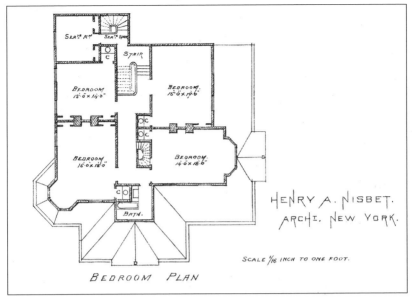

Fig. 3.9. Bedroom plan of Design #23 by Henry A. Nisbet from *Bicknell's Cottage and Villa Architecture,* illustrating relationship of servant bedroom to other bedrooms in the house. The servant room lies immediately above the kitchen, accessed by the service stair. Note that the servant's room—while isolated at the back—is not entirely cut off from the main portion of the house. This allowed servants to move throughout the family bedrooms to clean and also allowed mistresses a means of supervising them directly. From A. J. Bicknell, *Bicknell's Cottage and Villa Architecture* (New York: William T. Comstock, 1881), Plate 38.

middle-class houses. Victorian pattern-book writers praised this arrangement, since the family could lock the doors between service and family zones when they were away, thereby restricting servants' movements to their own zone.[23]

In many pattern-book designs, the butler's pantry acted as a mediating space between areas occupied chiefly by the family and those used principally by servants. Butler's pantries derived from English house plans of the eighteenth and nineteenth centuries. American homeowners rarely employed butlers but relied on the pantry as an area for storing dishes and for serving the meal, as well as to shield polite spaces from less genteel ones.[24] A plan from Louis Gibson's 1889 pattern book shows a common configuration (fig. 3.10).[25] In this plan the pantry divided the service and family zone from one another while still providing a controlled means of access between them.[26] Placement of the pantry between the two areas was only one way in which it served to buffer servant and served spaces from each other. When possible, Gibson and other plan book authors tried to stagger doors leading into and out of the pantry, keeping them a sufficient distance apart so as to minimize potential interactions

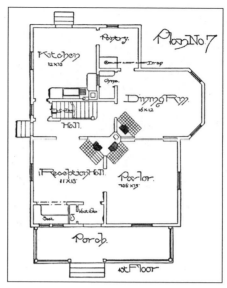

Fig. 3.10. First-floor plan of Plan No. 7 by Louis Henry Gibson. This plan shows a common strategy of buffering the kitchen from the dining room with a "butler's pantry," which would have kept the "sites, smells and sounds" of the kitchen at a remove from more polite spaces of the house. From Louis H. Gibson, *Convenient Houses, with 50 Plans for the Housekeeper . . .* (New York: Thomas Y. Crowell and Co., 1889), 121. Courtesy of Hagley Museum and Library.

between users of the kitchen and the dining room.[27] One pattern-book writer, C. Francis Osborne, explained: "When the kitchen is only separated from the dining room by the pantry itself, it is best to avoid, if possible, placing the pantry doors opposite each other, in order that a direct view from the dining room to the kitchen may not be had."[28] Furniture and built-ins could also be positioned in such a manner to help minimize views of the service quarter from polite areas of the house.

In the most elaborate house plans of the Victorian period, architects and builders went to great lengths to screen the service zone from the rest of the house so that it was almost completely self-contained. This separation occurred most often in affluent households where mistresses could afford to keep a hired housekeeper. In these cases the housekeeper assumed some of the supervisory duties from the mistress of the house, acting more or less as her proxy in the eyes of the servants.[29] Because of the housekeeper's perpetual presence among the domestics, architects and homeowners did not worry about a direct connection between the main block of the house and the service area. A house plan from Henry Hudson Holly's, *Modern Dwellings* of 1878 suggests how the presence of a housekeeper led to greater separation of servant and served zones (fig. 3.11). In this plan for a large house, Holly enclosed all service functions in a rear service ell extending off the back of the dwelling. This ell contained workspaces on the ground floor and sleeping chambers for domestics above. Movements of the servants through the house were almost entirely restricted to this zone. In this dwelling, as in most houses of this scale, Holly strategically sited the housekeeper's room (24) so that its occupant had considerable oversight of the service wing. In an ideal scenario, the housekeeper's room would have been

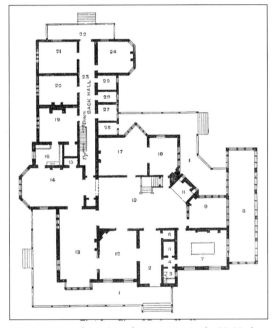

Fig. 3.11. First-floor plan of Design No. 22, by H. Hudson Holly. The service ell is located in the upper left corner, flanking the "back hall." Note the kitchen (19), laundry (20), servants' hall (21), and housekeeper's room (24). This plan suggests that the same principles underlie houses of all scales and sizes—for while this house is large, the same zonal organization used in smaller houses (by Downing and others) characterizes it. From H. Hudson Holly, *Modern Dwellings in Town and Country Adopted to American Wants and Climate* (New York: Harper and Brothers, 1873), 132. Courtesy of the University of Delaware Library, Newark, Delaware.

adjacent to the kitchen, rear entrance, and bedrooms of the domestics. In this case, though, sleeping quarters were in the upper quarters of the house—an arrangement that challenged direct oversight of these spaces. In Holly's mansion, the housekeeper's room stood between the kitchen, the servant's hall, and service entrance, positioning her at the threshold of movement between service spaces.[30] This compares with the positioning of managers' offices discussed earlier, which were located in such a position as to monitor workers' spaces as well as their movements through the workplace.

By the early twentieth century, changes in architectural styles as well as social practices led to significant modifications in house design that in some ways challenged these patterns. A reaction against Victorian excesses, both social and aesthetic, resulted in a radical reformulation of house styles and types as well as domestic lifestyles, largely around the time of the craze for efficiency in factories and workplaces. In a domestic context, the interest in efficiency meant downsizing and streamlining—of overall dwelling size, number of rooms, level of ornament, and interior furnishings. In addition new and efficient household technologies facilitated the ease with which laborious and time-consuming tasks could be done, such as washing dishes or laundering clothes. Coupled with the scarcity of people willing to work in domestic service, these new technologies contributed to a sizable decrease in the number of households that employed servants. New house types—namely, the one-and-a-half-story bungalow house (and its two-story vernacular counterpart, the four-square), the prairie houses of Frank Lloyd Wright, and colonial revival structures (such as the Cape Cod house)—all shared an emphasis on "structural simplicity, balanced proportions, and minimal decoration."[31]

Despite these changes, the zonal organization seen in nineteenth-century American middle-class houses continued to hold sway into the first few decades of the twentieth century. Examining house plans published by the Sears, Roebuck, and Company as part of their mail-order business between 1908 and 1940 suggests that divisions between the work zone and more polite spaces of the house endured after the turn of the twentieth century. In most house plans before 1930, some sort of buffer—be it a hallway, pantry, or dividing wall—separated the kitchen from other living spaces.[32] Moreover, although open planning—one of the hallmark features of domestic design during the early twentieth century—appeared more frequently in house plans developed by Sears and private architects such as Frank Lloyd Wright after World War I, many plans in the first decade of the twentieth century looked like smaller, more efficient versions of their nineteenth-century predecessors. These houses retained entrance halls and a sequence of formal rooms in the front part of the house, which were sharply demarcated from workspaces at the back of the dwellings. Though plans

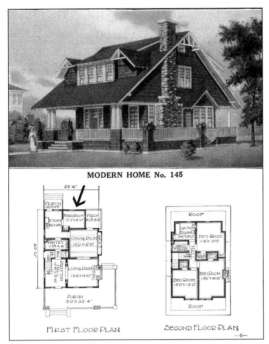

MODERN HOME No. 145

FIRST FLOOR PLAN

SECOND FLOOR PLAN

Fig. 3.12. "Modern Home No. 145," (also known as "The Arlington"), a house plan issued between 1913 and 1922 by the Sears® Roebuck and Company. While updated stylistically, the plan suggests how ideas from the late nineteenth century continued to inform house designs into the twentieth. Note the segregation of the "maid's room" at the back of the house abutting the kitchen. Image from www.searsarchives.com. Courtesy of Sears® Holdings Archives, Sears® Brands, LLC, Hoffman Estates, IL.

make fewer references to servants' rooms in early-twentieth-century designs of Sears and other mail-order house companies, abandonment of live-in service was gradual and by no means wholesale. As David Katzman has shown, the gradual transition from live-in to live-out service, especially after World War I, related partly to the ethnic makeup of the servant class, which shifted from immigrant groups to African American women.[33] But it also was tied to the rise of new household technologies that made housekeeping less time consuming. In addition shifts in cultural attitudes toward housekeeping upheld that progressive housewives managed their own homes, leading many to abandon hiring servants altogether.[34] Yet even with all of these changes, the possibility one might have servants continued to influence the layout of houses. In the plan for the Arlington, issued as "Modern Home #145" by Sears between 1913 and 1922, designers provided a maid's room off the kitchen on the first floor (fig. 3.12). This home was not extravagant; its three-bedroom size suggests that it was intended for a middle-class family. The presence of a maid's room suggests that traditions of having a room specially appointed for a maid continued to hold sway even as social practices changed.

Even Frank Lloyd Wright's prairie houses, with their relatively open floor plans, horizontal emphasis, and modern styling, preserved aspects of the zonal organization seen in late-nineteenth-century dwellings. The Robie House, located in Chicago and built in 1908–9, typifies Wright's mature prairie designs (fig. 3.13). Although conveying a sense of horizontality on the exterior intended to echo the flatness of the Midwestern landscape, the Robie House contained three floors. The organization of the three stories was itself zonal. Wright placed living spaces on the lower two floors and sleeping quarters in the upper story. The main floor (or second floor) exhibited the typically centripetal organization of Wright's homes. As the second-floor plan shows, the rooms seemed to spiral out from a central core, containing the chimney stack and main staircase (fig. 3.14). The core living area—containing the living room and dining room—remained largely open. No partitions divided the rooms from one another, just as the glazed outer walls and numerous porches suggest a blurring between exterior and interior. Despite the radical differences between Wright's main-floor plan and those of his nineteenth-century predecessors, segregation of work areas toward the back of the house remained. These work areas, which contained a kitchen and quarters for at least two live-in servants, were located in a separate wing off the dining room, well removed from

Fig. 3.13. Exterior view (looking northeast) of Frederick C. Robie House (Frank Lloyd Wright, 1908–09), ca. 1911 (photographer unknown). The innovative prairie style of this and other Wright houses of the period may be seen here with the low-lying appearance, cantilevered roofs, and large porch areas. Courtesy of The Frank Lloyd Wright Preservation Trust (Image No. 1983.11).

the central core of the house. Thus the zonal organization of domestic spaces that developed in the Victorian period persisted, even as the practice of hiring live-in domestic servants (and servants in general) declined and domestic lifestyles changed during the first two decades of the twentieth century.

Surveillance informed the zonal organization of late-nineteenth- and early-twentieth-century houses in several ways. At the most basic level, the arrangement of family to servant zones mirrored the hierarchical structure of the gaze from mistress to servant. The secondary position that service spaces occupied in these plans suggests how this relationship was spatially articulated. Pattern-book authors and Victorian homeowners also believed that keeping principal areas where servants lived and worked in a somewhat isolated zone would help mistresses more easily superintend their household help. By clustering servant spaces together in basements, back regions of the house, service ells, or attic spaces and restricting points of access between them and other parts of

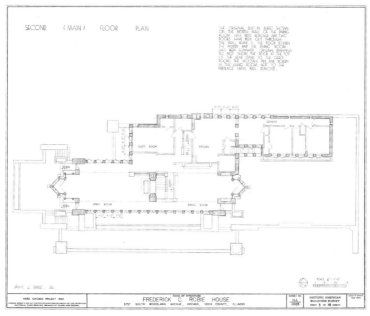

Fig. 3.14. Second (main) floor plan, Frederick C. Robie House (Frank Lloyd Wright, 1908–09), Chicago, Illinois, showing service wing off the kitchen in the upper right corner. This plan suggests that despite the changes Wright introduced to house design, many aspects of nineteenth-century house planning—namely, the hierarchical organization informing the relationship of family and servant spaces—remained in his dwellings. Courtesy of the Library of Congress, Prints and Photographs Division (Historic American Buildings Survey collection).

the household, servants' movements could potentially be restricted as well as more easily supervised. Putting the kitchen in the basement, a late-eighteenth- and early-nineteenth-century tradition that lingered in the Victorian period (though not without objection), was one strategy through which this containment was accomplished.[35] The survival of the practice stemmed from the fact that the arrangement isolated servants, thus permitting easier monitoring of their behavior. As one writer explained, putting service functions in the basement spatially reinforced the divide between servants and the rest of the house's occupants while simultaneously giving the mistress a single area rather than a series of spaces and a single point of access to oversee: "The cooking, eating, drinking, washing, ironing, churning, baking, brewing, yes, and the worrying and scolding, must all be kept on a common level. We can go down to them easily enough; we can't allow them to come up to us."[36] This writer warned that putting service areas throughout the house would make oversight of labor unsystematic. Keeping servant spaces in basements or ells facilitated supervision by limiting the extent of the principal domain mistresses oversaw as well as keeping the "sights and smells" removed from more polite spaces of the house.

Even more significant, the importance of surveillance in a domestic context may be seen in the fact that designers rarely cut off spaces designated for servants completely from the rest of the house. Although part of the reason for this may be attributed to the fact that servants had to move throughout the house in the course of their duties, writers also insisted that such connections helped keep the service zone within easy reach of the mistress's gaze. The rare exception may be found in plans for southern homeowners in pattern books, where kitchens and service quarters were completely freestanding. Even in these cases, direct communication was facilitated through strategic placement of windows and doors providing the mistress with access to the service quarters.[37] Architects and builders believed that connections between servant and served spaces allowed mistresses to traverse the boundary separating the two zones to oversee and direct the household help more easily—either through doors, hallways, or butler's pantries. They designed these buffers to mark the separation between zones so that they did not abut one another too directly while simultaneously providing a controlled means of access between servant and family spaces. Calvert Vaux, an American architect who worked closely with Downing, praised butler's pantries particularly for this mediating function, noting that "by this means convenience of access, without loss of privacy, is secured."[38]

The organization of middle-class houses aided surveillance above all by the way in which kitchen and service areas were positioned relative to other domestic spaces. In a majority of his plans, Downing located the kitchen so that mistresses could easily access it and thus monitor the actions of its occupants. He admonished his readers for choosing basement kitchens, specifically because of the problems with regards to surveillance of servants and their work: "The disadvantages are, that a basement kitchen is neither so convenient nor so economical for the mistress of a cottage; it is not so accessible, and therefore demands more personal attention, since it is not so directly under her own eye."[39] Instead Downing supported the idea of putting the kitchen on the main floor of the house. This meant the kitchen was more accessible, as well as "more completely under the *surveillance* of the mistress."[40] Later Victorian pattern-book writers heeded the warnings of Downing and Vaux, advising that workspaces be kept convenient for ease of oversight. In his 1882 book, *The House That Jill Built*, E. C. Gardner lauded one plan for isolating the servants' rooms at the back of the house but still close enough so that the mistress could have them under watch.[41] Even in elite houses, where work areas formed a self-contained zone under the oversight of a housekeeper, architects planned connecting spaces between the kitchen wing and other first-floor spaces. In Holly's mansion, discussed earlier, for example, what appeared to be a self-regulating service wing remained connected to the rest of the house via a back hall, thus keeping it accessible to the mistress's gaze (fig. 3.13).

Architects and house planners also took surveillance into account in terms of planning sleeping spaces for servants. Although Downing did not stress the need to keep servants' private quarters under watch with the same vehemence that he did with their workspaces, his plans and those of other pattern-book writers indicated that visual access to these spaces also was a factor to consider. Prior to the Civil War, designers allocated space for servants' sleeping quarters in attics; a staircase from the second floor provided easy access to the servants' quarters. Judging from plans in pattern books over the course of the Victorian period, it became increasingly common to position servants' bedrooms directly over their workspaces rather than in the garret. Although this practice conformed to the zonal organization of middle-class Victorian houses, it also revealed prevailing ideas about surveillance. The scheme ensured that servants' sleeping quarters, like their workspaces, always remained easily accessible to the family zone. Servants often had their own stair that led to their rooms, but typically their private domain also could be accessed from a door or hallway dividing the families' sleeping quarters from servant ones. This feature provided a means by which mistresses could easily access rooms used by their servants. As houses decreased in size during the early twentieth century, live-in servant spaces—where they existed—would have been even more accessible, although they remained clearly separate.

A design for a home from *Palliser's Model Homes* of 1878 (no. 19) illustrates how concerns about surveillance mediated the placement and arrangement of servants' bedrooms (fig. 3.15). Here Palliser Company designers placed the servants' bedroom on the second floor at the back of the house. Servants would have likely accessed their bedroom via a service stair that led to it directly from the kitchen. Designers did not entirely cut off the bedroom from the rest of the house, since mistresses could access the servant's room through a door off the main stairwell. Although servants would have used this door to enter the second-floor family zone when they needed to clean the family bedrooms, mistresses also took advantage of this provision to monitor the service quarter. Servants lamented that mistresses disregarded their privacy and regularly traversed boundaries separating their private chambers from the family zone. In a letter to a relative, one servant wrote that her quarters were always subject to her mistress's gaze: "I do not know what minute one or the other member of the family may pop in . . . & the door between the rooms does not lock."[42] Designing houses that isolated servant spaces while simultaneously keeping them easily accessible to the mistress posed ever-present challenges for architects and builders, who devised myriad architectural schemes in attempts to resolve these rather disparate aims.

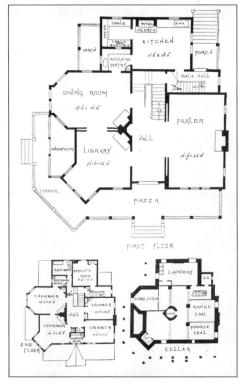

Fig. 3.15. First-, second-, and basement-floor plans of the "Underwood Residence" from *Palliser's Model Homes; Showing a Variety of Designs for Model Dwellings* (Bridgeport, CT: Palliser, Palliser, and Co., 1878), plate XIX. As with many plans, the kitchen occupies space at the rear but also allows easy access to the dining room by means of a butler's pantry. The servants' bedroom is distinguished from the chambers associated with the family zone of the house. While isolated, it is not cut off from the family sleeping quarters, and thus would have provided the mistress oversight of the servant's room. Courtesy, The Winterthur Library: Printed Book and Periodical Collection.

Another form of advice literature popular during the Victorian period, the house-planning guide, attempted to articulate the challenges in narrative form. These books, which gained popularity in the decades after the Civil War, focused on explaining principles behind good house design. Rather than offer full-scale plans as pattern-book authors did, writers of house-planning guides explored the social requirements of domestic spaces. Like pattern-book writers, authors of house-planning guides considered household organization in terms of zones, as can be seen in two British house-planning books that circulated widely in the United States during the Victorian period.[43] The authors of these books, Robert Kerr and John James Stevenson, divided household spaces into three broad categories: family living spaces, spaces for servants, and thoroughfares connecting the two. Although both books evinced similar attitudes about the hierarchical and zonal organization of houses, the authors differed in how they saw concerns about surveillance affecting the arrangement of domestic space. Throughout his book Kerr stressed the necessity of keeping family members and servants as spatially distinct from one another as possible. He advocated restricting passage completely between the two realms, because of the social gulf that separated the servant class from their employers: "The family constitute one community: the servants another. Whatever may be their mutual regard and confidence as dwellers under the same roof, each class is entitled to shut its door upon the other and be alone."[44] Writing fifteen years later, Stevenson questioned the extent of Kerr's division, fearing that removing service areas too much from family spaces might lead servants to challenge their mistress's authority:

> Is not this [Kerr's insistence upon division] carrying the separation a little too far? The days are gone when the whole household could dine at one table; but should the mistress not have the run of her own house? Should the master not know his own servants when he meets them? . . .

> I venture to doubt if a house should be planned as Mr. Kerr recommends, so that the servants may shut themselves off from the family in a separate establishment, where the mistress feels herself an intruder. She is responsible for their conduct, and should be able to encounter them at their work, and as they go to their rooms, without having to go prying after them. Some good housewives, therefore, like their store-room among the servants' offices, and object to the servants' bedrooms being isolated from the house.[45]

For Stevenson servants' quarters should be designed so that their occupants remain in their proper place. Servants must be out of general view of the family, but close enough so that the mistress could easily consult them as she went about managing household affairs. The one case where complete separation was permissible was when the family could afford to hire a housekeeper, who essentially acted as the mistress's proxy.[46] Stevenson preferred that the housekeeper's bedroom "be placed so as to command those of the female servants."[47]

American house-planning guides recall those of Kerr and Stevenson in focusing on keeping the servant realm separate but closely connected for ease of supervision. Osborne's 1888 book, *Notes on the Art of House-Planning*, appears to be modeled closely after Stevenson's guide in its general organization and argument.[48] Like his English predecessors, Osborne insisted on the absolute separation of the family and service zone as well as the thoroughfares within them, as diagrammed in his plan for the ideal house (fig. 3.16). But as rigorously as Osborne defended the zonal and hierarchical form of domestic organization, he guarded against removing the service domain entirely from the range of the mistress's gaze. His foremost maxim for the location of servant spaces such as the kitchen was that they should "be thoroughly, yet *conveniently*, separated from family rooms and thoroughfares."[49] Osborne inveighed against excessive separation of the two zones in English house plans. He denounced one design that separated the kitchen and dining room via a 130-foot-long corridor—which he felt removed the service zone too much. For Osborne and

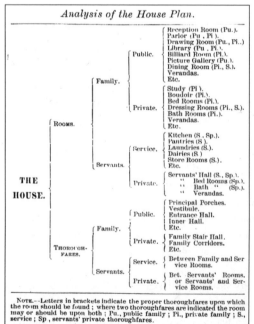

Fig. 3.16. "Analysis of the House Plan." Osborne's chart shows the degree to which many Victorian pattern book authors felt family and servant spaces (and public and private spaces) should be segregated. From Charles Francis Osborne, *Notes on the Art of House-Planning* (New York: William T. Comstock, 1888), 15. Courtesy, The Winterthur Library: Printed Book and Periodical Collection.

other house planners, the zonal organization of the home was mediated by ever-present concerns of household supervision.

Like pattern books, house-planning guides reflected their authors' faith that a well-designed home could create an efficient household. Read voraciously by middle-class Victorian Americans, these books also influenced their attitudes toward servants and the spaces they occupied. Such guides underscored the important role of supervision in middle-class Victorian houses in their emphasis on keeping the service zone isolated but accessible—something that remained consistent from the mid–nineteenth century into the early twentieth. Another form of prescriptive literature, directed toward teaching women how to manage their households, suggests what mistresses hoped to achieve through closely superintending the spaces where their servants lived and worked.

Household Surveillance

Advice literature on household management proliferated during the Victorian period and offers telling insights into mistresses' ambitious goals for surveillance as well as a means of considering how anxiety about resistance influenced their ideas. Previous scholarly accounts that recognize surveillance as a prominent theme in this body of literature have focused on trying to reconcile evidence in the prescriptive tracts with everyday life in the late-nineteenth- and early-twentieth-century home.[50] Such literature is more useful in terms of how it lays out expectations that Victorian Americans had for supervision (visual and otherwise) and for domestic management in general, as well as where they perceived pitfalls might occur. Numerous writers stressed that close oversight over servants provided women with assurance against potential problems in their households. Lengthy books and numerous articles urged mistresses to monitor their servants' activities regularly, particularly in the kitchen, where servants spent much of their day. Even if some authors recognized that visual surveillance alone was not foolproof, most texts stressed that mistresses' frequent intrusion into servant spaces offered a means by which they could assert their authority over their domestic help.

Catharine Esther Beecher, one of the best-known and influential domestic advice writers in nineteenth-century America, advocated surveillance as a part of a comprehensive strategy of household management.[51] Through a series of books on domestic economy, Beecher set out to refashion and reform the domestic realm as the special province of the housewife. For Beecher the mistress was in every way the manager of the domestic sphere. Her leadership had ramifications beyond the walls of the home, since Beecher linked the fate of American society to women's maintenance of healthy and moral domestic environments.[52] In her numerous writings Beecher addressed everything from the layout of houses to a housekeeper's responsibilities in general to the mundane details of cooking and cleaning, but a consistent theme was that a moral household is an efficiently administered one. For Beecher the housewife acted as a superintendent—whom she called a "chief minister"—whose charge involved ensuring that the home ran as efficiently as possible by whatever means necessary.

In *A Treatise on Domestic Economy, for the Use of Young Ladies at Home and at School*, originally published in 1841 and reissued repeatedly throughout the nineteenth century, Beecher emphasized the importance of supervision in the middle-class home. Beecher devoted an entire chapter to domestic service, in which she discussed a wide range of issues varying from treatment of servants to appropriate wages. She stressed how close monitoring of servants, the work they performed, and the spaces they occupied bore directly on the quality of their work. Benevolence and mentoring characterized Beecher's attitude toward household management. Under her model the mistress should instruct and teach as opposed to criticize and nitpick, or, in her words, to "forewarn" instead of "fault." For Beecher close supervision was most necessary on initially hiring a servant, but such watchfulness should continue, if less pervasively, throughout the servant's tenure.[53] In a revised edition of the book, published with her sister Harriet Beecher Stowe as *The American Woman's Home* in 1869, Beecher articulated more clearly the role of surveillance in a mentoring model of household management. Beecher and Stowe explained that the mistress recognized and subsequently corrected problems with servants that impinged on household efficiency: "If she [the mistress] understands her business practically and experimentally, her eye detects at once the weak spot; it requires only a little tact, some patience, some clearness in giving directions, and all comes right."[54]

Eunice White Bullard Beecher, Catharine Beecher's sister-in-law and herself an advice writer, placed even greater emphasis on surveillance in the maintenance of an efficient household. Unlike Catharine, who relied on a seemingly omnipresent gaze as a means of instruction and mentoring, Eunice Beecher upheld visual supervision as a primary strategy to prevent transgressions and to detect blatant abuses on the part of servants. She concerned herself with all aspects of running a household, but her call to arms was management and discipline. In all of Beecher's writings, she devoted extensive attention to maintaining order over domestics through perpetual supervision.[55] In the introduction to her book *The Law of a Household*, posthumously published in 1912 as a collection of essays based on earlier writings from across her career, Eunice Beecher describes many challenges women faced in running their households.

Although she recognized that becoming a successful manager took time, she stressed how success depended on the degree to which mistresses supervised their servants. Beecher related how she struggled with managing her domestics until she had an epiphany when standing with her husband watching their new house being built:

> I stood on the steps watching the men at work. They seemed so earnest and faithful and interested, that I remarked to my husband, "I wish I felt sure that the servants at home were doing their work as well. I can't stay there all the time watching them." And he answered, "Do you see that man standing by the gate? He is n't [*sic*] doing anything but watching; he's the boss." That night I saw the vision of woman's emancipation through system. Why should n't [*sic*] a woman conduct her household as a business, prepare herself for it as a man prepares for his life work—in other words, make a business of housekeeping. . . . I formulated a small system, wrote out my orders, and gave them to my few servants. I spent at least an hour a day, early in the morning, correcting, explaining, adjusting and inspecting the work done. I "laid down the law," and spent time in enforcing it.[56]

For Beecher good household management revolved around knowing where servants were and what they were doing at every moment. To do this, mistresses had to plan servants' schedules and follow up through regular visits to assess their progress. The above account suggests that Beecher envisaged the mistress's role as the equivalent of men in the more public sphere of the workplace. The language she used to describe housekeeping (as a business) in addition to the link she made between domestic spaces and workplaces indicates this. As was the case with the workplaces discussed earlier, according to Beecher, surveillance offered mistresses a means to enforce work discipline. "Laying down the law" meant visiting work areas regularly and monitoring servants' actions, as systematically as a foreman would in a factory.

In her 1879 book, *All Around the House,* Beecher described how a management philosophy based around perpetual supervision of servants and servant spaces could assure household efficiency. According to Beecher, a good housekeeper possessed a comprehensive knowledge of domestic duties as well as strategies of management. Only through mastering both could she have "peace and harmony" in her household.[57] Beecher felt that it was essential to train one's eye to spot servants' lapses. She noted that a good housekeeper must be able at a glance to notice servants' oversights and omissions, such as when servants only half-heartedly and incompletely dusted.[58] Beecher linked perpetual oversight to the organization of Victorian houses. Maintaining order meant that the mistress had to regularly move outside of the family zone and visit servants' workspaces to assert their command over this domain. Not only did this guarantee that the work was being conducted properly; it also reminded servants that they were always subject to the gaze even in their zone. Beecher used the case of making butter to illustrate her points. More than any other household task, she argued that this task required the mistress's presence in the service quarter. If servants were left unsupervised, Beecher feared servants would disregard the painstaking subtleties involved in the process:

> Of course, we do not mean that the labor may not be performed by the servants; but in no one department is the daily oversight of the mistress so indispensably necessary. This unfailing oversight is important in all the combinations that belong to domestic economy. Simply giving directions, without seeing that they are promptly and exactly followed, may possibly pass for good housekeeping, but it will not enable one to keep milk properly or make good butter.[59]

If the mistress only intermittently presented herself in the kitchen, Beecher explained, the butter would not set properly, given servants' propensity to use incorrect utensils and dirty towels and thus increase the likelihood of contamination of dairy products. Beecher argued that it was the presence of the mistress in the service quarter that ensured success.

For Beecher surveillance functioned less as a mechanism to detect wrongdoing than as a means of asserting the mistress's authority. Very much like the way the visual presence of a manager in a factory reminded workers of their place, the mistress needed to impress on servants that deviation from their assigned tasks or from proper methods would result in scolding or stronger forms of punishment: "It is the fault of the mistress if girls learn that they can hide or cover up their shortcomings. Let housekeepers teach those in their employ that they are never long unaware of neglected duties, and a better class of domestics will be the result."[60] To illustrate this point, Beecher offered a series of examples where a lack of oversight caused problems. For the most part, her examples occurred mainly in the service zone—the cellar, laundry, and kitchen—spaces that she castigated mistresses for visiting infrequently. If mistresses rarely asserted their gaze over these spaces, she warned, servants would take advantage. Beecher cautioned that without the potential of surveillance looming, servants might waste soap in the laundry or might leave clothespins out in the rain where they would rot. In the kitchen they might be inclined to discard leftover foodstuffs that could be stored away for later use, or, worse yet, they might pilfer them for their own consumption. Beecher asserted that exercising the gaze frequently reminded servants that mistresses had command over these spaces. It impressed on them that they were always subject to their employer's gaze, thereby minimizing the likelihood they would act in ways counter to her expectations for them. As was the case with the factory, the prominence of surveillance was believed to curtail attempts to shirk work.

Inherent in Eunice Beecher's tactic of preventing transgressions via surveillance is an anxiety about potential resistance—something that pervades domestic-advice literature during the late nineteenth and early twentieth centuries. Even under mentoring models of supervision such as that described by Catharine Beecher, authors endorsed surveillance as a preventative measure intended to assure that servants did not challenge limits set on them and their tasks. Although Catharine and Eunice Beecher differed in that the former used the gaze mainly as a first step in the training process whereas the latter relied on the gaze as the chief mechanism of household management, they both urged women to monitor servants closely to help prevent servants engaging in actions that might threaten order in the household. Eunice Beecher explicitly discoursed about her fears, contending at one point that the mistress must perpetually assume the role of a "looker on" to keep servants from finding shortcuts: "If a girl is tardy in rising in the morning, and feels the necessity of hurried preparations to start the washing or the breakfast—if she has learned that she need fear no detection from her mistress, she will probably fill her grate with kindling-wood, and, when fairly ignited, feed the fire with a larger size of hard-wood to expedite her work."[61] If a servant knew her misbehavior had no chance of being detected, Beecher worried, she would likely continue to choose to burn wood instead of the cheaper alternative of coal, eventually resulting in excessive expenditure as well as damage to the coal-burning stove. For Beecher the unremitting threat of surveillance minimized these kinds of transgressions and potentially might eliminate them altogether.

Most of all advice writers felt surveillance could guard against what they called "eye service." In the Bible (from which the term likely came), eye service referred to a tendency among the enslaved to work harder than they otherwise would when watched.[62] In domestic advice literature, writers used the term in a manner more akin to soldiering in a factory context, referring to cases where servants worked only when under watch. Use of the term *eye service* hints at the prominence of surveillance in household-management discourse, in that the quality of domestic service was linked to the presence or absence of the gaze. Although Eunice Beecher did not use the label, the forms of behavior she described accorded with actions that other writers on domestic economy labeled as "eye service."[63] Fears about eye service led many writers to question to what degree planning and foresight assured success in the domestic realm. The author of the 1885 book *The Housewife's Library* warned that although obtaining experienced help, planning their schedule, and dividing up tasks was important, careful planning alone would not ensure compliance: "Constant supervision is essential to securing good work. Eye-service is the bane of our laboring classes. See that orders are obeyed; see that things are put to proper uses; see that house-cloths do not become dish-cloths, or *vice-versa*. . . . Indeed, there is no end to the points that the housewife must supervise, if she be determined to have her work well done."[64]

Concerns about eye service appeared most strongly in instructive texts directed at servants. *Plain Talk & Friendly Advice to Domestics* (1855) admonished servants about practicing eye service. Through recounting a series of incidents, the author showed that eye servants, no matter how cunning, were always apprehended in the end, usually when the mistress discovered their abuses. "Your mistress has eyes," noted the writer, reminding servants to keep their areas neat and clean at all times.[65] The longtime editor of *Godey's Lady's Book,* Sarah Josepha Hale, also cautioned servants about the follies of eye service. Hale warned that transgressions would always be detected, if not by the mistress then by a higher power: "Act, in all these things, as you would if your employer was looking on you; and forget not that One, to whom you are more responsible than to any earthly master or mistress, is constantly watching you."[66]

In writings directed at servants, authors characterized the mistress's gaze as pervasive and omnipresent, just as tracts directed at mistresses urged women to move throughout the house extending their gaze over all of its spaces. Although Eunice Beecher firmly believed that servants' workspaces required the greatest attention, she believed that effective supervision left no region of the house unsupervised. To "spy on the land," Beecher insisted that the mistress must regularly move from genteel spaces such as the dining room or parlor to less polite ones such as the kitchen, making use of spaces such as the butler's pantry that kept the latter easily within the reach of her gaze. Other writers stressed that surveillance must be applied evenly throughout the house—for even if servants spent a great deal of time in the kitchen, they also needed to move throughout the house to clean it. In *The Young Housekeeper's Friend* (1871), "Mrs. Cornelius" advised her readers to visit each room every day to inspect servants' work. She explained that servants would learn over time to expect daily and unceasing inspection: "They will not be tempted to negligence or waste, by the idea that you will never discover it."[67] Mrs. E. F. Ellet urged in her 1873 book, *The New Cyclopedia of Domestic Economy,* that mistresses should "quietly exercise a general and regular surveillance over every part of her house and household."[68] In *The Expert Maid-Servant* (1904), Christine Terhune Herrick advocated a similar strategy of work discipline. She insisted that the mistress's gaze should assert and claim spatial authority: "From the first the mistress should have it clearly understood that there is no place in the house into which she may not penetrate."[69] Just as lookouts in all areas of the post office reminded workers of the ever-present possibility of inspection, mistresses felt their presence throughout the house reminded servants of their authority.

If the mistress's perpetual presence could minimize eye service, writers also recognized that the proximity of servants to the mistress could have other, more positive ramifications. Both Catharine and Eunice Beecher emphasized that the mistress's example might benefit their servants. Some of this may stem from their Christian background and allegiances with the Congregationalist Church. Harriet was the daughter of the famous Congregationalist minister, Lyman Beecher, while Eunice was married to Catharine's brother, Henry Ward Beecher, himself trained as a minister under Lyman's tutelage. Their experiences with benevolent societies and Christian aid organizations likely influenced their attitudes toward improving the lot of servants through their example.[70] Catharine Beecher's mentoring model shows this. Beecher advocated that mistresses teach servants, usually uneducated in polite middle-class ways, about gentility through their own model behavior.[71] Eunice Beecher likewise recognized that surveillance could be used to educate servants about etiquette in a kinder, gentler way, so that they could tend their own houses on leaving domestic service.[72] Mrs. Cornelius explained how her regular entrance into service work areas stimulated her servants to be neat and orderly in their own behavior. She told her readers that this might eventually reduce time spent overseeing them: "They will anticipate your daily inspection, and soon find themselves so much benefited by your habits of system and order, that their own convenience will dictate obedience to your directions and suggestions."[73] In this more positive vein, surveillance could (and did) serve as a mentoring tactic as much as a disciplinary one. But implicit in these discussions as well as more negative ones was a lingering, if often unstated concern, about servants' inclination toward potential resistance and the threat it posed to household hierarchies.

Surveillance and Hierarchy

A telling anxiety lies behind this advice literature: that surveillance, no matter how stringently exercised, was never total or complete. As the account at the beginning of this chapter illustrates, Mrs. Smith diligently supervised her young cook, but her failure to closely watch over the kitchen on the day of her dinner party led to disaster. Her trepidation on entering the kitchen suggested that Mrs. Smith feared what she might discover, and in this case her fears were apparently warranted. For middle-class readers, this kind of account likely reverberated with their experiences with servants and at the same time led them to fear potential acts of rebellion among their household help even more. In other words, reading such tales undoubtedly influenced the ways in which they managed their own homes and thought about their servants. Narratives such as these thus reveal how concerns about resistance influenced relationships between middle-class women and their hired help.

The account of the events in the Smith household typifies didactic fiction, a popular form of Victorian American literature that offered middle-class women advice with managing their households.[74] Didactic fiction differed from more instruction-oriented books such as those of the Beechers in offering guidance in the form of stories. Each tale had its own moral, which served to suggest ways in which women could reduce the likelihood of troubling incidents occurring in their own households. Didactic fictional accounts often detailed strategies for supervising servants. Whereas prescriptive household guides tended to focus on justifying surveillance as a strategy of household management, didactic fictional accounts suggested how surveillance (or, more commonly, the lack of it) could play out in a domestic context. Because didactic accounts were set in households, they offer interesting insights into how fears about resistance related to the layout of household spaces and mediated hierarchies between mistresses and servants.

Targeted at a middle-class audience, didactic tales appeared in articles in periodicals such as *Godey's Lady's Book* as well as in lengthy books, beginning in the 1830s and continuing into the early twentieth century. Illustrations often appeared alongside or, in a few cases, in lieu of narrative, themselves amounting to a visual form of didactic fiction. Part of the popularity of these representations—literary and visual—lay in the ways in which they reverberated with the kinds of events that occurred in Victorian American middle-class houses. Yet while instances recounted in works of didactic fiction may have resembled actual incidents that transpired in middle-class homes, such vignettes refer to, rather than describe, the kinds of encounters Victorian mistresses had with their hired help. These tales allude to an underlying and pervasive fear about servants' potential rebellion and its ramifications, shared by the authors of these tales as well as their middle-class and largely female audience. Such accounts served a complicated function in late-nineteenth- and early-twentieth-century American culture. At one level these stories offered their readers comfort through humor in allowing them to laugh at servants' behavior as well as in reminding them that their struggles with servants were shared ones. At another they offered advice about how to deal with trials, often through a moral at the end. Finally, they served to reinforce divisions Victorians wished to preserve between themselves and their hired help—largely through allusions to ways that servants sought to subvert their mistress's authority. Far from being mere diversions, these accounts encouraged their readers to assert authority over their homes to preclude resistant acts on the part of their domestics that might threaten household order.

A common theme in didactic fiction revolves around mistresses' fears that their supervision of the service zone was only intermittent. The account of Mrs. Smith's battles with Kitty is typical. Mrs. Smith's fear of Kitty's actions as she moves about the house drives her obsessive preoccupation with activities below stairs, largely because she worries that her supervision is not perpetual. The particular choice of behavior on Kitty's part—reading—appeared commonly in Victorian didactic fiction, likely because of the multiple levels at which such an action challenged household authority. As much as reading during work time represented slacking off, the particular choice to read also blurred the line between mistress and servant by suggesting aspirations to gentility. A common trope in didactic fictional accounts, the reading servant who seized on moments of leisure outside of her mistress's knowledge, suggested an abiding fear of what could happen if surveillance was not continually exercised.

Visual representations of reading servants produced during the Victorian period echoed sentiments found in written didactic accounts about the temporal limits of surveillance. In a 1910 painting, *The House Maid,* William McGregor Paxton, a Boston-based portraitist and genre painter, portrayed a young servant in profile, who reads a book to the neglect of her domestic duties (fig. 3.17). The servant stands in a domestic space, the precise nature

Fig. 3.17. William McGregor Paxton, *The House Maid,* 1910. Paxton's painting shows a common trope in Victorian-American literary and visual culture: the reading servant. In this case, the servant stands amid an assortment of polite artifacts as she engages in a polite activity, thus suggesting aspiration beyond her station. In the Collection of the Corcoran Gallery of Art, Washington, DC, Museum Purchase, Gallery Fund, Acc. No. 16.9, 30 ¼ x 25 ⅛ in., oil on canvas.

of which is unclear. Situated near the center of the composition in ¾ pose behind a marble top hall table, she is surrounded by an assortment of ceramic objects and an open file box. The graceful curves of her body echo those of the vessels around her, seeming to transform her into a commodity to be gazed on as well. Indeed, with her hair tied up and her genteel demeanor coupled with her choice of activity, reading, her status as servant is thrown into question. The only indication of her charge is the feather duster tucked idly beneath her arm. In many ways the image raises the question of "is she or isn't she?" that suggests the issue of the potential of boundaries to become blurred—a major concern amongst the Victorian American middle-class. The illustration accompanying the story of Mrs. Smith and Kitty is equally charged (fig. 3.1). As Kitty indulges herself in her book—identified in the text as *The Wandering Jew*—dinner literally burns on the stove. Her riveted fixation on her book suggests rather scandalous content, perhaps revolving around the protagonist's indiscretions. If the ambiguous status of Paxton's servant caused anxiety, so did the potential for a servant to descend into filth and squalor reading novels or other sensational tales. Mistresses worried that such books led servants down paths that compromised their domestics' virtue and threatened that of their household as well. Like written didactic accounts, these visual representations warned their readers of potential consequences of intermittent surveillance, particularly by honing in on servants' assertions of authority over their behavior during the workday.

Authors represented servants engaging in all sorts of activities—some sinister, some less so—when free from their mistress's supervision. In one fictional household, a servant simply stopped work periodically to stare out the window or look through magazines, knowing that she was but little watched.[75] A servant in another tale sneaks outside as soon as her mistress left the servants alone, now free to fraternize with men on the doorstep or in the back alley.[76] When mistresses left for the day or evening to attend social functions, more serious infractions often occurred. In one case a mistress came home unexpectedly to find a full-blown party going on in her parlor, even though she had issued a warning to her servants to stay in the kitchen.[77] As the supervisory gaze was only as effective as the length of time it was exercised, heroines portrayed in these stories had no recourse but to devote more time to keep watch or at the very least convey the impression that they would do so. More affluent mistresses hired housekeepers to act as their proxies when they were unable or disinclined to oversee their servants themselves. But some of these heroines discovered that housekeepers often needed watching as well, as Mrs. Harley, the heroine of Sarah Josepha Hale's 1845 novel, *Keeping House and Housekeeping*, had to learn the hard way. After struggling with a series of lazy, incompetent domestics, Mrs. Harley hires a housekeeper, Mrs. Hopkins, to oversee her cook and housemaid. Preferring to socialize rather than supervise her housekeeper, Mrs. Harley ignores Mrs. Hopkins for months, till the Harleys realize she has been stealing from them and also encouraging the other servants to do the same. After finding that Mrs. Hopkins has run up bills all over town, Mr. Harley takes actions into his own hands, excoriating his wife by telling her that "if you are never seen in your kitchen, they [your servants] become careless and indifferent."[78]

Other didactic writers portrayed servants taking advantage of the limited scope of the mistress's gaze, recognizing the remove of the service zone from domestic spaces frequented by their mistress. The zonal organization of houses during the late nineteenth and early twentieth centuries allowed some of the fictional servants to claim the kitchen as their exclusive domain. A series of cartoons published in *Harper's Monthly* in 1856 and 1857 entitled "The Miseries of Mistresses" show servants taking advantage of their freedom in the kitchen, where they were but infrequently watched. In one cartoon the mistress enters to find her servant hosting a gathering in the kitchen, replete with a sizable

"Who is them Fellows, did you say, Mum? Them Gentlemen's my Cousins, Mum, jist dropped in to kape me company, Mum!"

Fig. 3.18. Cartoon from "The Miseries of Mistresses," probably by Lossing-Barritt, from *Harpers Monthly* 13 (October 1856): 717. This cartoon suggests a common fear of mistresses in the Victorian period regarding potential trouble below stairs. Though servants often could entertain suitors or friends in the kitchen when free of their duties, mistresses worried about the potential disorder that could arise. The overturned chair and sheer number of guests in this image play on mistresses' worst fears about the kind of trouble that might occur.

"And so, Jane, this is Missis Jones's new Bonnet! Cost only ten Dollars! I'd be ashamed to be seen with such a thing on!"

Fig. 3.19. Cartoon from "The Miseries of Mistresses," by Lossing-Barritt, from *Harpers Monthly* 13 (October 1856): 718. This cartoon also played on mistresses' fears about servant behavior in their own spaces. Here servants neglect their work to try on and judge their lady's bonnet, which they deem tacky. For polite audiences, this image also had humorous content, since servants were thought to have poor taste and be unable to judge fashion.

and likely expensive ham that may have been intended for the family. The servant curtsies to her mistress, informing her that the six "gentlemen" are her cousins, who "jist dropped in to kape me company." The motley crew's respectability, however, is questionable. Several hide in the shadows, a couple of them seem particularly drunk, and the two in the foreground, one dressed in military attire, look particularly coarse. The overturned chair alludes to the rowdiness of this particular gathering and functions as a sign generally of disorder in the household (fig. 3.18).[79] Another illustration from *Harper's Monthly* shows three servants trying on their mistress's bonnets in the kitchen without any concern she might discover them (fig. 3.19). Their degree of freedom was apparently such that they criticize their mistress's tacky taste without fear of being heard, given the remove of the kitchen from the rest of the house.[80] In their private bedrooms, servants felt an even greater degree of freedom from surveillance. Several accounts described incidents where servants treated their chambers as private bars, while another tale describes a servant caught harboring the kitchen's stores in her room.[81]

Other didactic writers offered ways in which domestics exploited the limited range of surveillance as they moved throughout the house, performing their duties. Heroines in these stories complain of feeling that they cannot leave the parlor while dusting alongside their servants without coming back

MY MISTRESS'S BONNET.

Fig. 3.20. Engraving (likely by C. T. Hinckley), "My Mistress's Bonnet." From *Godey's Lady's Book* 37 (Sept. 1848): 119. Another image playing upon mistresses' fears, this one shows a mischievous servant who has stopped work to try on her mistress's bonnet and muff with a particularly smug degree of satisfaction on her face. Courtesy, The Winterthur Library: Printed Book and Periodical Collection.

to a broken valuable. A story in *The Biddy Club* revolves around a mistress trying to prevent this by telling her servants they have to pay for any items they break.[82] In other cases domestics merely disregard rules that they would abide by if under the gaze of their mistress, thereby acting out the eye service that advice writers warned of. An 1848 illustration from *Godey's Lady's Book* shows a servant trying on an elaborate bonnet and muff, presumably that of her mistress, while cleaning her employers' room. The idle broom signifies her failure to meet her charge (fig. 3.20). Displaying a sly grin as she admires herself in the mirror, the servant seems unconcerned that she may be discovered—a warning to middle-class mistresses not just of the conniving nature of servants but also of their lack of concern generally about authority.[83] A cartoon from *Harper's* displays a mistress entering her bedroom to discover one of her servants brushing her teeth with the mistress's perfume (fig. 3.21). To her horror (and likely also to the Victorian American middle-class viewer's amusement), the servant does not seem to understand the difference between perfume and tooth powder, as her vulgar response to her mistress's inquiry in the cartoon's caption suggests. As with didactic fictional accounts, including that of the Harleys discussed above, the cartoon implies that mistresses must always be vigilant in watching servants or risk jeopardizing their household's integrity and respectability.[84] Occasionally stories treat servants' transgressions

SALLY (*loquitur*).—"I wish Mr. Smith would get another bottle of Balm of a Thousand Flowers—it do give one such a sweet breath!"

Fig. 3.21. Cartoon from "The Miseries of Mistresses," by Lossing-Barritt, from *Harpers Monthly* 13 (Oct. 1856): 717. For nineteenth-century audiences, images such as this reassured them that despite their servants' aspirations to gentility and inclination to shirk work, they certainly had nothing serious to fear. This servant tries to use Mrs. Smith's perfume as tooth powder, much to her mistress's horror. Courtesy of the Libraries of the University of Wisconsin-Madison.

that occur outside the confines of the home, thus making a family's lack of decorum potentially visible to their neighbors.[85] Probably the most frightening case of eye service comes from a story about a mistress who discovers that her nursemaid, perfectly pleasant and responsible in front of her employers, often had taken the baby on walks into rather undesirable parts of town while she ignored the child to flirt with young men.[86] Most challenges to the limited scope of the mistress's gaze in written and visual accounts are less appalling, but all represent challenges on the part of servants to their mistresses' authority.

Authors of didactic accounts also represented servants rooting out places where the hierarchical gaze failed to see beneath the surface. Even if mistresses entered servant spaces regularly to assert their authority, fictional servants took advantage of the fact that their employers only cursorily inspected their domain. Eunice Beecher recounted a story of one woman who discovered her gaze's limitations after her servant had quit. On inspecting the kitchen, the woman was horrified to find that behind and beneath what appeared on the surface to be clean and neat, everything was dirty and disorderly.[87] A cartoon published in the May 1858 edition of *Ballou's Dollar Monthly Magazine* visually warns mistresses that they must look carefully to detect their servants' deceit (fig. 3.22). In this cartoon a rather haggard-looking mistress looks dead on into the face of her servant while she asserts there is a man in the house. Mary, meanwhile, holds her ground, spreading her skirt to conceal her beau, crouched behind her. The didactic message here seemed to be that only a scrupulous gaze will provide proper oversight. Here the mistress misses something that is quite literally hidden by her servant.[88]

For middle-class mistresses, these kinds of didactic tales operated at multiple levels. As a form of entertainment, didactic fictional accounts offered readers, at least some of the time, a humorous respite from household drudgery. Reading of the trials of fictional mistresses, women would also have been reminded that others shared their struggles. Even more important, such accounts gave women advice about superintending their homes. Instances of servant resistance, in

"Nonsense, Mary! I tell you it is my firm opinion there's a man in the house."

Fig. 3.22. Anonymous cartoon from *Ballou's Dollar Monthly Magazine* 7 (May 1858): 502. Mistresses of the period worried about their servants' deception, including their inclination to host guests when they should be working. This image plays upon that anxiety, while also reminding women that they should cast their gaze widely to maintain household authority. Courtesy of the Free Library of Philadelphia.

particular, served to warn mistresses about potential evils that could result from not attending to their duties as household managers. If at one level they offered precautionary advice, at another they supplied their readers a dose of realism in suggesting that even with all the best efforts, problems were inevitable. The heroine in *Trials and Confessions of an American Housekeeper* is an experienced, knowledgeable housekeeper who understands and welcomes her responsibilities, but even she fails to live up to the high standards set out in the advice literature on household management. Like much domestic advice literature in Victorian America, such accounts attempted to reassure mistresses that even if rigorous supervision could not prevent all transgressions, it gave them a strategy to help maintain authority over the domestic realm.

Anxiety about resistance in these accounts above all has to be understood in the broader context of the cult of domesticity that flourished in the Victorian period. With women as arbiters of the domestic sphere, maintaining authority over household affairs had ramifications beyond the walls of the home and on society at large. As Beecher and Stowe explained in *The American Woman's Home,* women had tremendous responsibility as moral leaders of the household: "Woman's profession embraces the care and nursing of the body in the critical periods of infancy and sickness, the training of the human mind in the most impressible period of childhood, the instruction and control of servants, and most of the government and economies of the family state. These duties of woman are as sacred and important as any ordained to man."[89] Victorian writers such as Beecher and Stowe urged women to manage the domestic sphere actively. Through their strict and disciplined eye, mistresses could support and nurture other members of the household and in the process serve the interests of society by keeping healthy and moral homes. Should they prove undisciplined as domestic managers, hierarchies on which the efficient maintenance of the home depended would collapse. This threatened their and their families' respectability as well as potentially jeopardized the moral order of Victorian society.

In account after account, didactic authors showed how more rigorous surveillance as part of a comprehensive approach to household management could help mistresses affirm their household's reputation and, in some cases, salvage it. In giving over all of her responsibilities to a rather surly and conniving housekeeper and refusing to oversee anything with regards to household affairs, the heroine of *Keeping House and Housekeeping* quickly loses control over her household. On her arrival the housekeeper takes over the finances, the menu, and many other duties that Mrs. Harley felt were outside a servant's domain. But more significant than the loss of power that Mrs. Harley comes to feel or the day-to-day problems that have resulted from her lack of oversight, she loses the respect of her friends and family. When the Harleys throw a dinner party, Mrs. Harley's inadequacies are on view for all to see. The menu has not been planned properly, the arrangements of the parlor and dining room are unacceptable, and the service does not meet the needs of her guests. Through her aunt's tutelage, Mrs. Harley ultimately realizes that she must supervise her servants closely if she is to maintain a genteel Victorian home, even though it takes some time to regain her husband's and friends' respect.[90]

Didactic fiction thus echoed the advice of domestic writers on the role surveillance could play in maintaining one's domestic virtue. In *American Woman's Home*, Beecher and Stowe emphasized that a genteel Christian home could be maintained only through a mistress's careful oversight of domestic affairs.[91] In *All Around the House*, Eunice Beecher linked the moral health of the household directly to the mistress's gaze:

> But are you not the mistress? Whose place but yours to watch their shortcomings and take active measures to prevent them? Servants are often great trials; but would they be half so troublesome if the mistress's eyes were more frequently over every portion of her house; if her maidens understood perfectly well that, while she was kind and in no wise [*sic*] overbearing, she was at the same time efficiently observant; that she was just to them and also to the interests committed to her charge? . . .
>
> If this course was pursued and fully understood in every family, should we not have better service, larger incomes, and much more quiet homes?[92]

Didactic accounts, meanwhile, suggest how actions around surveillance on the part of mistress and servant bore directly on the hierarchical relationship between them. Such stories stress how surveillance could help mistresses preserve their dominant position in the household hierarchy, maintain order in their homes, and assure their domestic virtue.

Though undoubtedly many mistresses relied on supervisory strategies (visual and otherwise) promoted by advice writers strictly as a strategy of asserting authority, others likely saw it as something they could use to mentor their employees in the event they might one day manage their own households. Although still hierarchical in nature, especially given that teaching servants proper ways of doing things directly evidenced the mistress's domestic virtue, this more benevolent form of surveillance ultimately worked as a means by which mistresses shared knowledge with their female companions in the home alongside whom they often worked. This kind of surveillance is certainly an aspect of the fictional Smith household described at the beginning of this chapter. Despite the dinner debacle, Mrs. Smith apparently appreciates Kitty's literary bent, electing to keep her around for some time. Perhaps the young cook's voracious appetite for reading has led Mrs. Smith to conclude that she might be a potentially good companion. Another of Mrs. Smith's struggles with Kitty suggests how surveillance could work in this vein. The story begins with Mrs. Smith again hearing a commotion below stairs. She "stepped lightly down" to "sneak a peek" through the cracked door, only to watch in disbelief as Kitty struggles to try to convince a lobster to lay on the fire to be cooked. Rather than scold Kitty, Mrs. Smith enters the kitchen to explain gently to her young cook that it is futile to try to cook a lobster in this manner. After both have had a good laugh, she instructs Kitty on how to cook a lobster easily by boiling, not broiling, it.[93] In this tale the author showed that Mrs. Smith has used surveillance less to castigate and more to instruct in a manner suggestive of a maternal relationship rather than one strictly of employer to employee.

Regardless of whether mistresses exercised surveillance in a vein of prevention, punishment, or maternalism, advice writers and their middle-class female audience recognized that the gaze involved two parties whose actions affected their hierarchical relationship to each other. Surveillance could affirm divisions, but it could also forge bonds—something the advice literature suggested even as it upheld the hierarchical divide between mistresses and servants. In the next chapter, I turn to another landscape, the religious camp meeting, where the fact that surveillance works between individuals took on even greater significance. At these Victorian American retreats, surveillance worked in multiple directions between different parties, who gazed on one another with purposeful intent, quite different from the one-way hierarchical gaze in late-nineteenth- and early-twentieth-century middle-class homes. In this context surveillance functioned as a means of forging divisions between campers and groups as well as a way of helping affirm bonds between members of a community united in a spirit of fellowship.

Chapter 4

FELLOWSHIP

The value of any camp meeting is not in the number of spectators who attend, but rather in the number of seekers who receive spiritual help. The skies are still full of Pentecost and whenever men assemble with one accord and one mind, marvelous is the response from above. What times of fellowship! What manifestation of the Divine Power!

—Description of Mission of God's Holiness Grove
Camp Meeting, founded 1920, from the
50th Year Anniversary Brochure

In early September of 1920, a group convened on the northwest bank of the Susquehanna River in central Pennsylvania for the first camp meeting at God's Holiness Grove (fig. 4.1). For ten days the devout gathered to worship, leaving behind everyday concerns to commune with fellow Christians, traveling ministers and exhorters, and God in this eight-acre wooded lot in rural Snyder County. Clearing the dense brush in early summer left them little time or money to erect permanent buildings. During the first year, they worshipped in a canvas tabernacle and slept in canvas tents. The next summer they erected a frame dining hall, as well as an open forty-by-sixty-foot frame tabernacle to protect campers from the elements during services. In 1925 they built a small house for the camp's caretaker near the main road and replaced some of the impermanent tents with framed, weatherboarded cabins, each averaging roughly thirteen by twenty feet in size. One by one these cabins, nearly identical in construction and level of finish, replaced their canvas predecessors. Campers expanded the tabernacle as the camp grew, first by extending its length to 105 feet, then by enclosing it in 1934, and finally by widening it

Fig. 4.1. View of entrance to God's Holiness Grove Camp Meeting, Hummels Wharf, Pennsylvania, at the first camp meeting on the grounds, September 1920. At this point, campers lived in makeshift canvas tents (seen in the background), which were arranged in neat rows surrounding the central brush arbor, located behind where most campers were standing. From Lodge W. Chappell, Harry J. Daniels, and John P. Campbell, *Camp Meeting Memories: A Short History of Holiness Camp Meetings in Central Penna* (Sunbury, PA: Sunbury Daily Item, 1951). Courtesy of *The Daily Item,* Sunbury, Pennsylvania.

approximately twenty feet on each side in the late 1940s. By 1947 God's Holiness had reached its largest extent, having ninety-nine frame tents laid out in parallel rows around the large centrally positioned tabernacle (fig. 4.2). The grounds remained fairly intact until the last service was held in 2001, prior to the demolition of the camp in 2003.[1]

The piecemeal construction of camps such as God's Holiness typified the development of many rural meeting grounds, the broader history of which extends back to around 1800, when the first camps appeared on the American landscape.[2] At these camps worshippers congregated annually to awaken, confirm, or advance their religious beliefs by attending a series of daily worship services and by socializing with other like-minded Christians. Although Presbyterians, Baptists, and Methodists attended early camp meetings, Methodists most enthusiastically embraced this form of outdoor revivalism. Methodist camps proliferated across the United States during the early Victorian period, drawing women and men of a variety of economic, social, and ethnic backgrounds for a week or more each summer.[3] The late-nineteenth-century Holiness movement breathed new life into camp-meeting revivalism. Originating

Fig. 4.2. Aerial photograph of God's Holiness Grove Camp Meeting, Hummels Wharf, Pennsylvania, ca. 1950. The canvas tents seen in the 1920 photograph have now been replaced by rows of frame cabins, which surround the centrally located frame tabernacle. Also visible are the caretaker's house (lower left), dining hall (lower center), and support buildings in the rear rows of tents, which included washrooms and restrooms (left and right). From archives at God's Holiness Grove Camp Meeting, now Willow Lake Wesleyan Camp, New Columbia, Pennsylvania. Courtesy of God's Holiness Camp Meeting Association.

as a trend within Methodism but quickly becoming interdenominational, the Holiness effort promoted the Wesleyan idea that after conversion, Christians sought sanctification, or holiness, a kind of second blessing which brought them closer to God. Besides holding Holiness services at Methodist camp meetings, Holiness leaders founded camps devoted to sanctification. God's Holiness represents an early-twentieth-century example.[4]

At Methodist and Holiness campgrounds built throughout the Victorian period, camp-meeting advocates envisioned surveillance as a critical part of the daily activities. Campers arranged the campsite to facilitate visual intercourse between and among worshippers, as the design of God's Holiness illustrates. The physical and symbolic nucleus of this camp—the central area where religious services occurred—aided the reciprocal forms of surveillance there in multiple ways. From a raised preaching stand—first in the open air, later in the tabernacle—the presiding minister or exhorter gazed over the entire camp. He could fix his gaze on worshippers intently listening on benches in front of him as well as look toward those who preferred to stay on the porches of their residential tents on the periphery (fig. 4.3). Likewise the benches and frame

Fig. 4.3. View of preaching stand inside tabernacle at God's Holiness Grove Camp Meeting, Hummels Wharf, Pennsylvania, prior to demolition. Photograph by the author, 1998.

tents faced inward, offering worshippers views of the pulpit and the religious proceedings that occurred there (fig. 4.4). Builders also took into account the natural slope of the land in arranging the campground. The minister's pulpit stood at the lowest point, creating a theatrical spatial configuration that directed the gazes of campers toward the symbolic heart of the campground. The compact arrangement of tents also brought campers into constant fellowship as did the design of individual tents. Multiple doors and large windows prompted occupants to gaze on others at the same time they invited surveillance by exposing the private sphere to onlookers.

Surveillance at Methodist and Holiness camp meetings of the late nineteenth and early twentieth centuries was of a complex nature. Although surveillance at these meetings was often visual, surveillance here—as elsewhere—could be multisensate, involving auditory as well as visual acts that both worked with the same transformative purpose. At camp meetings the layout of the grounds facilitated surveillance as participants moved about. From an elevated pulpit located at the center or at one end of the worship space, ministers and exhorters could oversee the congregation, delivering the gospel in hopes of saving the souls of their listeners. But equally significant, worshippers could return the speakers' gazes in hopes of reaching a higher religious plane, potentially looking beyond them toward a higher power. Worshippers at camp meetings

Fig. 4.4. View looking south toward tabernacle from rear row of circle of tents, God's Holiness Grove Camp Meeting, Hummels Wharf, Pennsylvania, prior to demolition. Photograph by the author, 1998.

also exchanged gazes as they moved throughout the camp-meeting grounds outside of religious services. Placed close together along streets or paths and each displaying many doors and windows, tents were arranged in such a manner that contact—visual and otherwise—with other campers was unavoidable. Pursuing and finding one's place in the camp involved knowing and scrutinizing others. The built environment conditioned all these complex forms of surveillance, in part by collapsing boundaries between public and private space and by directing gazes between and among campers. Here surveillance helped create a climate of ever-present censure ultimately oriented around creating a culture of conformity. Surveillance served as a means by which campers from different walks of life with different religious—and different nonreligious—goals formed and affirmed their relationships to others.

As shown previously, those in power would arrange the built environment to provide surveillance over others, be they prisoners, workers, or domestic servants. Such controlling gazes worked in one direction and from privileged vantage points and were closely tied to the physical organization of these spaces. Surveillance functioned somewhat differently at camp meetings. Partly this was because of the ways in which camp leaders designed the campgrounds as well as because of the way camp-meeting goers understood these environments. In this setting worshippers believed that the ordered, centralized layout of the grounds opened up multidirectional, highly visible, and often reciprocal gazes. In this context surveillance was intended to be omnipresent and ever-scrutinizing. Persons on either end of the gaze could become both its subject and its object.[5] This is not to say hierarchies did not exist, such as those between the minister and members of the congregation, but rather that in this environment surveillance could—and often did—transcend hierarchies demarcating those in power from those on whom power acted.

Surveillance at camp meetings typically involved two or more parties who simultaneously fixated on one another, each with a purposeful aim. By using the term *reciprocal* to describe this form of surveillance, I refer to two-way interchanges between camp-meeting goers. Such exchanges included gazes between worshippers, between them and the preachers, and between both and the omnipresent higher power that campers thought presided over camp meeting services. These complex reciprocal gazes held the potential to transform both seer and those seen, serving as a means by which both attempted to negotiate and establish their place in the camp-meeting community. Even when campers did not trade gazes reciprocally, surveillance often worked in multiple directions at camp meetings. This sharply contrasts with the more monocentric, autocratic modes of surveillance discussed earlier. With the blurring of lines between subject and object, then notions of control, authority, and domination associated with discourses about surveillance break down, even further than in settings where those under surveillance sought and sometimes found ways to resist the imposition of the gaze on them.

The multiple, reciprocal gazes at camp meetings functioned in what I call a context of fellowship. By fellowship I refer to the condition or relation of belonging to a group of like-minded individuals who feel connected on the basis of common goals, interests, or obligations. At Victorian-era camp meetings, participants came together out of a shared interest in and commitment to a set of religious beliefs. As they retreated into the woods for meeting, women and men came together to form self-sufficient, insular communities, which they intended to be opposed to those from which they came. An 1849 defender of camp meetings explained this: "The pride and pomp of the city, with the multiplied cares and distinctions of society, are laid aside, and all meet as members of one family, entitled to equal attention, and destined to the same immortality."[6] At these retreats everyday hierarchies waned as participants forged new relationships derived at least partly around Christian beliefs. However, living at the campsite did not automatically make one part of the camp-meeting fellowship. One's place in the camp-meeting family revolved around the degree to which one possessed religion. This in itself was constantly under negotiation, since one's religious status was at stake at camp-meeting services, where worshippers affirmed and often furthered their religious beliefs. Surveillance served campers as they sought to achieve conversion or sanctification, and thus helped shape the relationship of people and groups to one another within this tight-knit community.

Victor Turner's ideas of liminality, as first presented in his 1969 book, *The Ritual Process: Structure and Anti-Structure*, are helpful in understanding fellowship at camp meetings.[7] Turner suggests that in a liminal state of a ritual process—neither here nor there, betwixt or between—participants enter a condition of flux and uncertainty in which everyday customs, rules, and hierarchies are suspended. While the rituals Turner studied among tribal groups were temporally bound, the bonding effects of individuals in a liminal state—what Turner called communitas—make sustained liminality a vital, and even desired, component of the ritual process. He shows that the effects of communitas could, and often did, linger beyond the ritual occurrence itself.[8] Turner developed his ideas on liminality through his work on tribal cultures and their transformative rituals, but he also studied the modern incarnation of liminal experiences, or what he calls "the liminoid." According to Turner, liminoid experiences are found principally in modern Western leisure activities, which proliferated in Victorian America as a byproduct of industrial capitalism.[9] Because they are a product of choice and means, such leisure activities do not benefit every member of society and thus differ from mandatory rituals found in tribal cultures. In the liminoid state, participants act in their own self-interest more than for the community as a whole, as they would in a liminal state. Turner gave multiple examples of liminoid phenomena in modern Western culture, ranging from sporting events to rock concerts to hobby clubs, but he found one of the earliest manifestations in the rituals associated with Christian pilgrimages. According to Turner, these rites of passage, undertaken as early as medieval times, centered on individual transformation, even if the journeys were usually made collectively and bonds formed as pilgrims journeyed from shrine to shrine.[10]

Going to camp meetings functioned in many ways as a pilgrimage. Campers went seeking salvation through removing themselves to a holy place, thus freeing themselves from commitments in the everyday world at least temporarily. Retreating to the woods was liminoid in removing participants from everyday contexts at the same time that it kept them in an intermediate zone between this world and the eternal state to which they aspired. As they interacted on the grounds, everyday identities and traditional attributes of status ceased to function, just as rules governing everyday behavior relaxed and in some cases were suspended. The layout of the campgrounds and the design of the buildings contributed to the liminoid experience, alluding to the world that campers left behind but making it over in a miniaturized, ordered, and idealized manner that suggested a vision of an imagined heaven. Rather than having different areas where people lived in houses that varied according to their means and tastes, worshippers at camp meetings lived in tents or cabins that at least originally and always to some extent resembled one another and which occupied small, roughly equal-sized lots. These structures stood in close proximity to one another, reflecting values of fellowship at the heart of the camp-meeting experience. The appearance of these individual tents, often decorated in a fanciful manner, added to the otherworldly quality of the camp environment. At Methodist camps frame tents typically displayed abundant Victorian decoration, including bargeboard and scrollwork. In some cases bold paint and lavish decoration made them appear as if out of a dream. Frame tents at Holiness camps tended to be more understated but shared with their Methodist counterparts an ethereal quality. Much of this resulted from the proliferation of doors and windows that pierced the facades, which opened up the interiors to view as if to remind campers of the intimacy of their community. These features served to enhance the liminoid quality of camp meetings as betwixt and between everyday late-nineteenth- or early-twentieth-century urban spaces and unite a utopian Christian heaven of like-minded souls.

As a liminoid space, camp meetings also brought about suspension of rules for surveillance in everyday Victorian settings. Through the open design of the buildings and grounds, Victorian camp-meeting participants relaxed genteel customs that placed limits on unabashed stares and self-display, as surveillance was allowed and even encouraged. For example, women often assumed leadership at camp meetings as exhorters, a very visible public role that Victorian society would have condemned.[11] The way in which all the tents faced the preaching stand encouraged worshippers to gaze on the minister and the events occurring at the mourner's bench—a setting where campers believed that God's grace most strongly fell on the meeting and one that ministers and other camp-meeting goers hoped would spur onlookers' religious growth. The close-knit spatial relationships between buildings pushed campers into constant, daily interaction. The dense arrangement of buildings provided them with ample opportunities to survey and gauge one another's religious status. Architecture at camp meetings played a part in the ways in which customs and traditions governing relationships between public and private, notions of privacy, and genteel behaviors were distorted, moderated, and re-created. Omnipresent surveillance in this liminoid environment, which made one's actions constantly subject to scrutiny and judgment, helped campers forge and affirm their relationship to each other as part of the camp-meeting fellowship.

Surveillance at Methodist
and Holiness Camp Meetings

Methodist and Holiness groups responsible for building camp-meeting facilities during the Victorian period represented just a part of a longer camp-meeting tradition that cuts across Protestant denominations. Protestants attended modest camp meetings as early as the 1780s, and by 1800 and 1801 Christians organized large meetings on the Kentucky and Tennessee frontier.[12] Presbyterians and Baptists abandoned the practice of attending these summer revivals during the first quarter of the nineteenth century, but Methodists relied on camp meetings to gain members, founding hundreds of camps throughout the eastern and middle United States prior to the Civil War.[13] The rapid rate of growth of Methodism, from a denomination having only twenty-eight hundred listed members in 1800 to more than 1 million by 1844, has been attributed to camp meetings.[14] At these camps Methodists aimed to draw sinners into the Christian fold, and the increasing popularity of Methodism during the nineteenth century shows that camp meetings succeeded in this mission. Although exclusively Methodist camps continued to be built after 1850, it became more common during the Victorian period to build interdenominational holiness camps where Methodists and other Protestants worshipped together.[15]

Layouts for the grounds became standardized by the time of the Civil War, so that modern observers have identified patterns and relationships between camps.[16] Some of the similarities may be attributed to the fact that itinerant preachers took ideas about campgrounds with them as they traveled from site to site. It also related to a prescriptive literature on camp meetings. Like other forms of advice literature published during the second half of the nineteenth century, camp-meeting manuals and testimonials often contained a section providing recommendations about camp layout and design.[17] While they often provided minimal suggestions, writers typically stressed the importance of planning the grounds carefully to ensure utmost devotion from the throngs that would attend meetings. Patterns manifested in camp-meeting design and layout across the Victorian period suggest that campers followed these guidelines.

Writers of these manuals and others who wrote about camp meetings during the Victorian period paid particular attention to the main worship space, where camp-meeting goers convened for services. Typically located at the center of the grounds, worship spaces initially were open to the elements but by 1900 usually contained some sort of covered structure to shelter campers from the weather. Lodgings for campers surrounded the tabernacle. At most camps impermanent structures initially served to accommodate worshippers,

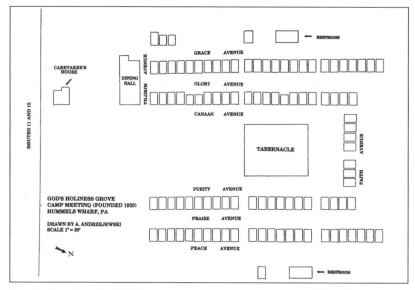

Fig. 4.5. Site plan, God's Holiness Grove Camp Meeting, Hummels Wharf, Pennsylvania, 1998, prior to demolition. Drawing by the author.

but campers gradually replaced them with sturdier tents, usually of frame construction. In some cases campers decorated these small tents with elaborate ornamentation, which served to enhance their heavenly quality. Tents sat along streets or paths, often named after prominent evangelical figures (such as John Wesley) or according to Christian terminology. Large boardinghouses and commercial spaces were rarely present, usually existing only at the largest camps. Facilities for overnight visitors, dining facilities, and commissary buildings where some items could be purchased were typically placed on the edges of the camp, often near the entrance. Man-made and natural boundaries, such as fences, tree lines, or creeks, surrounded most campgrounds, separating them physically from the outside world at the same time that they did symbolically, marking them off as sacred spaces.[18]

Variations in camps generally involved the spatial relationship of residential units and other support buildings to the communal worship space. The range of options may be gleaned from looking at a series of examples from east-central Pennsylvania built during the late nineteenth and early twentieth centuries. God's Holiness Grove Camp Meeting exemplified an early twentieth-example of the open-plan layout, which dominated Victorian-era camp-meeting design. In open-plan camps, all the tents faced toward the centralized worship space,

Fig. 4.6. View of one of the "double-cabins" at Elm Grove Camp Meeting, Center Valley, Pennsylvania. Fourteen of these were positioned around a central worship space in 1998, though several were deteriorating. Photograph by the author, autumn 1998.

which occupied an area at the open end of the row(s) of tents that surrounded it. At God's Holiness, ninety-nine frame tents, arranged in two rows, formed a rectilinear U-shape around the tabernacle (fig. 4.5). Besides the tents and the tabernacle, this campground included a dining hall and a caretaker's house, which are located toward the end of one of the arms of the U, and several other later buildings outside of the main core. Another Holiness camp meeting, Elm Grove Camp, founded during the 1920s near the village of Center Valley in Lehigh County, Pennsylvania, displayed a U-shaped layout on a much smaller scale, containing only fourteen double-cabins (fig. 4.6).[19] The row of cabins at Elm Grove was rounded at each of the corners, closer to a true horseshoe shape. Like God's Holiness, the dining hall stood on the end of one of the arms of the U.

Enclosing the tabernacle or worship space within a closed circle of tents was another popular option. Sometimes other communal spaces, such as the dining hall, were located inside the circle, while in other cases such facilities stood outside of it, often adjacent to the entrance to the grounds. In closed-plan camp meetings, the surrounding group of tents could be square, rectangular, circular, or semicircular in shape. Mt. Lebanon Camp Meeting, founded in 1892 by the United Brethren faith and located just north of Lebanon, Pennsylvania, displayed a rectangular variant of the closed plan (fig. 4.7).[20] At this camp canvas

Fig. 4.7. Aerial photograph of Mt. Lebanon Camp Meeting near Lebanon, Pennsylvania, taken by J. William Reddinger (2004) for the one hundredth anniversary of the construction of the Tabernacle (built by local carpenter and self-taught architect, John H. Cilley). The photograph shows the centrally located round tabernacle surrounded by cabins and other camp structures. Courtesy of Mt. Lebanon Campmeeting Association, Lebanon, Pennsylvania.

tents originally surrounded a centrally located open worship space containing a preaching stand. By 1900 campers had built a round tabernacle and permanent frame cabins where the original canvas tents once stood (fig. 4.8). Another camp meeting, Mountain Grove Campground, founded in the early 1870s in Luzerne County, Pennsylvania, employed another variation of the closed plan. No longer extant, its configuration is suggested by an illustration that appeared in a locally published atlas.[21] The camp meeting was semicircular in shape, with additional avenues lined with tents radiating out from the sides, probably necessitated by expansion. A semicircle of tents framed the open worship space. The pulpit stood at the center of a row of tents that formed the diameter of the semicircle. Both the closed and open layouts had limits in terms of expansion, since tents could not be added in the circle as the camp grew. Instead campers built later rows of tents immediately behind the first or along avenues radiating outward, as at Mountain Grove.[22] If the camp grew too large, worshippers erected new tents outside of the original scheme.[23]

A third popular layout scheme, the radial plan, appears to have been developed out of an anticipated need of expansion. Radially planned camps

Fig. 4.8. Historical photograph (taken by Harpels of Lebanon, Pennsylvania) of tabernacle and environs at Mt. Lebanon Camp Meeting near Lebanon, ca. 1914. Courtesy of Mt. Lebanon Campmeeting Association, Lebanon, Pennsylvania.

appeared on the American landscape during the last few decades of the nineteenth century, suggesting that they were an attempt to improve on the earlier open- and closed-plan layouts that dominated camp meetings prior to this.[24] A 1940s plan of Highland Park Camp Meeting, a Methodist camp founded in 1893 near Sellersville in Bucks County, Pennsylvania, showed that the original frame tents were to be built around the tabernacle in a square, but that later tents would be erected along eight avenues extending from the corners and sides of the main square.[25] The campground as it developed in the course of the early twentieth century proceeded roughly along these lines, although not to the scale that the founders hoped, as a plan from 1943 suggests (fig. 4.9). Not all of the eight planned rows were fully developed, but a few cabins lined several rows of tents that radiated outward from the main circle on the northeast, northwest, west, and south sides. The dining hall and an early boardinghouse at the camp stood at the end of two of these avenues. According to a former president of the camp, avenues followed this radial pattern so that campers would have unobstructed views of the tabernacle when they stood on their cabin porches.[26]

Regardless of the particular configuration, camp-meeting grounds shared a centralized organization that focused worshippers' attention away from the

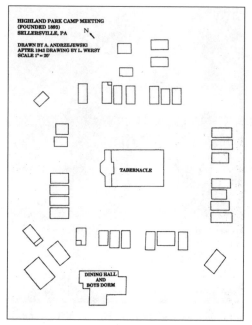

Fig. 4.9. Site Plan of Highland Park Camp Meeting, Sellersville, Pennsylvania. Drawing by the author after a 1943 plan by Lyman Werst in the camp office of Highland Park Camp Meeting Association in Sellersville, Pennsylvania.

outside world and the concerns of everyday life. Besides providing a physical separation, boundaries on the edges of camp-meeting grounds—whether tree lines, rivers, or fences—directed worshippers' attention inward toward the camp.[27] Residential tents either faced the worship space or tabernacle, except in the case of radial plans. In these plans, tents fronted the streets, which traveled toward the tabernacle, implying a direct, albeit collective, line of sight toward the spatial and symbolic heart of the camp meeting.[28] The elevated preaching stand, strategically located in a position in the central worship space to command views of as much of the camp as possible, afforded exhorters oversight of the campground. Like managers on elevated platforms in factories, they held a position that spanned the entire view—something not lost on campers. Campers in turn sat in a manner so that every seat yielded a view of the stand. The arrangement meant that actions of each were open for all to see, even if not clearly at all times.

The design of individual cabins and their compact arrangement on the grounds encouraged constant interactions between campers.[29] In her important book about Wesleyan Grove Camp Meeting in Martha's Vineyard, Massachusetts, Ellen Weiss observed how doors and windows dominated the facades of the cottages there. Although the abundance of doors and windows certainly provided some relief from the hot and humid summer air, Weiss showed how this also prompted campers to look inside individual cabins.[30] She quoted an 1867 article from the *New York Times* on Wesleyan Grove, which noted that the cabins appeared to have been designed to provide "a glimpse of all that transpires within."[31] Another commentator remarked on the openness of campgrounds at Wesleyan Grove in 1870:

> Here, even domestic life itself is as open as daylight. . . . Sauntering through the leafy lanes in close proximity to invitingly open doors and windows, one sees families at their meals, tempting larders in plain sight, and the processes of cooking, ironing, and other household duties, performed by the mothers or daughters themselves, with graceful unconsciousness or indifference to outside eyes. Occasionally, when curtains are not dropped, or sliding partitions closed, beds and even their inmates are disclosed. Everywhere ladies and children, in full or easy toilet, reading, writing, gossiping, amusing themselves at their discretion, unawed by spectators and as completely at home outside as inside their own doors.[32]

In addition to the prominence of doors and windows on the cottages, large balconies and porches encouraged campers to socialize with others at Wesleyan Grove. Even if not to the same degree of elaboration, tents at other camp meetings, Methodist and Holiness alike, displayed multiple doors and large windows. At God's Holiness the front and rear facades of each of the cabins had a central door flanked by two small windows (fig. 4.10). For tents on the front row, this meant that the back door acted almost as a second front door that opened into the tiny front yards of the tents in the row behind it. Benches outside many of the cabins encouraged campers to spend time in view of others at God's Holiness.

The close proximity of tents to each other and the lack of sizable yards, fences, and dense clusters of trees at many campgrounds made privacy all but impossible. A late-nineteenth-century lithograph of Patterson Grove Camp Meeting in Luzerne County, Pennsylvania, illustrates the density of the Victorian camp meeting. The main part of the image is devoted to the worship space, into which bodies are packed tightly. Flanking this space stand the cottages, themselves as condensed as are the campers listening to the orator. The detail in the lower right of an avenue within the grounds suggests the way that the concentration of cottages created a living environment that seems claustrophobic (figs. 4.11 and 4.12).[33] This arrangement echoes the experience at

Fig. 4.10. View of typical cabin at God's Holiness Grove Camp Meeting, Hummels Wharf, Pennsylvania, prior to demolition. Note the large portion of the façade given over to windows and doors. Most of the cabins have a centrally positioned door on the front and back, flanked by two large windows. Additional windows pierce the sides of the cabins, despite their close proximity to one another. Benches outside many cabins encourage campers to spend time in view (and viewing) others. Photograph by the author, 1999.

God's Holiness, where adjacent cabins were separated from one another by less than a foot. In such an environment, perpetual interaction with other campers would have been unavoidable.

Camp-meeting manuals, charters, and rulebooks stressed the importance of visibility on the campground and suggested how the design of the grounds and camp buildings supported it. The 1874 manual of the Denville Camp Ground of the Newark Conference Camp Meeting Association provided strict guidelines about building tents that included restrictions on their maximum size and placement on the grounds. Fences on the grounds were prohibited; the kind of privacy a fence provided was antithetical to the kind of close-knit communal environment the camp wished to foster.[34] Rules at most camps stipulated that at least a single light must be on in residential cabins at all times, enhancing the visibility of the interiors of the cabins.[35] Although this practice held symbolic significance, campers also believed it would prevent disorderly and sinful conduct by making one space where potentially illicit activities could occur open to view.[36] At Wesleyan Grove, rule no. 8 of the 1858 rulebook stipulated that a light should be kept burning all night in each of the cabins.[37] Rule no. 13 of the 1889 Manual of Crystal Spring Camp Meeting, a

Fig. 4.11. Unknown artist, *Patterson Grove Auditorium, Patterson Grove Camp Ground, Fairmount Township, Luzerne County, Pennsylvania,* last quarter of the nineteenth century, lithograph, 86.534. This lithograph suggests the close-knit nature of the camp meeting community. The tents are crowded close together, as are the worshippers in the main worship space, making the environment seem almost claustrophobic. Courtesy of Palmer Museum of Art, The Pennsylvania State University, partial gift and purchase from John C. O'Connor and Ralph M. Yeager.

Fig. 4.12. Detail of fig. 4.11, showing an avenue between the cabins. The scene suggests the environment's lack of privacy, with doors located on both ends of the cabins' gable ends, through which passersby could look into the cabins.

Methodist camp in Fulton County, Pennsylvania, stated that "Tent holders will be required to have lights in their tents during the night service and the front door open," exposing the private space of the camp-meeting home to the watchful gaze of other worshippers.[38]

An 1874 novel by Mary Harriott Norris entitled *Camp Tabor: A Story of Child Life in the Woods* suggests the degree to which campers sacrificed personal privacy.[39] Inspired by a camp meeting in Morris County, New Jersey, that Norris had attended, the novel revolves around four children and their daily experiences at the camp. The following scene, which takes place on one of the first mornings of camp meeting, describes the close contact between campers. Charlie, one of the young children, awakes to sounds of laughter next door. Curious about its origins, he peers out of his tent:

> Charlie thrust his curly head through his tent-curtains at the identical moment that Bentie looked out from hers. The black eyes, intent on seeing the new comers, looked straight into the gray ones, determined to take in all of their surroundings.
>
> The two children were so surprised at their relative positions that for a moment they gazed unabashed. Then each head disappeared, to come out a moment after for a second view.[40]

Throughout Norris's novel she repeatedly draws attention to the fact that one's actions were constantly open to view. On another morning, Trot, the youngest child, walks through camp "with no other object than to have a peep into the cottages." Trot views people making breakfast and cleaning up. While returning to her quarters, she notices a small tent set away from the others. Trot walks up to the tent and gazes in to see a disfigured and poverty-stricken woman saying her morning prayers, whom she later befriends.[41] Norris used these vignettes to show the children's naiveté and offer a fresh look at life at camp meeting by writing of their experiences, but such accounts also reveal how much the daily happenings at camp meetings depended on active gazes exchanged between worshippers.

Another kind of surveillance at camp meetings involved the gazes exchanged between worshippers and the exhorters who presided over the services. Such reciprocal acts of surveillance related to the religious end of camp meetings: to encourage camp-meeting goers toward higher spirituality. At Methodist camps founded before the Civil War, leaders focused on converting sinners. At camp meetings held later in the Victorian period, speakers hoped to prompt conversions as well as help the already-converted attain sanctification, a higher level of religious belief in which one renounced all sins and became holy in the eyes of God.[42] Thus at the camp meeting there were potentially multiple ritualistic transformations at stake for different campers and groups. Reciprocal gazes between speakers and worshippers helped to assure the latter's participation in services, thought to be critical to the success of religious exercises—whatever the ultimate goal might be.

Illustrations from ministers' biographies and camp-meeting manuals hint at how the physical layout of campgrounds furthered reciprocal gazes between worshippers and preachers. An engraving of Deal's Island Camp Meeting in Maryland from an 1861 biography depicts Joshua Thomas, a famous camp-meeting exhorter, preaching to worshippers who in turn gaze on him (fig. 4.13).[43] Although some campers on the fringes of the circle engage in conversation while a few others bow their heads in prayer, the eyes of most have dutifully focused on Thomas. The illustrator amplifies the preacher's centralized position by enclosing the figure within the supports of the preaching stand as if to frame his importance. The placement of the stand itself directs these gazes, as it occupies a central and elevated position on the grounds. Further, the benches on which the worshippers sit radiate outward from the stand. Behind them all the tents in the circle face the central preaching space. The frontispiece

DEAL'S ISLAND CAMP MEETING.

Fig. 4.13. Anonymous engraving, Deal's Island Camp Meeting, Deal's Island, Maryland. This image shows the elevated, centrally located preaching stand from which Joshua Thomas exhorts to worshippers, many of whom gaze intently at him. From Adam Wallace, *Parson of the Islands; A Biography of the Rev. Joshua Thomas* (Philadelphia, 1861). Courtesy of the University of Delaware Library, Newark, Delaware.

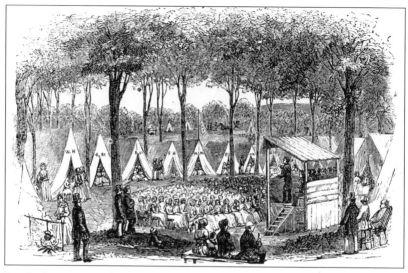

Fig. 4.14. Frontispiece from B[arlow] W[eed] Gorham, *Camp Meeting Manual: A Practical Book for the Camp Ground* (Boston: H. V. Degen, 1854). Gorham suggests the ideal camp meeting arrangement here, with a centrally located and elevated preaching stand, which facilitates gazes of worshippers toward it.

from Reverend B. W. Gorham's *Camp Meeting Manual*, published in 1854, also indicates how the layout of grounds could foster gazes between worshippers and ministers (fig. 4.14).[44] In this view most worshippers sit on benches or in front of their tents, which all face toward the central, conspicuously located stand. Their eyes appear fixed on the minister, who, from his privileged position, gazes back at his audience as he delivers his missive to them. Very much like the gaze in prisons, the gaze of minister to worshipper was as much symbolic as it was literal. These illustrations suggest that in actuality views would have been limited, given the size of the congregations. What mattered was the sense of surveillance, which the organization of the camp-meeting grounds helped to foster.

In his 1859 autobiography, William Henry Milburn, a blind Methodist preacher, discoursed on the importance of the minister-worshipper gaze. Milburn articulated his desire for eye contact with his audience asserting that the power of the minister, and through him the power of God, manifested itself as a result of this visual exchange. Stressing the importance of seeing the congregation and being seen by them, Milburn expressed anxiety about his own rhetorical prowess:

> Who has not felt the matchless power of the human eye? . . . Men not
> only see with their eyes, but hear; for the beaming eye and expressive face

speak a language that articulate sounds can never express—a language more moving, soft, and irresistible than ever entered the soul through the galleries of the ear. Through the eye, the speaker enters into sympathy with his audience, by it he perceives their capacity, reads their wants, appreciates their condition; by it they are persuaded of his simplicity, earnestness and faith . . . so true is it, here at least, "that seeing is believing."[45]

Milburn felt strongly that it was in and through the gaze that conversion of sinners and sanctification of believers occurred. Even if he could not see his worshippers with his own eyes, Milburn connected with his congregation through his words and his physical and symbolic position as minister while also functioning as the focus of their visual attention. The design and layout of Victorian-era Methodist and Holiness camp meetings of the type at which Milburn presided helped facilitate these multiple, and often reciprocal, gazes between camp-meeting participants.

Surveillance and Fellowship

Going to camp meeting involved a stepping out of sorts, in which campers separated from aspects of their everyday lives and entered—if only temporarily—a liminoid environment. Here everyday rules waned, as campers donned new mantles based on their religious status as sinner, saved, or sanctified, and united in pursuit of God. The idea of leaving the everyday world and entering a spiritual realm appeared throughout Methodist and Holiness literature on camp meetings.[46] In 1849 a Methodist writer described how retreating to the wilderness offered campers the opportunity to temporarily forsake everyday responsibilities and devote themselves fully to seeking God's blessing:

> Camp-meetings, like the Jewish feasts, take us away from the scenes of our conflicts, and abstract us from care. If we go to church on the Sabbath, it is often under a weight of responsibility which precludes the improvement that is desirable. But in going to camp-meeting we necessarily intrust [*sic*] our worldly cares to other hands. The intervals of public service may therefore be appropriated to prayer and meditation, whereas at home they would be occupied with the hurry and bustle of perplexing business. This is an advantage that cannot be too highly appreciated.
>
> . . . Camp-meetings taking men off many miles from their business and sinful amusements, and holding them to pointed and pathetic preaching and exhortation; and bringing them into immediate contact with the most effective Christians, some of whom were similarly situated to themselves when they were converted, they can but become sources of powerful conviction and impulse, and often of sound conversion.[47]

Holiness advocates saw coming together for a week to ten days as a way of leaving aside mundane concerns to devote attention to higher religious matters. A 1970 history of God's Holiness called the camp a "spiritual Sahara," a comparison that suggests the remoteness of the camp meeting from everyday Victorian American life in central Pennsylvania.[48]

Camp-meeting advocates during the Victorian period explained that campers assembled as one family devoted to shared religious concerns. One of the faithful participants at God's Holiness described how distinctions and divisions outside of a Christian context relaxed as worshippers bonded in a spirit of devotion: "The skies are still full of Pentecost and whenever men assemble with one accord and one mind, marvelous is the response from above. What times of fellowship! What manifestation of the Divine Power!"[49] Similar sentiments appear in earlier Methodist tracts. One writer conveyed the sense of unity experienced as worshippers came together with a shared purpose: "[Camp meetings] bring together members from different parts of the country, circumstanced [sic] variously, and in all possible states of religious interest, where, with friendly greetings, social songs, prayers, and conversation, they become fused and blended into a holy brotherhood, and resolve, with solemn purpose, to be faithful and meet in heaven."[50] Within the camp-meeting grounds, campers sought to unite in a spirit of fellowship. Descriptions of the camps from the Victorian period and beyond emphasized the special quality of these spaces and their distance from everyday life.

This shedding of everyday roles and concerns related to the camp-meeting space in a physical and conceptual sense. As Kenneth O. Brown and Steven D. Cooley have examined, camp-meeting grounds were seen as holy, hallowed, or sacred—whether Methodist, Holiness, or otherwise.[51] Often the entrance to camps was a fairly elaborate gate, suggesting to participants that crossing the gate meant entering a special place. Further, the orderly arrangement of the cabins on equally sized and spaced lots around a central meeting space helped to amplify the transcendental quality of the experience. The arrangement of the camp-meeting city exaggerated some elements of urban life (the density of communal living) and inverted others (by making private aspects of life public). The buildings and layout of the grounds remade and refashioned everyday modes of living in ways which accorded more with the Christian ideal of religious community that centered on shared devotion, unquestioned values, and the opening of oneself to the scrutiny of others.

Within this liminoid space where like-minded Christians gathered in a spirit of fellowship, surveillance (and the ever-present possibility of it) helped campers gauge the religious status of others and affirm their commitment to one another. The ubiquity of surveillance meant that campers knew others consistently judged their actions, leading them to comport themselves accordingly. The possibility of surveillance thus encouraged individuals to fashion their behavior in a manner they felt accorded with acceptable Christian standards or face the consequences. Campers who behaved fastidiously—for example, one who appeared before the mourner's bench in pursuit of sanctification—believed that their example would lead hedonists or lukewarm believers down a more religious path. In this context surveillance held potential to distinguish as well as unify, and to judge as well as affirm. It could sometimes work in divisive ways, however, as campers who did not share the religious goals of the camp meeting were ostracized and scorned. Yet the creation of hierarchies between campers through surveillance worked differently than in the Victorian American spaces discussed earlier, for here it ultimately furthered the sense of fellowship more than it weakened it. Limits and boundaries for acceptable and ideal behavior, judged through surveillance, brought people and groups together, since shared beliefs about inappropriate behavior served as something around which the community could bond. Gazes worked in the liminoid context of the camp-meeting grounds to shape individuals' relationships to one another in ways that ultimately strengthened the community as a whole.

Since the time of the earliest camp meetings, campers relied on surveillance in order to distinguish religious from nonreligious attendees. In his 1823 biography of the Reverend Jesse Lee, one writer articulated a distinction that became commonplace in descriptions of Methodist camp meetings: "The disorder originates from the disorderly spectators, and not from the orderly worshippers who assemble for the sole purpose of spiritual benefit."[52] Many nineteenth-century writers on camp meetings distinguished worshippers, who engaged in the religious activities of camp meetings, from spectators, who came for social reasons or entertainment. In his 1859 book, *Manna in the Wilderness,* the Methodist minister A. P. Mead also adopted this distinction. Mead explained qualities dividing worshipper and spectator through telling a story about his friend who claimed not to enjoy camp meetings:

> "Did you attend as a *spectator,* or as a *worshipper?* Perhaps you stood aloof and looked on, and thus you saw some incidental things which you could not approve, and which doubtless gave you pain. If so, you were like the man who ascended his neighbor's chimney, to observe the fire beneath; his eyes were soon filled with smoke, and he went away grumbling about his neighbor's miserable fire. . . .
> . . . did you take any part in the religious exercises, and thus identify yourself with the good work?"[53]

Mead's friend claimed that he had behaved at camp meetings, explaining that he had not been one of those who came to be disruptive or gawk at the proceedings, as a spectator would have. But for this minister, participation meant more than behaving properly. Joining in required going to camp meetings with a mind to partake deliberately and actively in the rituals there, which his friend conceded he never intended to do.

In using the term spectator to refer to those who did not actively participate in camp meeting activities, these Methodist ministers tied participation (or non-participation) at camp meetings to surveillance. The degree to which campers participated in transformative events occurring on the grounds determined their level of religious commitment and ultimately their degree of involvement in the camp community. In his 1854 *Camp Meeting Manual,* Reverend Gorham warned that one should not go to camp meeting merely to observe (as a spectator), but to engage with the events: "He that goes to church [camp meeting] merely to see or be seen, accomplishes that object and returns home. He that goes to be entertained with the intellectual qualities of a discourse, listens to it in a corresponding temper of mind, and is acted upon accordingly; but he that goes to church [camp meeting] 'hungering and thirsting after righteousness shall be filled.'"[54]

In Methodist discourse about camp meetings, a spectator looked on the events with a passive eye, intent on merely witnessing the striking show of events and refraining from a participatory role. This type of gaze contrasted with the active, transformational gazes of worshippers within the camp-meeting circle, whose gazes sought to influence the behavior of both themselves (to remind them of their religious devotion) and those they judged (to bring them further along the religious path).

Whether one participated in camp-meeting events as a spectator or as a worshipper depended on the spatial position that these different types of campers occupied on the grounds. At services spectators took seats at the back of the worship space or tabernacle, or they stood outside it. Usually they stayed on the grounds only for the day or two. If they stayed overnight, they resided in cabins, tents, or boardinghouses at the margins of the grounds. Worshippers, on the other hand, sat in good seats on benches in the tabernacle and lived in tents on the circle.[55] In an account of the first religious service at the Landisville Camp Meeting for the Promotion of Holiness of 1873 in Pennsylvania, the writer explained the distinctions, noting how worshippers crowded around the stand while the rest of the congregation filled in behind. At this service the Reverend J. S. Inskip warned idle visitors lingering on the outskirts that it might become "too hot" for them in the circle; he encouraged them to "move out into the moonlight" rather than disturb the proceedings.[56] An account of a Holiness meeting in 1869 details how it became too hot for one spectator. Despite his position on the fringes of the grounds, watching the services led to his subsequent conversion. In this account the author expressed surprise about his conversion, noting that his position on the outside of the circle led him to believe it was impossible. The writer's testimony suggests the degree to which one's physical position at camp meetings bore on their degree of involvement in camp-meeting services.[57]

Visual representations of camp meetings illustrated the kinds of distinctions between worshippers and spectators described in written accounts. In these images worshippers are depicted close to the preaching stand, looking intently at the speaker, while spectators stand outside of the worship space and appear to be paying little attention to the religious activities. In an illustration from a nineteenth-century history of Wesleyan Grove (fig. 4.15), the behavior of spectators is very prominent. Several rather disinterested dandies linger on the fringes of the meeting while three others rest against trees in the foreground.[58] One of these, who sits on the ground, appears to be yawning, a sign of his nonparticipation that would have marked him as a spectator

Fig. 4.15. Image of Wesleyan Grove Camp Meeting, Martha's Vineyard, Massachusetts, ca. 1858. Note the contrast between the yawning spectator in the left foreground (as well as the men chatting to his right on the other side of the tree) and the attentive worshippers in the middle ground. Frontispiece, H. Vincent, *A History of the Wesleyan Grove, Martha's Vineyard, Camp Meeting: From the First Meeting Held there in 1835 to that of 1858* (Boston: G. C. Rand and Avery, 1858). Courtesy of Murphy Library, University of Wisconsin–La Crosse.

Fig. 4.16. *Interior View of West Branch Camp Meeting, Clinton County, Pennsylvania* (Philadelphia: W. H. Rease, 1872). In this image, worshippers positioned nearer the preaching stand appear more involved in the service than those on the outskirts, who seem more interested in socializing. Courtesy of the Library of Congress, Prints and Photographs Division.

in the eyes of Victorian viewers. In an 1872 color lithograph of a meeting in Clinton County, Pennsylvania (fig. 4.16), several finely dressed male and female spectators dawdle about on the edges of the grounds, in sharp contrast to the vast majority of the campers, who are seated and gazing toward the preaching stand.[59] They seem preoccupied with displaying their finery, in many cases standing with their backs (and their gazes) turned away from the religious center. As in everyday Victorian society, camp-meeting goers would have read appearances as a means of knowing others. But at camp meetings, campers believed appearances to be less deceiving than in society at large. In this context campers perceived an interest in fashion as a sign of spiritual malaise and ultimately marked the fashionable as spectators only marginally committed to the camp-meeting fellowship.[60]

Camp-meeting manuals and testimonials from campers suggest that worshippers went to meetings accepting that their actions were always open to judgment. They recognized, then, that surveillance could serve as a means of affirming their commitment to one another while at the same time bringing others into the Christian fold. An anonymous 1849 essay by a devout Methodist suggested the power that surveillance could have in transforming behavior. The writer explained the ways in which surveillance could lead spectators along a more righteous path: "And this is common sense—it is philosophical—*right*. God has made us capable of influencing each other. This may be done, to some degree, by writing, meeting in our respective neighbourhoods [*sic*], &c., but cannot be carried to its greatest practicable extent without these imposing conventions [camp meetings]."[61] The author stressed that the influence of good

Christians on less fervent ones pushed the latter toward spiritual growth. He felt that camp meeting provided the perfect forum for spectators to mend their ways, since it offered them the possibility of meeting Christian worshippers to emulate:

> They need to *see* and *hear* a higher order of Christians, [*sic*] and feel their regenerating influence. Reading about them is not enough. The evil is great, and will require the most direct and powerful agency of man to effect its removal.
>
> Camp-meetings bring together the best spirits within a large circumference. Those who possess most of the divine influence, and are best informed in the science of salvation, are much inclined to such meetings. They love to retire from the world, to commune with God and his people. They delight to talk of his word and works—of the blessedness of religion; to sing his praise and tell of his goodness. How appropriate then is the place for the stupid and the impenitent![62]

The author asserted that worshippers, especially those who had been converted or sanctified, had a duty at camp meeting almost as important as that of the preacher. They had responsibility to bring "the difficulties out of the sinner's way . . . and bring him under the most powerful stimulants to duty possible," by which the author meant their own pious behavior.[63] If worshippers did not behave, he knew spectators, who "watched for evil" and "seized upon the slightest impropriety," would notice: "Great care should be exercised in regard to our *general deportment*. . . . The rules of the ground are to be strictly observed. If *we* [model Christians] violate them, how can we enforce them upon others?"[64] Within the camp-meeting environment, where one's actions were perpetually subject to the scrutinizing gaze of others, the author's analysis of the power of influence was telling. His anxiety reveals the degree to which relationships between Methodists at mid-nineteenth-century camp meetings depended on surveillance between worshippers.

At Holiness meetings, hierarchical distinctions between worshippers became more complicated than at Methodist camp meetings held through the early 1860s. At Methodist meetings, campers understood gazes between worshippers and spectators in the context of having the potential to push sinners toward Christian conversion, thus moving toward creating a community of the saved. Therefore religious hierarchies depended on whether one had been converted or not, and one's position, both in a physical sense (in terms of one's location on the grounds) and a religious one, turned on this distinction. But at Holiness camps, new categories emerged: to the categories of sinners and saved were added seekers of Holiness and the sanctified.[65] Although the worshipper-spectator distinction remained in use, in the context of these later camp meetings the label of spectator often referred to the believer who came to camp with no intention of seeking the second blessing as much as it did to the sinner. Rev. R. V. Lawrence, a Holiness preacher, explained:

> The mere fact of being on the camp-ground in the midst of all these holy persons and influences will not make you more holy. . . . The most heavenly scenes of the camp-ground, witnessed as a spectator, but not engaged in as a participant, will harden and disgust. The mere spectator had better hurry off the ground before the devil of ridicule and dislike creeps into his soul.[66]

Knowing who had received the second blessing, who sought it, and who attended merely as a spectator was important at Holiness camp meetings. Through contact with those who had found holiness, the already-sanctified confirmed their beliefs, and seekers moved closer to attaining holiness, all of which furthered the sense of communitas.

The already-sanctified and seekers of holiness had responsibilities besides confirming and advancing their own religious beliefs at Holiness camp meetings. As Reverend Lawrence explained, they needed to use their divine influence to lead others toward sanctification: "Be active in helping others. What! were [*sic*] you so selfish as to come all the way to this Camp Meeting for your own sole benefit? How unlike Jesus! . . . Be active. There is a blessing here for you; find it."[67] By attracting the gaze of others, those who had attained Holiness led by their own holy example. A Holiness preacher working at the 1873 National Camp Meeting for the Promotion of Holiness in Landisville urged seekers of the second blessing and those who possessed holiness to "win a soul for Jesus" by focusing on campers who needed to be converted and bring them along in their quest.[68] Another minister at this camp, L. C. Matlock, reiterated his colleague's words, stressing how the sanctified should exercise special powers of persuasion, recognizing their potential to influence others through their own model behavior, conspicuous for all to see: "These souls become magnetic centres of attraction. Filled with God's gracious power, their light shines, and is seen of men. They radiate pious influences over a vast circumference. Instrumentally they fulfill the Savior's words, 'I, when lifted up, will draw all men unto me.'"[69] At Holiness camp the creation of another religious category—the sanctified—produced an even more complicated fellowship of believers than at earlier Methodist camp meetings, but one that also depended on gazing as a means of forging relationships between campers.

Even more than model worshippers, ministers and exhorters at Methodist and Holiness camp meetings led by example. They served as the focus of aspiring believers' attention while simultaneously exercising powerful gazes themselves. At home in their churches, the faithful typically relied on one minister as their spiritual leader. Methodist and Holiness camp meetings, meanwhile, attracted multiple itinerant preachers who took turns leading religious exercises. At these camp meetings, exhorters served as guiding forces, regardless of who occupied the pulpit at a particular time. During services the elevated preaching stand housed multiple ministers, which reinforced their position as leaders of the meeting, as an 1859 description of a scene around a pulpit suggests: "Hundreds of worshippers, occupying the rude benches, are listening. . . . Nearly a score of ministers occupy a seat directly back of the speaker, and in full view of the congregation. . . . The lights are burning brightly. . . . nothing here to divert attention."[70] The prominent physical position of the speakers dovetailed with their duties as leaders of camp meetings. In his 1854 manual, Reverend Gorham emphasized the need to keep distinctions between ministers and worshippers in place: "On the Camp ground, as in the army, and for similar reasons, there must be a general Head."[71] Through their leadership, itinerant preachers and exhorters assured that worshippers focused on spiritual goals—namely, worship, conversion, and sanctification.

Descriptions of Victorian-era Methodist camp meetings suggest the important role that ministers and exhorters played by converting souls through their moral presence. These accounts emphasized how conversions involved the facility with which worshippers gazed on the preacher and how successfully he returned their gaze, as an 1861 account of a camp meeting at Deal's Island, Maryland, reveals. One visitor to the camp reported how the Reverend Joshua Thomas attracted the attention of the congregation during his exhortation:

> At first I thought the man [Thomas] was a fool, and the preachers were to blame for asking him up. I was about leaving my seat in disgust and indignation, and retiring from the ground; for, though I was not a professor of religion, I respected its order too much, to see it caricatured in that manner. I finally concluded to stand it out, rather than attract attention by my departure. I took a steady look at him, and in that instant one of the strangest sensations I ever had experienced, came over me. I felt that the Spirit of the Lord was there, actuating the man in what he said and did, and for the first time in all my life, I trembled from head to foot, under a new and overpowering conviction that I was a lost sinner.[72]

In this vignette the narrator's conversion took place through the very act of fixing his attention on the minister in his central and elevated position on the stand.[73] At Holiness camp meetings, defenders explained that reciprocal gazes between ministers and worshippers propelled those seeking sanctification toward their goal of attaining holiness. Although some sanctifications occurred at camp-meeting services, in many cases, the beneficiary did not secure the second blessing until several days or weeks later. However, holiness was a lifelong pursuit, and advocates believed that attending to preachers or exhorters during camp-meeting services helped push seekers toward their sanctification, even if they did not achieve it during the orations. An 1873 description of the exhortations of Holiness pastor R. V. Lawrence illustrates his persuasive power, through which he led many in his congregation toward holiness: "Brother Lawrence *employed largely the power of description, and illustration.* . . . he understood human nature well enough to know that a successful pulpit must arrest attention, hold it, and concentrate the thoughts of the hearer upon the great truths of salvation." Through gazing on this man of God, many in Lawrence's crowd had joy awoken in their hearts, while others moved closer to holiness.[74]

Victorian American writers stressed that the reciprocal gaze between worshippers and ministers at Methodist and Holiness services furthered religious piety—for the latter as much as the former. Discoursing on the power of reciprocal surveillance, the blind Reverend Milburn articulated how he received inspiration when he captured the attention of his congregation: "The secret of eloquence is to be found in the eye of the audience, and through it the orator gains his highest inspiration—through it they lend him attention, interest, sympathy—their best thoughts and passions. He is reinforced by their strength, and his powers are enriched by the unrestrained gift of their sensibilities. Thus, it seems, the true power of the speaking man consists in the balanced and serene movement of his intellect and his near and living connection with his hearers through the eye."[75] Milburn described the feeling of realizing that he had arrested the attention of his audience during a sermon, which in turn spurred him to greater depths in preaching God's word. Beverly Carradine, a Holiness evangelist, recounted how, at a camp meeting in 1911, he felt he saw into the souls of people looking back at him. This impelled him to preach his holiness message to them more emphatically, thus helping to unite a congregation devoted to a shared pursuit of sanctification.[76]

However prominent their role at camp meetings, ministers and exhorters ultimately served as conduits to a higher power in this liminoid space. A Methodist preacher explained his purpose as God's agent in a sermon directed at sinners, when he invoked Isaiah 45:22, demanding "look unto me and be ye saved, all ye ends of the earth; for I am God, and there is none else."[77] Looking at the figure in the pulpit, Holiness worshippers also hoped to connect with God and in the process find sanctification. Through gazing on the Holiness reverend John Lakin Brasher, seekers explained how his powers of illustration helped them see God, as J. Lawrence Brasher wrote in his biography of the famous minister:

Letters from Brasher's listeners testify to "eyes opened only in spiritual vision" during his preaching. After hearing him in 1907 at White Cross Camp Meeting near Oneonta, Alabama, Eloway Hurst wrote, "The sermon you preached Sunday was the *richest* I had heard for awhile. It seemed to me sometimes my poor little narrow contracted soul would burst out of its fetters . . . and soar into the heavenlies." A listener in Conneaut, Ohio, told Brasher that his eloquence brought her, "face to face with God Himself." A broadside advertising the camp meeting at Sharon Center, Ohio, announced: "Brasher's flights of oratory carry his hearers very near the gates of heaven."[78]

Gazes at Methodist and Holiness camp meetings extended beyond reciprocal gazes traded between worshippers and between the ministers and their congregation to involve a third, if noncorporeal, player: the spirit that reigned above them who spoke through the ministers and exhorters and to whom the worshippers looked for guidance. God's presence—however ethereal—was a critical part of the camp-meeting fellowship. Seeking his blessing had brought campers to the grounds in the first place and undoubtedly helped motivate the gazes they exchanged as they united in pursuit of salvation and grace.

At Methodist and Holiness camp meetings, annual ceremonies typically closed with a circular procession around the campground. This ritual celebration allowed worshippers a final opportunity to affirm their commitments to one another and God before returning home to their everyday lives. Reverend Mead described the ceremony at a Methodist camp: "The procession starts from the right of the stand, and passes on within the inner circle of tents. . . . We are marching to the music of Zion! We are in the grove! . . . How touching is the scene! Here is manhood with its strength and hope; but who can resist the current of sympathy that flows from heart to heart?"[79] Mead explained that campers at the closing ceremony identified with others in the circle and came together as part of a Christian family. Reverend Edgar Levy recalled the Christian unity that brought campers together in the closing ceremony at the National Camp Meeting at Landisville in 1873, stressing how the meeting had brought together a brotherhood: "As it is the nature of sin to separate, disintegrate and repel, it is nature of holiness to unite, adjust and harmonize."[80]

Surveillance at the closing ceremony worked to remind campers one final time of the liminoid quality of the camp-meeting experience and the communitas they had pursued there. In this ritual everyone's actions were once again on view for all to see. Gazes were encouraged and welcomed as a means of reminding camp-meeting goers that they were part of a united community. Just as the design of the camp fostered constant interaction and encouraged campers to come together, their circular parade around the grounds cultivated feelings of fellowship. As they looked at one another across the circle, campers felt their bonds strengthened. Seeing fellow worshippers gazing back at them, they recalled their role as part of the camp-meeting family united in their commitment to their religious beliefs. Thus despite their different degrees of religion, hierarchies waned through these last acts of surveillance as campers joined in their celebration of God.

CONCLUSION

This book has suggested how concerns about surveillance have shaped buildings and landscapes ranging from the public to the private, the religious to the secular, and the spaces of work to those of leisure during the late nineteenth and early twentieth centuries. Because surveillance seemingly cuts across and through the Victorian American landscape, it is tempting to accept Michel Foucault's claim that modern society "is one not of spectacle, but of surveillance."[1] Indeed, to read discourses of surveillance through the built environment of the United States during this time reveals a preoccupation with the gaze and its potential to transform behavior of individuals and groups. Yet attempting to account for the modern fascination with surveillance by looking at buildings and landscapes through which it worked complicates, rather than affirms, Foucault's reading of it as uniformly and absolutely disciplinary. Understanding how surveillance relates to architecture involves taking into consideration different kinds of gazes and the diverse contexts in which they acted.

These case studies of American buildings and landscapes elucidate different ways in which builders and their principal users enlisted surveillance to shape the relationships of people and groups to one another. They reveal that a variety of gazes acted through the built environment for transformative purposes, some highly visible and others less so. Whereas some people exercised surveillance from privileged positions of power and a singular vantage point, in other cases individuals exchanged gazes reciprocally, as study of camp meetings illustrated. If prison wardens, postal officials, entrepreneurs and managers, middle-class women, and camp-meeting exhorters held faith in the potential of surveillance to shape the behavior of those under their control, fears of resistance to the gaze nonetheless held sway. This anxiety had potential to transform the behavior of those on whom surveillance was exercised as well as those who enacted it. However much disciplinary concerns motivated those imposing surveillance, equating surveillance with discipline fails to account fully for the ways in which it influenced how people and groups related to one another in Victorian America.

An examination of buildings and landscapes and the discourse surrounding them greatly adds to our understanding of surveillance and its role in American culture during the later nineteenth and early twentieth centuries. Evidence about prisons, post offices, factories, middle-class houses, and camp meetings collected here has expanded prevailing interpretations of these building types by revealing how concerns about surveillance informed their design and use. In addition to showing how architecture provides evidence for reframing the ideology of surveillance, this book has laid out frameworks through which other kinds of spaces might be interpreted. The organization of the book's core chapters has been thematic, based on the concepts of discipline, efficiency, hierarchy, and fellowship. These case studies are meant to suggest a much broader landscape of surveillance that could be examined. As scholars continue to probe surveillance and how it has been incorporated into the built environment, the frameworks in this book may serve as a convenient point of departure.

It is also hoped that this book can provide a springboard to extending and enriching Foucault's work by adding nuances to his findings about the associations among architecture, surveillance, and modernism. There are three highly profitable avenues of investigation that future researchers might explore. The first undoubtedly lies in continuing to extend the range of spaces through which we understand surveillance to have operated—in the United States and elsewhere, such as through explorations of banks, parks, hospitals, and churches. More important, as these and other kinds of spaces are examined, a second, and even more profitable, avenue of investigation may emerge. This book has focused principally on the *ideology* behind surveillance, whereas a great deal remains to be written about practice. Buildings and landscapes offer a rich source of evidence for learning about this as well. Changes made over time, for example, signal responses to failures in surveillance—something that was discussed briefly in chapter 1, but which could be explored through spaces discussed elsewhere in this book and in the larger cultural landscape. Moreover, looking to particular types of environments provides us a means of looking deeper at forms of resistance to surveillance. Chapter 3 explored resistance as a prominent theme that motivated and shaped exercise of surveillance in the Victorian middle-class home, but how resistance has worked out in practice deserves more scholarly attention. Looking to the built environment might help us document strategies of resistance—in the Victorian American house and elsewhere—and thus enrich understanding of surveillance as process. The historical record may be impossible to reconstruct precisely, but teasing out aspects of the past from the viewpoint of both viewer and the viewed remains a highly profitable endeavor.

Such work would be important in part because it might build understanding of our contemporary situation and our continued reliance on surveillance.

A third, and in many ways the most critical, avenue of continuing research might probe the links between the past and the present. As a historian, my interest has been in the buildings and landscapes of the past. I focused on the late nineteenth and early twentieth centuries because it was a period in the United States when great faith was placed in buildings and the organization of space as a means of influence (the emphasis here on post office buildings is perhaps the strongest example). I relied on historical evidence to help ground ideas about surveillance and to refine more philosophical and theoretical interpretations by Foucault and others. But continuing to explore the ways surveillance structured the built environment and experience of it—in the Victorian period and after—may help us come to grips with our continued reliance on it as a means through which we as individuals interact with others in an increasingly global culture. I ended my analysis with buildings erected during the first two decades of the twentieth century, a time when surveillance began to achieve new forms under the impact of technology and was thus less manifest in the built environment. But clearly surveillance has continued to shape experiences of spaces during the later twentieth and twenty-first centuries.

My interest in surveillance in the past directly relates to concerns I share with many others about the asymmetries of power in our contemporary culture. Historians of modernity working under the influence of Marxist theory have focused for decades on elucidating the gap between those who exercise power and those on which it is exercised, many out of the belief that exposing such inequities might bring about a more egalitarian way of life. However noble such aims may seem, to reduce the history of modern culture to a struggle between the bourgeoisie and the proletariat now seems problematic and somewhat naive. But this in no way negates the fact that relationships of power structured the way many in the so-called modernizing societies have lived over the past several centuries, and indeed throughout history. Many contemporary historians have contributed to complicating and elucidating aspects of this history, not only to correct the historical record but also (and it might be said a Marxist social agenda lingers here) to come to grips with a rapidly changing world that cannot be easily divided between urban and rural, male and female, east and west, primitive and civilized, culture and nature. This book should be understood in this context. It has contributed to our historical knowledge about power as an integral part of modern culture by complicating its workings. I hope it will lead readers to reflect on how concerns about surveillance continue to affect how we relate to one another—spatially and otherwise—in an ever-changing and significantly more complicated global landscape.

NOTES

Preface

1. David Lyon, "Surveillance Studies: Understanding Visibility, Mobility and the Phenetic Fix," *Surveillance and Society* 1 (2002): 1-7, at http://www.surveillance-and-society.org/articles1/editorial.pdf (accessed December 13, 2007). Lyon's other notable studies of surveillance as a phenomenon of contemporary culture include *Surveillance Society: Monitoring Everyday Life* (Buckingham: Open Univ. Press, 2001), and *Surveillance after September 11* (Cambridge, UK: Polity; Malden, MA: Blackwell, 2003).

2. "Surveillance studies" is the label given to a rapidly developing transdisciplinary endeavor; its practitioners seek to explain and analyze historical and contemporary manifestations of surveillance. See http://www.surveillance-and-society.org (accessed December 13, 2007).

Introduction

1. Michel Foucault, *Discipline and Punish: The Birth of the Prison,* trans. Alan Sheridan (New York: Pantheon, 1977), 177–78; originally published as *Surveiller et punir: Naissance de la prison* (Paris: Gallimard, 1975).

2. Ibid., 228.

3. Critical sources on Foucault are numerous. Representative examples include essays in Colin Jones and Roy Porter, eds., *Reassessing Foucault: Power, Medicine, and the Body* (London: Routledge, 1994); essays in Mike Gane, ed., *Towards a Critique of Foucault* (London: Routledge, 1986), especially that by Michael Donnelly, "Foucault's Genealogy of the Human Sciences," 15–32; and the essays in Jan Ellen Goldstein, ed., *Foucault and the Writing of History* (London: Basil Blackwell, 1994), especially the introduction by the editor, 1–15.

4. Notable critiques include Norman Bruce Johnston's *Forms of Constraint: A History of Prison Architecture* (Urbana: Univ. of Illinois Press, 2000); Thomas A. Markus, *Buildings and Power: Freedom and Control in the Origin of Modern Building Types* (London: Routledge, 1993); David Garland, *Punishment and Society: A Study in Social Theory* (Chicago: Univ. of Chicago Press, 1990), esp. chapter 7; and various essays on Foucault and prisons in Norbert Finzsch and Robert Jütte, eds., *Institutions of Confinement: Hospitals, Asylums, and Prisons in Western Europe and North America, 1500–1900* (New York: Cambridge Univ. Press, 1996).

5. See Johnston, *Forms of Constraint;* Markus, *Buildings and Power;* and Carla Yanni, *The Architecture of Madness: Insane Asylums in the United States* (Minneapolis: Univ. of Minnesota Press, 2007).

6. Examples include Jeffrey Rosen's essay "A Cautionary Tale for a New Age of Surveillance," in the *New York Times Magazine,* 7 Oct. 2001, as well as his popular book *The Unwanted Gaze: The Destruction of Privacy in America* (New York: Random House, 2000); Derrick Jensen and George Draffan, *Welcome to the Machine: Science, Surveillance, and the Culture of Control* (White River Junction, VT: Chelsea Green Pub., 2004); FOX's reality program *Caught on the Job;* and the motion pictures *Enemy of the State* (1998) and *Minority Report* (2002), based on Phillip K. Dick's short story.

7. Foucault, *Discipline and Punish,* and Mike Davis, *City of Quartz: Excavating the Future in Los Angeles* (London: Verso, 1990).

8. Foucault elaborated on the voyeuristic and sexualized implications of the gaze in *The History of Sexuality,* trans. Robert Hurley (New York: Pantheon, 1978). Other explorations of the voyeuristic and scopophilic gaze include Laura Mulvey, "Visual Pleasure and Narrative Cinema," *Screen* 16 (Autumn 1975): 6–18; Peter de Bolla, "The Visibility of Visuality," in *Vision in Context: Historical and Contemporary Perspectives on Sight,* ed. Teresa Brennan and Martin Jay (New York: Routledge, 1996), 63–81; and Parveen Adams, "Father, Can't You See I'm Filming?," in *Vision in Context,* 203–16.

9. David Lyon, *The Electronic Eye: The Rise of Surveillance Society* (Minneapolis: Univ. of Minnesota Press, 1994), ix.

10. See, for example, Lyon, *The Electronic Eye;* Oscar H. Gandy, *The Panoptic Sort: A Political Economy of Personal Information* (Boulder, CO: Westview, 1993); and Gary T. Marx, "The Surveillance Society: The Threat of 1984–Style Techniques," *Futurist* 19 (June 1985): 21–26.

11. Norman Bryson, *Vision and Painting: The Logic of the Gaze* (New Haven: Yale Univ. Press, 1983).

12. Foucault, *Discipline and Punish,* 216–17.

13. Jonathan Crary, *Techniques of the Observer: On Vision and Modernity in the Nineteenth Century* (Cambridge, MA: MIT Press, 1990).

14. Daniel Joseph Singal, "Towards a Definition of American Modernism," *American Quarterly* 39 (Spring 1987): 7–26.

15. This argument about modern building types follows that of Markus in *Buildings and Power.*

16. Besides Foucault's ideas on this, the idea of invoking surveillance as a means by which one could gain knowledge echoes Dell Upton's ideas about the ordering of the landscape of the early American city as an effort on the part of those in power to assert and maintain order; see "Another City: The Urban Cultural Landscape of the Early Republic," in *Everyday Life in the Early Republic,* ed. Catherine E. Hutchins (Winterthur, DE: Henry Francis du Pont Winterthur Museum, 1994), 61–117.

17. Daniel Walker Howe, "Victorian Culture in America," in *Victorian America,* ed. Daniel Walker Howe (Philadelphia: Univ. of Pennsylvania Press, 1976), 3–28. Also see Walter Edwards Houghton, *The Victorian Frame of Mind, 1830–1870* (New Haven: Yale Univ. Press, 1957) and Masao Miyoshi, *The Divided Self: A Perspective on the Literature of the Victorians* (New York: New York Univ. Press, 1969).

18. Singal, "Towards a Definition of American Modernism," 12.

19. See T. J. Jackson Lears, *No Place of Grace: Antimodernism and the Transformation of American Culture, 1880–1920* (New York: Pantheon, 1981) for a discussion of the transition from Victorian- to twentieth-century culture. Also see Stanley Coben's *Rebellion against Victorianism: The Impetus for Cultural Change in 1920s America* (New York: Oxford Univ. Press, 1991) on the demise of American Victorian culture by the 1920s.

20. Sources that discuss the problems with distinguishing different categories of architecture are numerous; see Dell Upton's book, *Architecture in the United States* (Oxford: Oxford Univ. Press, 1998); editorial introductions to all volumes of the Perspectives in Vernacular Architecture series; Upton, "The VAF at 25: What Now?," in *Perspectives in Vernacular Architecture* 13, no. 2 (2007): 7–13; and my own essay "*Perspectives in Vernacular Architecture,* the VAF, and the Study of Ordinary Buildings and Landscapes in North America," *Perspectives in Vernacular Architecture* 13, no. 2 (2007): 55–63.

21. Spiro Kostof, *A History of Architecture: Settings and Rituals* (New York: Oxford Univ. Press, 1985).

22. Paul Erling Groth's state of the field article on vernacular architecture illustrated that although the movement grew out of a study of common buildings, it has greatly expanded to include all kinds and scales of buildings. See Groth, "Making New Connections in Vernacular Architecture," *Journal of the Society of Architectural Historians* 58 (Sept. 1999): 444–51. Because of the expanded scope of study, Dell Upton has distinguished the current study of vernacular architecture as an approach to buildings rather than a category of subject matter—a "social history" of architecture. See Upton, "The Power of Things: Recent Studies in American Vernacular Architecture," *American Quarterly* 35, no. 3 (Bibliography 1983): 262–79, as well as Thomas Carter and Bernard L. Herman "Introduction: Toward a New Architectural History," *Perspectives in Vernacular Architecture*

IV, ed. Thomas Carter and Bernard L. Herman (Columbia: Univ. of Missouri Press, 1991), 4–5. Examples of the so-called new architectural history are too extensive to list here, but notable works include Dell Upton, *Holy Things and Profane: Anglican Parish Churches in Colonial Virginia* (New York: Architectural History Foundation; Cambridge, MA: MIT Press, 1986); Bernard L. Herman, *The Stolen House* (Charlottesville: Univ. Press of Virginia, 1991) and *Architecture and Rural Life in Central Delaware, 1700–1900* (Knoxville: Univ. of Tennessee Press, 1987); Thomas C. Hubka, *Big House, Little House, Back House, Barn: The Connected Farm Buildings of New England* (Hanover, NH: Univ. Press of New England, 1984); Abigail Ayres Van Slyck, *Free to All: Carnegie Libraries and American Culture, 1890–1920* (Chicago: Univ. of Chicago Press, 1995); Alison K. Hoagland, *Army Architecture in the West: Forts Laramie, Bridger, and D. A. Russell, 1849–1912* (Norman: Univ. of Oklahoma Press, 2004); and Richard W. Longstreth, *City Center to Regional Mall: Architecture, the Automobile, and Retailing in Los Angeles, 1920–1950* (Cambridge, MA: MIT Press, 1997). Also see articles in previously published volumes of the Perspectives in Vernacular Architecture series.

23. Examples of work in this vein are numerous; they include Upton, *Architecture in the United States;* Upton, "The City as Material Culture," in Anne Elizabeth Yentsch and Mary C. Beaudry, eds. *The Art and Mystery of Historical Archaeology: Essays in Honor of James Deetz* (Boca Raton: CRC Press, 1992), 51–74; Bernard L. Herman, *Town House: Architecture and Material Life in the Early American City, 1780–1830* (Chapel Hill: Omohundro Institute of Early American History and Culture and the Univ. of North Carolina Press, 2005); Gretchen Townsend Buggeln, *Temples of Grace: The Material Transformation of Connecticut's Churches, 1790–1840* (Hanover, NH: Univ. Press of New England, 2003), and J. Ritchie Garrison, *Two Carpenters: Architecture and Building in Early New England, 1799–1859* (Knoxville: Univ. of Tennessee Press, 2006).

24. Although there is no one source that describes the "material culture approach," helpful sources include the anthology edited by Ann Smart Martin and J. Ritchie Garrison, *American Material Culture: The Shape of the Field* (Winterthur, DE: Henry Francis du Pont Winterthur Museum, 1997) and the introduction to Jules David Prown and Kenneth Haltman, eds., *American Artifacts: Essays in Material Culture.* (East Lansing: Michigan State Univ. Press, 2000). Early statements about studying American material culture are still some of the most resonant. See Cary Carson, "Doing History with Material Culture," in *Material Culture and the Study of American Life,* ed. Ian M. G. Quimby (New York: W. W. Norton, 1978), 41–64; James Deetz, *In Small Things Forgotten: The Archaeology of Early American Life* (Garden City, NY: Anchor Press/Doubleday, 1977); assorted articles in Thomas J. Schlereth, ed., *Material Culture: A Research Guide* (Lawrence: Univ. Press of Kansas, 1985) and *Material Culture Studies in America* (Nashville, TN: American Association for State and Local History, 1982); and Jules David Prown, "Mind in Matter: An Introduction to Material Culture Theory

and Method," *Winterthur Portfolio* 17 (Spring 1982): 1–19. Studies of material culture in this vein are far too numerous to list here; for bibliographical sources, see references in the works cited above, particularly Martin and Garrison, as well as articles in *Winterthur Portfolio, Material Culture,* the Perspectives in Vernacular Architecture series of books, and the journal *Perspectives in Vernacular Architecture* (now *Buildings and Landscapes*).

1. Discipline

1. On development of the Pennsylvania system, see LeRoy B. DePuy, "The Triumph of the 'Pennsylvania System' at the State's Penitentiaries," *Pennsylvania History* 21, no. 2 (April 1954): 128–44; Eugene E. Doll, "Trial and Error at Allegheny: The Western State Penitentiary 1818–1838," *Pennsylvania Magazine of History and Biography* 81 (Jan. 1957): 3–27; Adam Jay Hirsch, *The Rise of the Penitentiary: Prisons and Punishment in Early America* (New Haven: Yale Univ. Press, 1992); Norman Bruce Johnston et al., *Eastern State Penitentiary: Crucible of Good Intentions* (Philadelphia: Philadelphia Museum of Art, 1994); Johnston, *Forms of Constraint,* especially 69–74; Blake McKelvey, *American Prisons: A History of Good Intentions* (Montclair, NJ: P. Smith, 1977); and Negley K. Teeters and John D. Shearer, *The Prison at Philadelphia, Cherry Hill: The Separate System of Penal Discipline, 1829–1913* (New York: Columbia Univ. Press, 1957).

2. John Haviland, *A Description of Haviland's Design for the New Penitentiary Now Erecting near Philadelphia* (Philadelphia: R. Desilver, 1824), 3–4.

3. Minutes of the Building Commission, reproduced in Teeters and Shearer, *Prison at Philadelphia,* 59.

4. Precedents are discussed in Teeters and Shearer, *Prison at Philadelphia,* 62 and Johnston, *Forms of Constraint,* 55–63, 70, and 175 (n. 17).

5. W. Barksdale Maynard, *Architecture in the United States, 1800–1850* (New Haven: Yale Univ. Press, 2002).

6. See Damie Stillman, *English Neo-Classical Architecture* (London: A. Zwemmer, 1988), 2:381–86, and Johnston, *Forms of Constraint,* 70.

7. A good discussion of Howard's place in English penal reform may be found in Michael Ignatieff, *A Just Measure of Pain: The Penitentiary in the Industrial Revolution, 1750–1850* (New York: Pantheon, 1978), especially chapters 3 and 4.

8. Bentham, *Panopticon; or, The Inspection-House* (London: T. Payne, 1791). Reprinted as *The Panopticon Writings,* ed. Miran Bošovič (London: Verso, 1995).

9. On the panopticon and the relation of Bentham's ideas to those of Howard, see Janet Semple, *Bentham's Prison: A Study of the Panopticon Penitentiary* (Oxford: Oxford Univ. Press, 1993), especially chapter 4.

10. On the system of punishment prior to the Enlightenment, see Foucault, *Discipline and Punish,* 3–69, and David J. Rothman, *The Discovery of the Asylum:*

Social Order and Disorder in the New Republic, rev. ed. (Boston: Little, Brown, 1990), 48–63.

11. See Rothman, *The Discovery of the Asylum,* 30–78.

12. On the history of the Philadelphia Prison Society, see Negley K. Teeters and Albert Gray Fraser, *They Were in Prison; A History of the Pennsylvania Prison Society, 1787–1937, Formerly the Philadelphia Society for Alleviating the Miseries of Public Prisons* (Philadelphia: John C. Winston Co., 1937); Teeters and Shearer, *Prison at Philadelphia,* especially 5–32; and LeRoy B. DePuy, "The Walnut Street Prison: Pennsylvania's First Penitentiary," *Pennsylvania History* 18 (Apr. 1951): 130–44.

13. The Massachusetts State Prison, originally built in the early nineteenth century, was renovated in 1829 along the lines of the New York State Prison at Auburn, a typical pattern among nineteenth-century prisons. On this see Johnston, *Forms of Constraint,* 74–75 and 138–39, and Hirsch, *The Rise of the Penitentiary.*

14. Other prisons that adopt the configuration include Haviland's New Jersey Prison at Trenton (1833–36); the Philadelphia County Prison at Holmesburg (1895–96); and the penitentiary in Fort Leavenworth, Kansas (1896–1928). The plan was also influential in Europe; see, for example, London's Pentonville Prison (opened in 1842) as well as prisons in Berlin (1844–46) and Madrid (1877). For more on Eastern State's influence, see Norman Bruce Johnston, *The Human Cage: A Brief History of Prison Architecture* (New York: Published for the American Foundation, Institute of Corrections by Walker, 1973), 31–38.

15. Johnston, *Forms of Constraint,* 55.

16. On Trenton State Prison, see Gresham M. Sykes, *The Society of Captives: A Study of a Maximum Security Prison* (Princeton, NJ: Princeton Univ. Press, 1958); Johnston, *Forms of Constraint,* 74–75; and United States Bureau of Prisons, *Handbook of Correctional Institution Design and Construction* (Washington: GPO, 1949), 37–39.

17. On Western State, see DePuy, "The Triumph of the Pennsylvania System at the State's Penitentiaries," 128–44; Doll, "Trial and Error at Allegheny," 3–27; and McKelvey, *American Prisons,* 14–18.

18. Other prisons laid out in this arrangement, such as the Virginia State Penitentiary designed by Benjamin Henry Latrobe in 1797, more closely adhered to the panoptic scheme by having tiered cellblocks around a central tower. See Paul W. Keve, *The History of Corrections in Virginia* (Charlottesville: Univ. Press of Virginia, 1986).

19. Another quasi-panoptic prison, designed by Benjamin Latrobe, opened in Richmond, Virginia, in 1800. Most other derivations were in Europe; ideas about these made their way to the United States and undoubtedly informed, if only indirectly, designs of American Victorian prisons. On panoptic prisons, see Johnston, *Forms of Constraint.*

20. On Stateville, see Johnston, *Forms of Constraint,* 143–44; McKelvey, *American Prisons,* 282–83; and U.S. Bureau of Prisons, *Handbook,* 69–70.

21. On Auburn and its influence, see McKelvey, *American Prisons,* 11–17, and W. David Lewis, *From Newgate to Dannemora: The Rise of the Penitentiary in New York, 1796–1848* (Ithaca, NY: Cornell Univ. Press, 1965), especially 81–135.

22. See William Crawford, *Report of William Crawford, Esq., on the Penitentiaries of the United States, Addressed to His Majesty's Principal Secretary of State for the Home Department* (London, 1834), 17, and Lewis, *From Newgate to Dannemora,* 117–18.

23. On the "congregate" or silent system, see Lewis, *From Newgate to Dannemora,* 111–35. On the arrangement of work spaces in congregate prisons built during the first half of the nineteenth century such as the State Penitentiary in Massachusetts, see Elaine Jackson-Retondo, "Manufacturing Moral Reform: Images and Realities of a Nineteenth-Century American Prison," in *People, Power, Places: Perspectives in Vernacular Architecture, VIII,* ed. Sally Ann McMurry and Annmarie Adams (Knoxville: Univ. of Tennessee Press, 2000), 117–37.

24. See Haviland, *A Description of Haviland's Design for the New Penitentiary,* 3–4. These were later torn out when doors were installed in the corridor walls.

25. Prison Discipline Society, *First Annual Report of the Board of Managers of the Prison Discipline Society, Boston, June 2, 1826* (Boston: T. R. Marvin, 1826), 7, and Crawford, *Report on the Penitentiaries,* appendix page 24.

26. See Haviland, *A Description of Haviland's Design for the New Penitentiary,* 4.

27. Prison Discipline Society, *Second Annual Report of the Board of Managers of the Prison Discipline Society, Boston, June 1, 1827* (Boston: T. R. Marvin, 1827), 112, reproduced in Upton, "The City as Material Culture," 69.

28. Crawford, *Report on the Penitentiaries,* 24

29. Lewis, *From Newgate to Dannemora,* 117. Also see Gustave de Beaumont, Alexis de Tocqueville, and William B. Sarsfield, *Origin and Outline of the Penitentiary System in the United States of North America* (London: J. and A. Arch, 1833), 12, and Jackson-Retondo, "Manufacturing Moral Reform," 117–37.

30. Robin Evans, *The Fabrication of Virtue: English Prison Architecture, 1750–1840* (Cambridge: Cambridge Univ. Press, 1982). The cataloging impulse that Evans discusses has also been explored as a defining feature of modern (Western) culture. On this desire to "put the world in order" in the modern period see Robert Darnton, *The Great Cat Massacre and Other Episodes in French Cultural History* (New York: Basic Books, 1984). Also see Upton's study of the grid in nineteenth-century American cities in "The City as Material Culture," 51–74.

31. Evans explained how the proliferation of prison designs in Britain in the late eighteenth and early nineteenth centuries was closely tied to surveillance. Comparing the origin of the centrifugal plan in the Maison de Force at Ghent (begun 1772) with early nineteenth-century English prisons, Evans showed how centrifugal

planning meant to *symbolize* power was replaced in later buildings that used centralized planning to *enable* discipline via the gaze. See Evans, *The Fabrication of Virtue,* 294–95.

32. Rothman, *The Discovery of the Asylum,* 82–83.

33. Ibid. Along with the population explosion of the nineteenth century came a rapid rise in delinquency and crime, or at the least a perceived threat of it. In the face of these changes, Americans sought to recover a sense of community they felt had been lost in myriad ways, many of which had material ramifications and which can be seen in the material record. As Upton has shown, one way to combat the chaos was through a more careful ordering of the city through imposing and reasserting the concept of the grid. Through classification and organization of bodies-in-space and the buildings they occupied, the urban grid offered republican Americans the possibility of attaining a semblance of order in an increasingly chaotic landscape. See Upton, "The City as Material Culture," 53–56.

34. Rothman, *The Discovery of the Asylum,* especially 79–108. Also see Upton, "The City as Material Culture," 51–74.

35. Haviland, *A Description of Haviland's Design for the New Penitentiary,* 7.

36. Gershom Powers, *A Brief Account of the Construction, Management, and Discipline of the New York State Prison at Auburn, Together with a Compendium on Criminal Law* (Auburn, NY: Printed by U. F. Doubleday, 1826), 75.

37. Charles Bulfinch, *Report of Charles Bulfinch on the Subject of Penitentiaries* (Washington: Gales and Seaton, 1827), 6.

38. Neither a history of incarceration nor an architectural history of prison buildings, Foucault's work deals with architecture only to the extent that he sees surveillance in buildings as a marker of modernity. See Michael Donnelly, "Foucault's Genealogy of the Human Sciences," *Economy and Society* 11 (Nov. 1982): 363–80, reproduced in Jones and Porter, eds., *Reassessing Foucault,* 15–32.

39. Foucault, *Discipline and Punish,* 249.

40. Teeters and Shearer, *Prison at Philadelphia,* 79.

41. Ibid.

42. Ibid., 67.

43. Ibid., 79.

44. Warden Nimrod Strickland noted this in his journal on 3 September 1855, according to Teeters and Shearer, *Prison at Philadelphia,* 78–79. They contend that hoods/masks were used as late as 1904.

45. See the report by Thomas B. McElwee, *A Concise History of the Eastern Penitentiary of Pennsylvania* (Philadelphia: Neall & Massey, 1835). The findings of McElwee's report and its consequences are discussed in Teeters and Shearer, *Prison at Philadelphia,* 93–107.

46. Excerpts from Warden's Annual Report of 1830 as reproduced in Doll, "Trial and Error at Allegheny," 18–19.

47. Doll, "Trial and Error at Allegheny," 14.

48. Ibid., 19–20.

49. See Powers, *Brief Account,* 10; Prison Discipline Society, *First Report* (1826), 7; Crawford, *Report on the Penitentiaries,* 17; and Lewis, *From Newgate to Dannemora,* 117–18.

50. Gershom Powers, *Brief Account,* 14–15; this is also discussed in Lewis, *From Newgate to Dannemora,* 117–19.

51. See Lewis, *From Newgate to Dannemora,* 121.

52. U.S. Bureau of Prisons, *Handbook,* 32–34, and Johnston, *Forms of Constraint,* 138–39.

53. U.S. Bureau of Prisons, *Handbook,* 37–38.

54. Ibid., 33.

55. Alfred Hopkins, *Prisons and Prison Building* (New York: Architectural Book Publishing, 1930), 46–47.

56. Ibid., 50, 52.

57. The plan appears in Henry Grattan Tyrrell, *A Treatise on the Design and Construction of Mill Buildings and Other Industrial Plants* (Chicago: Myron C. Clark Publishing, 1911), 3.

58. Hopkins, *Prison and Prison Building,* 49.

59. Ibid., 55–56.

60. Ibid., 135–36.

2. Efficiency

1. A. P. Frederick, James A. Small, Rush D. Simmons, and I. S. N. Gregg, postal inspectors, to Col. William T. Sullivan, inspector in charge, Denver, CO, Feb. 17, 1901; volume covering Jan. 17, 1901–Apr. 16, 1901, pp. 373–79; Records of the Inspection Office, Denver, CO, 1879–1907; Office of the Postmaster General, Division of Post Office Inspectors; Records of the Post Office Department, Record Group 28, National Archives Building, Washington, DC (hereafter NAB).

2. Inspector's comments in Marshall Henry Cushing, *The Story of Our Post Office: The Greatest Government Department in All Its Phases* (Boston: A. M. Thayer, 1893), 647.

3. T. J. Zimmerman, "The Chalk Line of Business; I. The System of General Inspection," *System* 10 (Oct. 1906): 353.

4. Sources on the theory and development of capitalist modes of production in the United States are numerous. Some of the most useful are Alfred D. Chandler, Jr., *The Visible Hand: The Managerial Revolution in American Business* (Cambridge, MA: Belknap Press, 1977); Richard Edwards, *Contested Terrain: The Transformation*

of the Workplace in the Twentieth Century (New York: Basic Books, 1979); Harry Braverman, *Labor and Monopoly Capital: The Degradation of Work in the Twentieth Century* (New York: Monthly Review Press, 1975); and William H. Lazonick, "Technological Change and the Control of Work: The Development of Capital-Labor Relations in U.S. Mass Production Industries," in *Managerial Strategies and Industrial Relations: An Historical and Comparative Study,* ed. Howard F. Gospel and Craig R. Littler (London: Heinemann Educational Books, 1983), 111–36.

5. Karl Marx, *Capital: A Critique of Political Economy,* vol. 1 (1867; reprint, New York: International Publishers, 1967), 167.

6. Edwards, *Contested Terrain,* 17.

7. On Taylor and the "labor problem," see Lazonick, "Technological Change and the Control of Work," 111–36.

8. The function of the gaze as a means of "possessing" labor parallels the argument of John Locke in his *Second Treatise on Civil Government* in the way ownership acquires "property" in the form of labor. I thank Bernie Herman for pointing out the comparison.

9. Cushing, *The Story of Our Post Office,* 15.

10. For information on the mail boom of the late nineteenth century, see James H. Bruns, *Great American Post Offices* (Washington, DC: Preservation Press; New York: Wiley, 1998); Daniel C. Roper, *The United States Post Office, Its Past Record, Present Condition, and Potential Relation to the New World Era* (New York: Funk and Wagnalls, 1917); and Vern K. Baxter, *Labor and Politics in the United States Postal Service* (New York: Plenum Press, 1994), especially 39–44.

11. The relationship between the Post Office Department and the Office of the Supervising Architect is not entirely clear if one judges by the documentary record. There are correspondence records located in various parts of the Records of the Public Buildings Service, Record Group 121 (hereafter RG 121), NACP. But these records fail to elucidate the actual exchange that occurred between the two offices. Regarding look-outs, it appears that the impetus for installing them would have come from the Post Office Department, which provided guidance to Treasury Department architects as to what spaces the look-outs had to observe. For information on the Office of the Supervising Architect, see Rufus H. Thayer, *History, Organization, and Functions of the Office of the Supervising Architect of the Treasury Department, with Copies of Reports, Recommendations, etc.* (Washington, DC: GPO, 1886); Darrel Hevenor Smith, *The Office of the Supervising Architect of the Treasury: Its History, Activities, and Organization* (Baltimore: Johns Hopkins Univ. Press, 1923); and Antoinette J. Lee, *Architects to the Nation: The Rise and Decline of the Supervising Architect's Office* (New York: Oxford Univ. Press, 2000).

12. On the history of federal buildings (which often included postal facilities), a good source is Daniel Bluestone's essay "Civic and Aesthetic Reserve: Ammi Burnham Young's 1850s Federal Customhouse Designs," *Winterthur Portfolio* 25 (Sum-

mer/Autumn 1990): 131–56. Also see Lee, *Architects to the Nation,* and Bruns, *Great American Post Offices.*

13. First floor plan, Wilmington, Delaware, Post Office and Courthouse, 1896; Wilmington, Delaware, Post Office and Courthouse Records, Drawing #30; Consolidated File, Construction of Federal Buildings; Records of the Public Buildings Service, RG 121; National Archives Building, College Park, Maryland [hereafter NACP].

14. Ibid.

15. My conclusions about these three types of look-outs is based on my perusal of architectural plans for more than thirty post offices, mainly in the mid-Atlantic region, in the Consolidated File, Construction of Federal Buildings; Records of the Public Buildings Service, RG 121; NACP. The three types remained dominant through at least 1948, when the first book-length monograph on standardized designs for post offices was published by the federal government for building contractors. This 1948 book used these terms, and thus I adopt them retroactively here. See United States Public Building Administration, *United States Post Offices* (Washington, DC: The Administration, 1948).

16. Second floor plan, New Castle, Pennsylvania, Post Office, Nov., 1904; New Castle, Pennsylvania, Post Office Records, Drawing #8; Consolidated File, Construction of Federal Buildings; Records of the Public Buildings Service, RG 121; NACP.

17. The post office in Baltimore, Maryland, contained a look-out gallery that was designed in 1888 and installed around 1890. See Plan of Inspection Gallery and Details, Baltimore, Maryland, Post Office and Courthouse, 1888; Baltimore, Maryland, Post Office and Courthouse Records, Drawing #284; Consolidated File, Construction of Federal Buildings; Records of the Public Buildings Service, RG 121; NACP.

18. Twelve post offices out of thirty that I examined (or 40 percent) contained hanging galleries at some point.

19. First Floor Plan, Wilmington, Delaware, Post Office and Courthouse (extension), April, 1911; Wilmington, Delaware, Post Office and Courthouse Records, Drawing #96; Consolidated File, Construction of Federal Buildings; Records of the Public Buildings Service, RG 121; NACP.

20. Basement Plan, Wilmington, Delaware, Post Office and Courthouse (extension), ca. 1911; Wilmington, Delaware Post Office and Courthouse Records, Drawing #131; Consolidated File, Construction of Federal Buildings; Records of the Public Buildings Service, RG 121; NACP.

21. Observation of these spaces became increasingly common in post offices after 1900. Look-outs in restrooms were ordered to be sealed in December of 1964 because of right-to-privacy legislation. However, surveillance of swing rooms has continued through the present day. See George Alan White, "Issues and Answers: The Post Office Observation Gallery Controversy," M.A. thesis, George Washington Univ., 1965.

22. Basement and First Floor Plans, Milford, Delaware, Post Office, Oct., 1908; Milford, Delaware, Post Office Records, Drawing #4; Consolidated File, Construction of Federal Buildings; Records of the Public Buildings Service, RG 121; NACP.

23. Longitudinal and Cross Sections, Milford, Delaware, Post Office, Oct., 1908; Milford, Delaware, Post Office Records, Drawing #7; Consolidated File, Construction of Federal Buildings; Records of the Public Buildings Service, RG 121; NACP. Although not common, this scheme was also adopted at Perth Amboy, New Jersey, suggesting it was not an anomaly either.

24. Basement and First Floor Plans, Danville, Virginia, Post Office (extension), ca. 1909; Danville, Virginia, Post Office Records, Drawing #79; Consolidated File, Construction of Federal Buildings; Records of the Public Buildings Service, RG 121; NACP.

25. Horace Samuel Merrill, *William Freeman Vilas, Doctrinaire Democrat* (Madison: State Historical Society of Wisconsin, 1954).

26. See Post Office Department, *Report of the Postmaster-General of the United States,* 50th Cong., 1st sess., 1887, H.exdoc.1, Part 4 (*Serial Set* 2540), 18–23.

27. Ibid., 21.

28. Post Office Department, *Report of the Postmaster-General of the United States,* 51st Cong., 2d sess., 1890, H.exdoc.1, Part 4 (*Serial Set* 2839), 4. On Wanamaker's impact on the department, see Gerald Cullinan, *The Post Office Department* (New York: F. A. Prager, 1968).

29. Post Office Department, *Report of the Postmaster-General of the United States,* 51st Cong., 1st sess., 1889, H.exdoc.1 (*Serial Set* 2723), 9.

30. On these measures, see Roper, *The U.S. Post Office;* Cushing, *The Story of Our Post Office;* and Herbert Adams Gibbons, *John Wanamaker* (New York: Harper and Brothers, 1926), 1:262–320.

31. Wanamaker's attack on lavish buildings may partly stem from his frustration in having to deal with architects in the Treasury Department. Taking control of post office architecture would have assured more control, something that Wanamaker certainly desired. His frustration with this may be found in his discussion of the need for a new post office in New York City in Post Office Department, *Report of the Postmaster-General of the United States,* 52nd Cong., 1st sess., 1891, H.exdoc.1 (*Serial Set* 2932), 74–77.

32. Post Office Department, *Report of the Postmaster-General of the United States,* 51st Cong., 2d sess., 1890, H.exdoc.1, Part 4 (*Serial Set* 2839), 46–48.

33. Gibbons, *Wanamaker,* 2: 36–39.

34. John N. Makris, *The Silent Investigators: The Great Untold Story of the United States Postal Inspection Service* (New York: E. P. Dutton, 1959), and Elinore Denniston, *America's Silent Investigators: The Story of the Postal Inspectors Who Protect the United States Mail* (New York: Dodd, Mead, 1964).

35. Post Office Department, *Report of the Postmaster-General of the United States,* 45th Cong., 3d sess., 1878, H.exdoc.1, Part 4 (*Serial Set* 1849), 12.

36. See Post Office Department, *Report of the Postmaster-General of the United States,* 46th Cong., 2d sess., 1879, H.exdoc.1, Part 4 (*Serial Set* 1909), 17; Cushing, *The Story of Our Post Office,* 313, and Post Office Department, *Report of the Postmaster-General of the United States,* 57th Cong., 1st sess., 1901, H.doc.4 (*Serial Set* 4288), 912. Numbers of inspectors are rarely given in early-twentieth-century reports, but clues are given as to percentages of increases in staff that can help one glean the relative rates of increase.

37. Duties of inspectors are described in the Report of the Fourth Assistant Postmaster General in the Post Office Department, *Report of the Postmaster-General of the United States,* 52nd Cong., 2d sess., 1892, H.exdoc.1 (*Serial Set* 3086), 987.

38. Gibbons, *Wanamaker,* 1: 212.

39. Gibbons, *Wanamaker,* 2: 35–36.

40. Post Office Department, *Report of the Postmaster-General of the United States,* 53rd Cong., 2d sess., 1893, H.exdoc.1 (*Serial Set* 3208), 577.

41. The Post Office Department insisted that the spotter system was intended to weed out inefficient carriers, but letter carriers have historically perceived its mission as an attempt to get rid of the postal unions. See M. Brady Mikusko, *Carriers in a Common Cause: A History of Letter Carriers and the NALC* (Washington, DC: NALC, 1989).

42. Post Office Department, *Report of the Postmaster-General of the United States,* 54th Cong., 1st sess., 1895, H.exdoc.4 (*Serial Set* 3380), 124.

43. Post Office Department, *Report of the Postmaster-General of the United States,* 63rd Cong., 2d sess., 1913, H.doc.712 (*Serial Set* 6629), 42.

44. On Burleson's significance, see Baxter, *Labor and Politics in the USPS;* Sterling Denhard Spero, *The Labor Movement in a Government Industry: A Study of Employee Organization in the Postal Service* (New York: George H. Doran, 1924); and Murray B. Nesbitt, *Labor Relations in the Federal Government Service* (Washington, DC: Bureau of National Affairs, 1976).

45. See various annual *Reports of the Postmaster-General,* and United States Post Office Department, *Manual of Instructions for Post Office Inspectors* (Washington, DC: GPO, 1941).

46. G. C. Holden, acting inspector in charge, to the Honorable M. D. Wheeler, chief inspector, Washington, DC, July 12, 1897; volume covering Aug. 28, 1896–April 28, 1899, pp. 409–11; Records of the Inspection Office, Philadelphia, PA, 1896–1909; Office of the Postmaster General, Division of Post Office Inspectors; Records of the Post Office Department, Record Group 28 (hereafter RG 28), NAB.

47. G. C. Holden, inspector, to M. C. Fosnes, inspector in charge, Philadelphia, Nov. 17, 1899; volume covering April 12, 1899–Dec. 1, 1900, pp. 260–62;

Records of the Inspection Office, Philadelphia, PA, 1896–1909; Office of the Postmaster General, Division of Post Office Inspectors; Records of the Post Office Department, RG 28, NAB.

48. G. C. Holden, inspector, to M. C. Fosnes, inspector in charge, Philadelphia, March 8, 1900; volume covering April 12, 1899–Dec. 1, 1900, pp. 435–36; Records of the Inspection Office, Philadelphia, PA, 1896–1909; Office of the Postmaster General, Division of Post Office Inspectors; Records of the Post Office Department, RG 28, NAB.

49. Warren Edgarton, inspector in charge, to chief post office inspector, Philadelphia, PA, March 22, 1892; Volume covering June 25, 1889–Aug. 5, 1893, pp. 297–98; Records of the Inspection Office, Philadelphia, PA, 1889–1893; Office of the Postmaster General, Division of Post Office Inspectors; Records of the Post Office Department, RG 28, NAB. A sketch of Edgarton's proposal for floor-type look-outs in Pittsburgh is found in a letter from Edgarton to the Chief Postal Inspector, March 22, 1892; Pittsburgh, PA Post Office; Letters Received, 1843–1910; Records of the Public Buildings Service, RG 121, NACP.

50. In advising another inspector, Edgarton explained how essential it was for him to impress on clerks that they were always subject to watch. See Warren Edgarton, inspector, to W. W. Dickson, inspector, Sept. 22, 1893; volume covering June 25, 1889–Aug. 5, 1893, pp. 393–94; Records of the Inspection Office, Philadelphia, PA, 1889–1893; Office of the Postmaster General, Division of Post Office Inspectors; Records of the Post Office Department, RG 28, NAB.

51. Warren Edgarton, inspector in charge, to chief post office inspector, Philadelphia, May 11, 1892; Volume covering June 25, 1889–Aug. 5, 1893, pp. 312–13; Records of the Inspection Office, Philadelphia, PA, 1889–1893; Office of the Postmaster General, Division of Post Office Inspectors; Records of the Post Office Department, RG 28, NAB.

52. W. S. Ryan and M. C. Duryea, inspectors, to W. W. Dickson, acting inspector in charge, Philadelphia, March 14, 1901; volume 1 covering Jan. 29, 1900–Jan. 19, 1903, pp. 33–35; Records of the Inspection Office, Philadelphia, PA, 1896–1909; Office of the Postmaster General, Division of Post Office Inspectors; Records of the Post Office Department, RG 28, NAB.

53. Warren Edgarton, inspector, to chief postal inspector, Washington, DC, March 22, 1892; Pittsburgh, Pennsylvania, Post Office; Letters Received, 1889–1892; Records of the Public Buildings Service, RG 121, NACP.

54. See especially Lindy Biggs, *The Rational Factory: Architecture, Technology, and Work in America's Age of Mass Production* (Baltimore: Johns Hopkins Univ. Press, 1996); Margaret Crawford, *Building the Workingman's Paradise: The Design of American Company Towns* (London: Verso, 1995); and William Littmann, "Designing Obedience: The Architecture and Landscape of Welfare Capitalism, 1880–1930," *International Labor and Working Class History* 53 (Spring 1998): 88–114. Studies of white-collar settings that discuss the layout of workspaces

also reveal similar trends. See in particular Angel Kwolek-Folland, *Engendering Business: Men and Women in the Corporate Office, 1870–1930* (Baltimore: Johns Hopkins Univ. Press, 1994), and Olivier Zunz, *Making America Corporate, 1870–1920* (Chicago: Univ. of Chicago Press, 1990).

55. See Frederic Smith, *Workshop Management: A Manual for Masters and Men, Comprising a Few Practical Remarks on the Economic Conduct of Workshops, and c.* (London: Wyman and Sons, 1879), 3. Also see J. Slater Lewis's description of raised platforms in *The Commercial Organisation of Factories* (London: E. and F. N. Spon; New York: Spon and Chamberlain, 1896), 161. The practice appears to date back to the 1830s in New England textile mills. See Thomas Dublin, *Women at Work: The Transformation of Work and Community in Lowell, Massachusetts, 1826–1860* (New York: Columbia Univ. Press, 1979), 69. The presence of a platform in an eighteenth-century mill is referenced in Robert B. Gordon and Patrick M. Malone, *The Texture of Industry: An Archaeological View of the Industrialization of North America* (New York: Oxford Univ. Press, 1994), 298–99.

56. "Mill Engineering (Part 3): Cotton-Mill Planning," in *Yarns, Cloth Rooms, Mill Engineering, Reeling and Baling, Winding,* vol. 78 of the International Library of Technology (Scranton, PA: International Textbook, 1906), 22–27.

57. A larger setting where a raised platform was used is provided by the Armour Company; see T. J. Zimmerman in "The System of the Armours," *System* 5 (Apr. 1904): 234–47.

58. "Piloting a Shop from the 'Bridge,'" *Factory* 14 (Apr. 1915): 244.

59. Austin Company, *Austin Standard Factory-Buildings* (Cleveland, OH: The Company, 1919). On the history and influence of the Austin Company, see Martin Greif, *The New Industrial Landscape: The Story of the Austin Company* (Clinton, NJ: Main Street Press, 1978).

60. Ernest Hexamer and Sons, *Hexamer General Surveys, 1866–1896* (Philadelphia: E. Hexamer and Sons, 1866-95), in the Map Collection, the Free Library of Philadelphia (also available online at http://www.philageohistory.org/rdic-images/ HGS/index.cfm [accessed July 10, 2007]). Partitioned supervisory spaces appear in all kinds of facilities in the surveys, including machine shops and metalworks. For example, see Hexamer and Sons, "Moore and White Machine Works, Northeast Corner of 15th St., and Lehigh Avenue, 28th Ward, Philadelphia," vol. 27 of the *Hexamer General Surveys* (1892), Plate 2625 and "Ellwood Ivins Tube Company, Montgomery County, PA," vol. 29 of the *Hexamer General Surveys* (1895), Plate 2776.

61. Hexamer and Sons, "Powhatan Cotton Mill, Powhatan Manufacturing Company, owner; Powhatan, 2nd District, Baltimore County, Maryland," vol. 23 of the *Hexamer General Surveys* (1889), plate 2235.

62. Enclosing these offices within fireproof walls in the middle of the plant or at one end of it had the advantage of providing a physical break that would have prevented fires, quite common in factories, from spreading. See Betsy W. Bahr,

New England Mill Engineering: Rationalization and Reform in Textile Mill Design, 1790–1920 (Ann Arbor, MI: UMI Press, 1988), and Gary Kulik, "A Factory System of Wood: Cultural and Technological Change in the Building of the First Cotton Mills," in *Material Culture of the Wooden Age,* ed. Brooke Hindle (Tarrytown, NY: Sleepy Hollow Press, 1981), 300–335.

63. Similar arrangements occur in plans of "Rose Glen Mills, Booth and Brother, Montgomery County, PA," vol. 26 of the *Hexamer General Surveys* (1892), plate 2510, and "Penn Cordage Company," vol. 28 of the *Hexamer General Surveys* (1894), plate 2740.

64. Hexamer and Sons, "Hoopes and Townsend's Bolt, Nut, and Rivet Works," vol. 19 of the *Hexamer General Surveys* (1884), plates 1756–57, and vol. 29 of the *Hexamer General Surveys* (1895), plates 2796–97.

65. Biggs, *The Rational Factory,* and Gordon and Malone, *The Texture of Industry.*

66. Hugo Diemer, *Factory Organization and Administration,* 3rd ed. (New York: McGraw-Hill, 1921), especially 80–87.

67. Interior view of No. 1 Machine Shop at the Essington, Pennsylvania, plant of the Westinghouse Electric Corporation, ca. 1918. From Westinghouse Electric Corporation, Power Generation Division, Lester, Pennsylvania, Photographic Collection, Acc. No. 69.170, Photograph #12743, Hagley Museum and Library.

68. View of operators at work in the Blade Shop at the Essington, Pennsylvania plant of the Westinghouse Company (near Philadelphia, Pennsylvania), ca. 1930s, Westinghouse Electric Corporation, Power Generation Division, Lester, Pennsylvania, Photographic Collection, Acc. No. 69.170, Photograph #28791, Hagley Museum and Library.

69. See photograph of stenographers at NCR in Dayton, OH, as part of the series, "The Battlefields of Business," in *System* 12 (July 1907): 53. The layout of a branch office of the Sherwin Williams Company in Montreal looked similar to the office at NCR, except that the clerks' desks were turned away from the manager rather than toward him. See "The Battlefields of Business," *System* 15 (Jan. 1909): 30.

70. Kwolek-Folland, *Engendering Business,* 110. Also see R. H. Goddell, "Saving 42% on Routine Work," *System* 37 (June 1920): 1184–86.

71. *System* 8 (Oct. 1905): n.p.

72. Biggs, *The Rational Factory.* Biggs relies upon an extensive prescriptive literature written by factory owners, managers, and self-proclaimed industrial reformers in order to trace the impact of new ideas about efficiency on factory buildings. Although this literature is critical to understanding the "rational factory" ideal (and most importantly, for the purposes of this study, the place of surveillance within it), Biggs's analysis of it is less helpful because she fails to account fully for their ideological character; see Wayne Lewchuk, review of *The Rational Factory: Architecture, Technology, and Work in America's Age of Mass Production,* by Lindy

Biggs, *Economic History Review* 50, no. 4 (November 1997): 846. Moreover the reform literature did not translate easily into practice, for financial reasons and otherwise, further suggesting the need to treat such prescriptive literature carefully as a form of evidence.

73. Joseph A. Litterer, "The Emergence of Systematic Management as Shown by the Literature of Management from 1870–1900," M.A. thesis, Univ. of Illinois, 1954.

74. Industrial engineering emerged as a profession around this time. On the development of the industrial engineering profession and its relation to the efficiency movement, see Biggs, *The Rational Factory,* 36–54; Howard P. Emerson and Douglas C. E. Naehring, *Origins of Industrial Engineering: The Early Years of a Profession* (Norcross, GA: Industrial Engineering and Management Press, Institute of Industrial Engineers, 1988); and George M. Parks and Roger B. Collins, "200 Years of Industrial Engineering," *Industrial Engineering* 8 (July 1976): 14–25.

75. Moritz Kahn, *The Design and Construction of Industrial Buildings* (London: Technical Journals, 1917), 1.

76. Ibid., 11.

77. Hugh [Hugo] Diemer was one of the strongest advocates for the one-story configuration (discussed below). Ralph Currier Davis also liked the one-story configuration; see *The Principles of Factory Organization and Management* (New York: Harper and Brothers, 1928); also see Edward David Jones, *The Administration of Industrial Enterprises, with Special Reference to Factory Practice* (New York: Longmans, Green, 1916); Edward M. Stradley, "Economy by Centralized Control," *Factory* 2 (Nov.–Dec.–Jan. 1908–9): 105–07; and Henry Hess, "Works Design as a Factor in Manufacturing Economy," *Engineering Magazine* 27 (July 1904): 498–520. Those that remained neutral included Leon Pratt Alford, in *Management's Handbook, by a Staff of Specialists* (New York: Ronald Press, 1924); Ralph Mosser Barnes, *Industrial Engineering and Management, Problems and Policies* (New York: McGraw-Hill, 1931); Arthur G. Anderson, *Industrial Engineering and Factory Management* (New York: Ronald Press, 1928); Perley F. Walker, *Management Engineering: The Design and Organization of Industrial Plants* (New York: McGraw-Hill, 1924); D. C. Newman Collins, "The Design and Construction of Industrial Buildings," *Engineering Magazine* 33 (Sept. 1907): 906–30; and O. M. Becker and William J. Lees, "Building a Factory V—Plans and Materials for Construction," *System* 11 (Jan. 1907): 28–35.

78. Tyrrell, *A Treatise on the Design and Construction of Mill Buildings,* 30.

79. Hugo Diemer, "The Planning of Factory Buildings and the Influence of Design on Their Productive Capacity," *Engineering News* 50 (24 Mar. 1904): 293.

80. Diemer, *Factory Organization and Administration,* 87, and "The Planning of Factory Buildings," 294.

81. Diemer, *Factory Organization and Administration,* 87.

82. Herbert F. Simpson, "The Design and Construction of Industrial Buildings, Part II," *Engineering Record* 59 (5 June 1909): 716–18.

83. Lewis, *The Commercial Organisation of Factories*, 161.

84. Oscar E. Perrigo, "Economical Arrangement of Machinery," *System* 8 (Sept. 1905): 261–65.

85. F. A. Scheffer's plan is discussed in Tyrrell, *A Treatise on the Design and Construction of Mill Buildings*, 3.

86. Stradley, "Economy by Centralized Control," 105–6.

87. Hess, "Works Design as a Factor in Manufacturing Economy," 511.

88. Advertisement in *Factory* 14 (Jan. 1915): 40.

89. Standard Sanitary Manufacturing Company, *Factory Sanitation* (Pittsburgh, PA: The Company, 1913).

90. Anderson, "Industrial Engineering and Factory Management," 228.

91. Joseph French Johnson et al., *Office Management*, vol. 19 of Modern Business: A Series of Texts Prepared as Part of the Modern Business Course and Service of the Alexander Hamilton Institute (New York: Alexander Hamilton Institute, 1919), 19.

92. Ibid., 30. Also see John William Schulze, *The American Office: Its Organization, Management and Records* (New York: Ronald Press, 1914).

93. Zimmerman, "The System of the Armours," 234–47. The Armour "method," as this author called it, was not unique to this firm. Many business owners employed this management strategy of "benevolent paternalism" during the late nineteenth century.

94. Lewis, *The Commercial Organisation of Factories*, 165.

95. Frederick Winslow Taylor, *Shop Management* (New York: Harper and Brothers, 1911), 30–32.

96. Biggs, *The Rational Factory*, 16–25. At the textile mills at Lowell, Massachusetts, for example, overseers' desks and offices were prominently positioned for management to oversee workers on the mill floor and for mill workers to recognize this fact. See Chandler, *The Visible Hand*, 68–69 and Dublin, *Women at Work*, 58–69.

97. Litterer, "The Emergence of Systematic Management"; Sanford M. Jacoby, *Employing Bureaucracy: Managers, Unions, and the Transformation of Work in American Industry, 1900–1945* (New York: Columbia Univ. Press, 1985), 13–20; Edwards, *Contested Terrain;* Lazonick, "Technological Change and the Control of Work"; Biggs, *The Rational Factory;* Zunz, *Making America Corporate;* Daniel Nelson, *Managers and Workers: Origins of the New Factory System in the United States, 1880–1920* (Madison: Univ. of Wisconsin Press, 1975); and Chandler, *The Visible Hand.*

98. Edwards, *Contested Terrain*, 23–25, and Chandler, *The Visible Hand*, especially 14–78. Chandler cites the McLane Report of 1832, which showed only 36 busi-

ness enterprises having over 250 employees in the U.S., of which 31 were textile mills.

99. Edwards, *Contested Terrain*, 25.

100. See Chandler, *The Visible Hand*. While scholars have debated the origins, timing, and reasons behind these changes, there is little disagreement that significant changes occurred.

101. For a Marxist interpretation of deskilling, see Lazonick, "Technological Change and the Control of Work," especially 112–15.

102. On early unions and other labor movements, see Milton J. Nadworny, *Scientific Management and the Unions, 1900–1932* (Cambridge, MA: Harvard Univ. Press, 1955); Jacoby, *Employing Bureaucracy;* Hugh G. J. Aitken, *Taylorism at Watertown Arsenal: Scientific Management in Action, 1908–1915* (Cambridge, MA: Harvard Univ. Press, 1960); and David Montgomery, *The Fall of the House of Labor: The Workplace, the State, and American Labor Activism, 1865–1925* (Cambridge: Cambridge Univ. Press, 1987).

103. On labor unions and their effect on management, see Nadworny, *Scientific Management and the Unions;* Aitken, *Taylorism at Watertown Arsenal;* Montgomery, *The Fall of the House of Labor;* and Jacoby, *Employing Bureaucracy.* On Pullman, see Stanley Buder, *Pullman: An Experiment in Industrial Order and Community Planning, 1880-1930* (New York: Oxford Univ. Press, 1967).

104. On the history of postal unions see Mikusko, *Carriers in a Common Cause;* Baxter, *Labor and Politics in the USPS;* Spero, *The Labor Movement in a Government Industry;* and Nesbitt, *Labor Relations in the Federal Government Service.*

105. I borrow the phrase from Edwards, *Contested Terrain*, 51. Also see Stephen Meyer, *The Five Dollar Day: Labor Management and Social Control in the Ford Motor Company, 1908–1921* (Albany: State Univ. of New York Press, 1981), 3–5.

106. The literature on systematic management is limited. The only comprehensive sources on the movement are by Litterer, especially his thesis, "The Emergence of Systematic Management." See also Chandler, *The Visible Hand;* Lazonick, "Technological Change and the Control of Work"; Biggs, *The Rational Factory,* 37–38; and Jacoby, *Employing Bureaucracy.*

107. On Litterer's distinction between "systematic" and "scientific" management, see "The Emergence of Systematic Management," 258–61.

108. Ibid., 78–101.

109. Ibid., 69–70.

110. John Tregoning, *A Treatise on Factory Management, Being a Comprehensive and Practical Scheme for the Better Management of Factories* (Lynn, MA: Press of Thomas P. Nichols, 1891), iii, reproduced in Litterer, "The Emergence of Systematic Management," 117–18.

111. Jacoby, *Employing Bureaucracy,* 43–44, and Nelson, *Managers and Workers,* 48–53. These writers argue that even though the foremen still retained supervisory

power, their lack of power to punish the workers by cutting their rates or dismissing them reduced the supervisory potential.

112. Taylor first presented his piece-rate incentive system, a key component of his philosophy of scientific management, in 1895 to the American Society of Mechanical Engineers (ASME); see "A Piece Rate System, Being a Step Toward Partial Solution of the Labor Problem," in *Transactions of the American Society of Mechanical Engineers* 16 (1895): 856–903. More developed examinations of his philosophy may be found in *The Principles of Scientific Management* (New York: Harper and Row, 1911), and *Shop Management.*

113. Taylor, *Shop Management.*

114. Ibid., 95–103.

115. On welfare capitalism, see Littmann, "Designing Obedience"; Stuart D. Brandes, *American Welfare Capitalism, 1880–1940* (Chicago: Univ. of Chicago Press, 1976); Nelson, *Managers and Workers,* especially 101–20; and David Brody, *Workers in Industrial America: Essays on the Twentieth Century Struggle* (New York: Oxford Univ. Press, 1980), 48–81.

116. Littmann, "Designing Obedience," 104.

117. Articles in *Factory* or *System* from the first two decades of the twentieth century provide a representative sampling of the kinds of record-keeping systems that were developed.

118. On welfare programs at General Electric, see Littmann, "Designing Obedience."

119. Edwards, *Contested Terrain,* especially 112–29.

120. Johnson et al., *Office Management,* 284–85.

121. Post Office Department, *Report of the Postmaster-General of the United States,* 51st Cong., 1st sess., 1889, H.exdoc.1 (*Serial Set* 2723), 17. See also Cushing, *The Story of Our Post Office,* 310.

122. Zimmerman, "The System of the Armours," 234.

123. See William Judson, "Cashing the Manpower in Business," *System* 13 (Jan. 1908): 4–7; "What's the Matter with the Employer, III—Overworking Men—Result: Under-Production," *System* 11 (May 1907): 491–94.; and "Automatic Assistant Managers—How Machinery Aids in Supervision," *Factory* 14 (Apr. 1915): 233–34, 288, 290.

124. *Factory* 17 (May 1916): 438.

125. *System* 8 (July 1905), n.p.

126. *System* 37 (Mar. 1920): 579.

127. Henry T. Noyes contended that the area under supervision should be "300 feet square or less." See Noyes, "Planning for a New Manufacturing Plant," *Annals of the American Academy of Political and Social Science* 85 (Sept. 1919): 76.

128. On the rise of personnel departments in the 1910s and 1920s, see Edwards, *Contested Terrain;* Littmann, "Designing Obedience"; Jacoby, *Employing Bureaucracy,* especially 147–54; and Nelson, *Managers and Workers,* 148–56. On the rise of

cost accounting, see Littmann, "Designing Obedience"; H. Thomas Johnson and Robert S. Kaplan, *Relevance Lost: The Rise and Fall of Management Accounting* (Boston, MA: Harvard Business School Press, 1987); and Joseph Litterer, "Systematic Management: Design for Organizational Recoupling in American Manufacturing Firms," *Business History Review* 37, no. 4 (Winter 1963): 369–91, and "The Emergence of Systematic Management." Such measures became increasingly popular after 1900; see John Whitmore, "Factory Accounting as Applied to Machine Shops," *Journal of Accountancy* 2 (Oct. 1906): 430–41, and G. Harvey Porter, "The Cost Accountant, an Essential to Management," *Journal of Accountancy* 45 (May 1928): 351–56. I thank Phil Scranton for his suggestion that the decline of visual surveillance as a means of control corresponds with the rise of the other systems and William Littmann for his helpful references on cost accounting.

129. Meyer, *The Five Dollar Day,* 37–61.

130. See the annual *Reports of the Postmaster General* from the 1910s and 1920s.

131. Warren P. Edgarton, inspector in charge, to chief post office inspector, March 22, 1893; Box 1, Vol. 1, June 25, 1889–August 5, 1893, p. 297–98; Records of the Inspection Office, Philadelphia, PA, 1896–1909; Office of the Postmaster General, Division of Post Office Inspectors; Records of the Post Office Department, RG 28, NAB.

132. See records of the Office of Division of Inspectors, especially in case files where Inspectors discuss their discoveries of the clerks' stealth methods.

133. Taylor, *Shop Management* and *Principles of Scientific Management.* Typical articles dealing with soldiering include "How to Prevent 'Soldiering,'" *System* 8 (Dec. 1905): 572–75, and "How Loafing of Employees Was Stopped," *System* 13 (Jan. 1908): 55–56.

3. Hierarchy

1. T. S. Arthur, *Trials and Confessions of an American Housekeeper* (Philadelphia: Lippincott, Grambo, 1854), 21–28.

2. On Arthur's popularity, see Donald A. Koch, "T. S. Arthur," in Joel Myerson, ed., *Antebellum Writers in New York and the South,* vol. 3 of Dictionary of Literary Biography (Detroit: Gale Research, 1979), 3–7. Arthur's book was reprinted at least three times in the 1850s (1853, 1854, 1859) and by 1860, his books had sold more than a million copies.

3. This chapter focuses on domestic environments of the northeastern United States. As Kenneth L. Ames has noted in his work on Victorian America, the North in the Victorian period can be discussed relatively easily given its homogeneity in the period whereas the South was a "distinctive subculture," with its own traditions and rules governing domestic spaces. See Ames, "Meaning in Artifacts: Hall Furnishings in Victorian America," *Journal of Interdisciplinary History* 9 (Summer 1978): 19–46.

4. My thinking about everyday resistance comes from several sources, but especially James C. Scott's pioneering study *Weapons of the Weak: Everyday Forms of Peasant Resistance* (New Haven: Yale Univ. Press, 1985). Though Scott's ideas about the actual impact of everyday resistance have been challenged, the concept remains a useful one, at least in terms of how anxieties about potential acts of resistance have affected relationships between classes. Other sources on everyday resistance include Nicole Constable, *Maid to Order in Hong Kong: Stories of Filipina Workers* (Ithaca, NY: Cornell Univ. Press, 1997), especially 7–16; Eugene D. Genovese, *Roll, Jordan, Roll: The World the Slaves Made* (New York: Pantheon Books, 1974); and Lila Abu-Lughod, "The Romance of Resistance: Tracing Transformations of Power through Bedouin Women," *American Ethnologist* 17, no. 1 (February 1990): 41–55. I thank Rebecca Ginsburg for directing my attention to this literature.

5. Critiques include Michael Brown, "On Resisting Resistance," *American Anthropologist* 98 (Dec. 1996): 729–35; Sherry B. Ortner, "Resistance and the Problem of Ethnographic Refusal," *Comparative Studies in Society and History* 37 (Jan. 1995): 173–93; and Marshall Sahlins, *Waiting for Foucault* (Cambridge: Prickly Pear, 1993). Robert Fletcher offers a balanced critique, suggesting while the concept of everyday resistance has been given too much causal status, it remains viable. See Fletcher, "What Are We Fighting For? Rethinking Resistance in a Pewenche Community in Chile," *Journal of Peasant Studies* 28 (Apr. 2001): 37–66.

6. Foucault, *Discipline and Punish,* especially 195–228.

7. Helen Campbell, *Prisoners of Poverty: Women Wage-Workers, Their Trades and Their Lives* (Boston: Roberts Brothers, 1887), 230.

8. Numerous historians who have written on domestic service have struggled with this. David M. Katzman is among the most successful in finding evidence, but he, too, notes the challenges involved. See Katzman, *Seven Days a Week: Women and Domestic Service in Industrializing America* (New York: Oxford Univ. Press, 1978), chapter 1.

9. Lucy Maynard Salmon, *Domestic Service* (New York: Macmillan, 1897), 108–9.

10. Typical explanations of mistresses' complaints about servants may be found in Blaine Edward McKinley, "'The Stranger at the Gates': Employer Reactions toward Domestic Servants in America, 1825–1875," Ph.D. diss., Michigan State Univ., 1969, and Daniel E. Sutherland, *Americans and Their Servants: Domestic Service in the United States from 1800 to 1920* (Baton Rouge: Louisiana State Univ. Press, 1981), 26–39. Examples of period literature that make such references include Harriet Prescott Spofford, *The Servant Girl Question* (Boston: Houghton, Mifflin; Cambridge: Riverside Press, 1881); Nicholas A. Griffith [Elizabeth Strong Worthington], *The Biddy Club: And How Its Members . . . Grappled with the Troublous Servant Question to the Great Advantage of Themselves, and, as They Hope, of Many Others* (Chicago: A. C. McClurg, 1888); Charles Chamberlain,

Jr., *The Servant-Girl of the Period, the Greatest Plague of Life: What Mr. and Mrs. Honeydew Learned of Housekeeping* (New York: J. S. Redfield, 1873); Augustus Mayhew et al., *The Greatest Plague of Life; Or, The Adventures of a Lady in Search of a Good Servant* (London: D. Bogue, 1847); and Susan Anna Brown, *Home Topics: A Book of Practical Papers on House and Home Matters* (New York: Century, 1881).

11. On challenges with using pattern books as evidence, see Dell Upton, "Pattern Books and Professionalism: Aspects of the Transformation of Domestic Architecture in America, 1800–1860," *Winterthur Portfolio* 19, no. 2/3 (Summer-Autumn 1984): 107–50, and James L. Garvin, "Mail-Order House Plans and American Victorian Architecture," *Winterthur Portfolio* 16 (Winter 1981): 309–34.

12. In some cases late nineteenth-century pattern books illustrate designs of houses already built—but even in these cases, designs should be considered as prescriptive. Presentation of these designs was intended, in these later books, to provide ideas for future homebuilders, not simply to illustrate existing house designs. Examples of pattern books presenting realized house designs include A. J. Bicknell, *Bicknell's Cottage and Villa Architecture* (New York: William T. Comstock, 1881); Arnold William Brunner and William Paul Gerhard, *Cottages; Or, Hints on Economical Building* (New York: William T. Comstock, 1884); William T. Comstock, *American Cottages* (New York: William T. Comstock, 1883); William T. Comstock, *Victorian Domestic Architectural Plans and Details* (New York: William T. Comstock, 1881); and E. C. Gardner, *Illustrated Homes: A Series of Papers Describing Real Houses and Real People* (Boston: J. R. Osgood, 1875).

13. As Clifford Edward Clark deftly showed in his 1986 book, *The American Family Home,* house plans in these books collectively reflect and embody a set of domestic ideals to which Victorian men and women subscribed in varying degrees when building or remodeling their houses. See Clark, *The American Family Home, 1800–1960* (Chapel Hill: Univ. of North Carolina Press, 1986), especially xiv–xv.

14. Ibid., 64.

15. See Clark, *The American Family Home;* David P. Handlin, *The American Home: Architecture and Society, 1815–1915* (Boston: Little, Brown, 1979); and Gwendolyn Wright, *Building the Dream: A Social History of Housing in America* (New York: Pantheon Books, 1981).

16. I borrow the idea of the *social molecule,* developed by Dell Upton, as a means of thinking about typology in terms of function, from his essay "Vernacular Domestic Architecture in Eighteenth-Century Virginia," *Winterthur Portfolio* 17 (Summer/Autumn 1982): 95–119. Upton devised the social molecule to explain underlying similarities between houses that showed little similarity of form.

17. Wright noted that as early as 1843 household reformers such as Lydia Sigourney and Catharine Beecher were arguing that houses needed to be divided such that different areas of the dwelling were reserved for social functions, personal privacy,

and household production—a trend that Wright found accelerated as the Victorian period wore on. Clark meanwhile stressed two principal zones in the Victorian house—the "public," which referred to spaces where the family communed and entertained guests, and the "private," which included all other areas of the house that were to be kept out of view of public spaces. See Wright, *Building the Dream,* 76–78, 111–12, and Clark, *The American Family Home,* 42.

18. A. J. Downing, *The Architecture of Country Houses* (New York: D. Appleton, 1850). Downing was one of the first and most vocal advocates for creating a domestic architecture appropriate for the middle-class American family. On Downing's influence, see Clark, *The American Family Home,* 16–23; see also George Bishop Tatum, "Andrew Jackson Downing: Arbiter of American Taste," Ph.D. diss., Princeton Univ., 1949, and David Schuyler, *Apostle of Taste: Andrew Jackson Downing, 1815–1852* (Baltimore: Johns Hopkins Univ. Press, 1996).

19. Downing, *The Architecture of Country Houses,* 166–70.

20. Ibid., 257.

21. Ibid., 334. Downing does not provide a plan of the servants' quarters on the second floor, but he describes their location and placement.

22. Bicknell, *Bicknell's Cottage and Villa Architecture,* plates 37 and 38.

23. See Henry Hudson Holly, *Modern Dwellings in Town and Country Adapted to American Wants and Climate* (New York: Harper and Brothers, 1878), 112–13; Louis H. Gibson, *Convenient Houses, with Fifty Plans for the Housekeeper Architect and Housewife* (New York: T. Y. Crowell., 1889), 60; and Palliser, Palliser, and Company, *Palliser's Model Homes: Showing a Variety of Designs for Model Dwellings* (Bridgeport, CT: Palliser, Palliser, 1878), 62–63.

24. Russell Lynes, *The Domesticated Americans* (New York: Harper and Row, 1963), 179.

25. Gibson, *Convenient Houses,* 121.

26. Sutherland briefly discussed the mediating function of the butler's pantry in *Americans and Their Servants,* 32, as does McKinley in "'The Stranger at the Gates,'" 248–49, and Lynes in *The Domesticated Americans,* 179. Besides serving as an intermediate zone between kitchen and dining room, the butler's pantry typically contained items to help servants prepare the meal (for example, condiments, serving dishes), thus dividing "preparation" and "cooking" and therefore keeping with the Victorian notion of specialization of rooms by function.

27. Gibson, *Convenient Houses,* 39–44, 122. Also see Brunner, *Cottages; Or, Hints on Economical Building,* 17, and E. C. Gardner, *The House That Jill Built, After Jack's Had Proved a Failure* (New York: Fords, Howard, and Hulbert, 1882), 82–85.

28. Charles Francis Osborne, *Notes on the Art of House-Planning* (New York: William T. Comstock, 1888), 46.

29. The role of housekeepers and how they help (and hinder) housekeeping is a frequent topic in advice literature. Many Victorian pattern books, including that by

Holly, *Modern Dwellings* and Calvert Vaux et al., *Villas and Cottages: A Series of Designs Prepared for Execution in the United States* (New York: Harper & Brothers, 1857), make reference to houses with housekeepers. On advantages and drawbacks, see Sarah Josepha Buell Hale, *Keeping House and House Keeping: A Story of Domestic Life* (New York: Harper and Brothers, 1845), and Brown, *Home Topics*.

30. Holly, *Modern Dwellings*, 129–37.

31. Clark, *The American Family Home*, 132. For more on these changes, see Clark's chapter 5 and Gwendolyn Wright, *Building the Dream*, chapter 9.

32. My analysis is based on examination of the 450 house plans in Katherine H. Stevenson and H. Ward Jandl, *Houses by Mail: A Guide to Houses from Sears, Roebuck and Company* (Washington, DC: Preservation Press, 1986). More than 94 percent of the single-family houses in this book have one of these buffer spaces.

33. Katzman, *Seven Days a Week*, especially chapter 2.

34. Wright, *Building the Dream*, 158–76.

35. Downing inveighed against the practice, adopting it (reluctantly) in only one of his plans in *The Architecture of Country Houses*, 115–16. Also see Holly, *Modern Dwellings*, 114, and Gardner, *Illustrated Homes*, 146.

36. Gardner, *Illustrated Homes*, 136, 139.

37. Examples of houses identified as "Southern" are found in many pattern books, including Downing, *The Architecture of Country Houses*, 312–17, and Gervase Wheeler, *Homes for the People, in Suburb and Country* (New York: C. Scribner, 1855), 253–55. Herman also discusses this in southern plantation homes and their view of the quarter in chapter 4 of *Town House*.

38. Vaux, *Villas and Cottages*, 162.

39. Downing, *The Architecture of Country Houses*, 115–16.

40. A. J. Downing, *Cottage Residences* (New York: Wiley and Putnam, 1842), 3.

41. Gardner, *The House That Jill Built*, 45.

42. Letter from Libbie to Margaret Scott, 14 May 1887, as quoted in Sutherland, *Americans and Their Servants*, 117. Another servant lamented the loss of privacy when she was reprimanded for reading in the service quarters; see Lillian Pettengill, *Toilers of the Home: The Record of a College Woman's Experience as a Domestic Servant* (New York: Doubleday, Page, 1903), 18.

43. John James Stevenson, *House Architecture* (London: Macmillan, 1880), and Robert Kerr, *The Gentleman's House; Or, How to Plan English Residences*, 2nd ed. (London: J. Murray, 1865). On the influence of these books on American house-planning guides and American architecture in general, see Handlin, *The American Home*, 333.

44. Kerr, *The Gentlemen's House*, 68.

45. Stevenson, *House Architecture*, 2: 79.

46. Ibid.

47. Ibid., 102.

48. Osborne, *Notes on the Art of House-Planning*. Other examples include Gardner's books, in particular *Illustrated Homes* and *The House That Jill Built*, and his essay, "Model Homes for Model Housekeeping, IV," *Good Housekeeping* 1, no. 6 (25 July 1885): 1–5; Isabel Bevier, *The House: Its Plan, Decoration and Care* (Chicago: American School of Home Economics, 1907); and O. S. Fowler, *A Home for All; Or, The Gravel Wall and Octagon Mode of Building* (New York: Fowler and Wells, 1854).

49. Osborne, *Notes on the Art of House-Planning*, 82–89.

50. See Faye E. Dudden, *Serving Women: Household Service in Nineteenth-Century America* (Middletown, CT: Wesleyan Univ. Press, 1983), especially pages 155–92; Sutherland, *Americans and Their Servants*, 30–33; and McKinley, "'Stranger at the Gates,'" chapter 6.

51. On Catharine Beecher's influence on the American home and the ideal of domesticity, see Kathryn Kish Sklar, *Catharine Beecher: A Study in American Domesticity* (New Haven: Yale Univ. Press, 1973); Nancy Ann Holst, "'The Wise Woman Buildeth Her House': Catharine Beecher and Nineteenth-Century House Pattern Books," M.A. thesis, Univ. of Delaware, 1996; and Jeanne Boydston et al. *The Limits of Sisterhood: The Beecher Sisters on Women's Rights and Women's Sphere* (Chapel Hill: Univ. of North Carolina Press, 1988).

52. Sklar, *Catharine Beecher*, especially 151–67.

53. Catharine Esther Beecher, *A Treatise on Domestic Economy, for the Use of Young Ladies at Home, and at School* (Boston: Marsh, Capen, Lyon, and Webb, 1841), 210–13.

54. Catharine Esther Beecher and Harriet Beecher Stowe, *The American Woman's Home; Or, Principles of Domestic Science* (New York: J.B. Ford, 1869), 314. Also see Catharine Esther Beecher, *Letters to Persons Who Are Engaged in Domestic Service* (New York: Leavitt and Trow, 1842), especially 92, which discusses the role of the "overseer" in the household.

55. In particular see the following books by Eunice White Bullard Beecher (Mrs. Henry Ward Beecher): *The Law of a Household* (Boston: Small, Maynard, 1912); *All Around the House; Or, How to Make Homes Happy* (New York: D. Appleton, 1879); and *Motherly Talks with Young Housekeepers* (New York: J. B. Ford, 1875).

56. Beecher, *The Law of a Household*, 3–4.

57. Beecher, *All Around the House*, 4–5.

58. Ibid., 32–36.

59. Ibid., 101.

60. Ibid., 119.

61. Ibid., 337.

62. See Ephesians 6:5–6 and Colossians 3:22.

63. In *Motherly Talks,* Beecher described the inclination among Irish servants to slack if not under watch, in contrast to English and Scottish servants, who worked "as faithfully . . . when left in charge alone, as when the master and mistress are near them." See *Motherly Talks,* 249.

64. George A. Peltz, *The Housewife's Library* (Boston, MA: E. R. Curtis, 1885), 360–61.

65. *Plain Talk and Friendly Advice to Domestics, with Counsel on Home Matters* (Boston: Phillips, Sampson, 1855), 31.

66. Sarah Josepha Buell Hale, *The Good Housekeeper; Or, The Way to Live Well and To Be Well While We Live* (Boston: Weeks, Jordan, 1839), 116. A similar argument is advanced in C. H. Fowler and William De Puy, *Home and Health and Home Economics: A Cyclopedia of Facts and Hints for All Departments of Home Life, Health, and Domestic Economy* (New York: Phillips and Hunt, 1880), 31.

67. Mrs. [Mary H.] Cornelius, *The Young Housekeeper's Friend,* rev. ed. (Boston: Thompson, Brown, 1871), 15.

68. Mrs. E. F. Ellet, ed., *The New Cyclopedia of Domestic Economy, and Practical Housekeeper Adapted to All Classes of Society, and Comprising Subjects Connected with the Interests of Every Family* (Norwich, CT: Henry Bill Publishing, 1872), 31. Also see a later version of this book, Florence K. Stanton, *The Practical Housekeeper and Cyclopedia of Domestic Economy* (Philadelphia: Keeler and Kirkpatrick, 1898), 31.

69. Christine Terhune Herrick, *The Expert Maid-Servant* (New York: Harper and Brothers, 1904), 41.

70. On the Beecher family and religion, see Marie Caskey, *Chariot of Fire: Religion and the Beecher Family* (New Haven: Yale Univ. Press, 1978), and Sklar, *Catharine Beecher,* part 1.

71. Beecher, *A Treatise on Domestic Economy,* 209–12.

72. Beecher, *All Around the House,* 276.

73. Mrs. Cornelius, *The Young Housekeeper's Friend,* 15. Also see Brown, comp., *Home Topics,* especially 75.

74. On the flourishing of didactic fiction in antebellum America, see Blaine Edwards McKinley, "Troublesome Comforts: The Housekeeper-Servant Relationship in Antebellum Didactic Fiction," *Journal of American Culture* 5 (Summer 1982): 36–44.

75. Hale, *Keeping House and House Keeping,* 25–27.

76. Mayhew et al., *The Greatest Plague of Life,* 88–89, and American Sunday-School Union, *Parlour and Kitchen; Or, The Story of Ann Connover* (Philadelphia: American Sunday-School Union, 1835), 125–28.

77. "Trials of an English Housekeeper: High Life Below Stairs," *Godey's Lady's Book* 55 (Dec. 1857): 531–33. Also see Hale, *Keeping House and House Keeping,* 35–37, and Chamberlain, *The Servant Girl of the Period,* 159.

78. See Hale, *Keeping House and House Keeping,* 111.
79. See "The Miseries of Mistresses," *Harper's Monthly* 13 (Oct. 1856): 716.
80. Ibid., 717.
81. Stories where servants imbibed in alcohol in their rooms are found in *Parlor and Kitchen: The Greatest Plague of Life,* 41–43, and Chamberlain, *The Servant Girl of the Period,* 93. The story of "borrowing" food is found in Arthur, *Trials and Confessions,* 23.
82. Griffith, *The Biddy Club,* 64.
83. *Godey's Lady's Book* 37 (Sept. 1848): 181.
84. "The Miseries of Mistresses," 716.
85. Hale, *Keeping House and House Keeping,* 93.
86. Alice B. Neal, "Fetch and Carry," *Godey's Lady's Book* 54 (Feb. 1857): 112–17.
87. Beecher, *Motherly Talks,* 29–30.
88. See *Ballou's Dollar Monthly Magazine* 7 (May 1858): 502, reproduced in Elizabeth L. O'Leary, *At Beck and Call: The Representation of Domestic Servants in Nineteenth-Century American Painting* (Washington, DC: Smithsonian Institution Press, 1996), 129. O'Leary juxtaposes this illustration with another that she claims shows a mistress discovering a male caller hiding beneath her servant's bed. In this case, the mistress's gaze discovers her servant's indiscretion—but the same dynamic of the potential of the gaze *not* to see is at work here. For this other cartoon, see *Harper's Weekly* 2 (9 Jan. 1858): 21.
89. Beecher and Stowe, *The American Woman's Home,* 14.
90. Hale, *Keeping House and House Keeping.*
91. Beecher and Stowe, *The American Woman's Home,* 18–19, 220–21, 314–15.
92. Beecher, *All Around the House,* 340.
93. Arthur, *Trials and Confessions,* 147–149.

4. Fellowship

1. Information about the camp's history comes from two locally published sources. See Lodge W. Chappell, Harry J. Daniels, and John P. Campbell, *Camp Meeting Memories: A Short History of Holiness Camp Meetings in Central Penna.* (Sunbury, PA: Sunbury Daily Item, 1951), and God's Holiness Grove Camp Meeting Association, *Fifty Years of Spiritual Ministry* (Hummel's Whart, PA: The Association, 1969). Also helpful were conversations with persons associated with the camp, including Al and Sue Carroll, G. Edwin Lint, Scott Schambach, and Rev. James Leininger. Also see the memorial Web site at http://www.diskbooks.org/camp.html (accessed June 15, 2007), which describes the camp's last flourishes, its demise, and the relocation of the meeting.
2. There is some debate about when the first camp meetings were held. The oft-cited example of the first camp meeting is the one at Cane Ridge, Kentucky,

in 1801. Kenneth O. Brown has taken issue with the prevalent chronology in camp-meeting studies that assume camp meetings emerged spontaneously in the wake of the success of Cane Ridge, though certainly it helped encourage the broader camp-meeting movement during the nineteenth century. See Brown, *Holy Ground: A Study of the American Camp Meeting* (New York: Garland, 1992). Other scholarly sources on the history of the camp meeting movement include Ellen Eslinger, *Citizens of Zion: The Social Origins of Camp Meeting Revivalism* (Knoxville: Univ. of Tennessee Press, 1999); Dickson D. Bruce, *And They All Sang Hallelujah: Plain-Folk Camp-Meeting Religion, 1800–1845* (Knoxville: Univ. of Tennessee Press, 1974); Charles A. Johnson, *The Frontier Camp Meeting: Religion's Harvest Time* (Dallas: Southern Methodist Univ. Press, 1955); Ellen Weiss, *City in the Woods: The Life and Design of an American Camp Meeting on Martha's Vineyard* (New York: Oxford Univ. Press, 1987); and Ray McKinzie Goodrow, "From Sacred Space to Suburban Retreat: The Evolution of the American Camp Meeting Ground," M.A. thesis, Univ. of Virginia, 1994.

3. The racial, class, and ethnic make-up of camp meeting attendees is not entirely clear. Bruce has discussed camp meetings in terms of plain folk religious culture in the South in *And They All Sang Hallelujah.* Weiss has discussed the rise of camp meetings during the Victorian period as part of a trend toward vacation retreats for the middle class in *City in the Woods;* and John Lawrence Brasher in *The Sanctified South: John Lakin Brasher and the Holiness Movement* (Urbana: Univ. of Illinois Press, 1994) has looked at the place of camp meetings within the religious climate of the South. Most scholars agree that a variety of people attended camp meetings during the Victorian period, a conclusion that seems largely based on descriptions of camp meetings that reveal persons of all backgrounds being converted or sanctified at them.

4. On camp meetings and the holiness revival, see Melvin Easterday Dieter, *The Holiness Revival of the Nineteenth Century* (Metuchen, NJ: Scarecrow Press, 1980), especially 96–155; Charles Edwin Jones, *Perfectionist Persuasion: The Holiness Movement and American Methodism, 1867–1936* (Metuchen, NJ: Scarecrow Press, 1974); and Brasher, *The Sanctified South.*

5. This kind of reciprocal gaze recalls Jacques Lacan's analysis of the interrelationship between subjectivity and visuality, as he discussed throughout his writings but especially in *The Four Fundamental Concepts of Psycho-Analysis,* trans. Alan Sheridan (Harmondsworth: Penguin Books, 1977). My account of reciprocity in the field of vision, however, derives from a consideration of how the built environment structures gazes between viewing parties and how the gazes facilitated through design worked in specific historical, social, and cultural contexts. This has little to do with how the reciprocal gaze bears upon psychoanalytic theories of subject formation, which is the focus of Lacan's work and many others that deal with the reciprocal gaze. For an illustration of the difference between my emphasis and that of those focused on subjectivity and the gaze, see de Bolla, "The Visibility of Visuality," 65–81.

6. James Porter, *An Essay on Camp Meetings* (New York: Lane and Scott, 1849), 20–21.

7. Victor Witter Turner, *The Ritual Process: Structure and Anti-Structure* (London: Routledge and K. Paul, 1969).

8. Ibid., 95–97.

9. See Turner, "Variations on a Theme of Liminality," in *Secular Ritual,* ed. Sally Falk Moore and Barbara G. Myerhoff (Assen: Van Gorcum, 1977), 36–52 and in his "Introduction: Pilgrimage as a Liminoid Phenomenon," in *Image and Pilgrimage in Christian Culture: Anthropological Perspectives,* ed. Victor Witter Turner and Edith L. B. Turner (New York: Columbia Univ. Press, 1978).

10. See Turner, "Introduction: Pilgrimage as a Liminoid Phenomenon," 1–39.

11. On the anxiety about gazing in the nineteenth century, see Karen Halttunen, *Confidence Men and Painted Women: A Study of Middle-Class Culture in America, 1830–1870* (New Haven, CT: Yale Univ. Press, 1982), and John F. Kasson, *Rudeness and Civility: Manners in Nineteenth-Century Urban America* (New York: Hill and Wang, 1990). The different roles women assumed at Methodist and holiness camp meetings are discussed in Bruce, *And They All Sang Hallelujah,* especially 73–132, and Joe L. Kincheloe Jr., "Women at Camp Meetings and Political Rallies," *Tennessee Historical Quarterly* 40 (Summer 1981): 158–69.

12. Scholarly sources on the history of the camp-meeting movement include Bruce, *And They All Sang Hallelujah;* Johnson, *The Frontier Camp Meeting;* and Goodrow, "From Sacred Space to Suburban Retreat." A good study of early camp meetings in Kentucky may be found in Eslinger, *Citizens of Zion.*

13. Johnson emphasized the importance of camp meetings to Methodism, discussing how they became a weapon through which the denomination gained adherents during the early nineteenth century, in *The Frontier Camp Meeting,* especially 84–85.

14. Statistics on the rapid rate of growth of Methodism may be found in many standard histories, but these statistics are reproduced in Weiss, *City in the Woods,* 3.

15. On camp meetings and the holiness revival, see Dieter, *The Holiness Revival of the Nineteenth Century,* especially 96–155; Jones, *Perfectionist Persuasion;* and Brasher, *The Sanctified South.*

16. In a much earlier study focused on the early nineteenth century, Charles Johnson laid out a typology of sorts for Methodist camp meetings, noting three basic forms: the circular, the oblong, and the horseshoe. My findings differ in part because of the period and denominational differences and also because the camps of the later nineteenth and twentieth centuries were considerably larger than their early-nineteenth-century Methodist counterparts.

17. Two good examples of these manuals include Rev. B[arlow]. W[eed]. Gorham, *Camp Meeting Manual: A Practical Book for the Camp Ground; in Two Parts* (Boston: H. V. Degen, 1854) and Amos. P. Mead, *Manna in the Wilderness; Or, The*

Grove and Its Altar, Offerings, and Thrilling Incidents (Philadelphia: Perkinpine and Higgins, 1859).

18. Brown and Cooley have examined the idea of the grounds as holy, sacred spaces symbolically separate from the everyday world, though neither specifically discusses this relative to design. See Kenneth O. Brown's books *Holy Ground* and *Holy Ground, Too: The Camp Meeting Family Tree* (Hazleton, PA: Holiness Archives, 1997), as well as Steven D. Cooley, "Manna and the Manual: Sacramental and Instrumental Constructions of the Victorian Methodist Camp Meeting during the Mid–Nineteenth Century," *Religion and American Culture* 6 (Summer 1996): 131–59.

19. Another example of a Methodist camp meeting that employs the U-shaped layout is Perkasie Park Camp Meeting, located in Perkasie, Bucks County, Pennsylvania, which began in 1882.

20. On Mt. Lebanon, see Jeanne Jacoby Smith, *An Altar in the Forest: A History of Mt. Lebanon Campmeeting, 1892–1992* (Lebanon, PA: Mt. Lebanon Campmeeting Association, 1992), 2–3, as well as http://www.mtlebanoncampmeeting.org (accessed December 18, 2007). Another excellent example of the circular plan is Indian Fields Methodist Campground (ca. 1848), in Dorchester County, South Carolina. On this camp meeting, see Indian Fields Methodist Campground documentation, Records of the Historic American Buildings Survey (HABS), No. SC-595, Department of Prints and Photographs, Library of Congress, Washington, DC.

21. On the history of Mountain Grove, see Craig A. Newton, "Of Piety's Pleasure: The Mountain Grove Camp Meeting," *Pennsylvania Heritage* 11 (Spring 1985): 12–17.

22. At Balls Creek Camp Meeting Ground, a Methodist camp located in Catawba County, North Carolina, several rows of cabins surrounded the tabernacle. For information on Balls Creek, see Goodrow, "From Sacred Space to Suburban Retreat."

23. This was the case at Northeast Nazarene Camp Meeting, in Northeast, Maryland, located just south of the Pennsylvania border. In an interview I conducted in January 1997 with one of the caretakers of the camp, I learned that initially all of the original cabins flanked the tabernacle in an oval shape. Later an additional row of cabins was added behind the first, and additional cabins were subsequently built outside the original plan.

24. On the history of the radial form, see Weiss, *City in the Woods,* and Goodrow, "From Sacred Space to Suburban Retreat," 25–26. Goodrow follows Weiss's contention in *City in the Woods,* 32, that the radial plan at Wesleyan Grove was one of the first and was enormously influential on later camp-meeting designs. He also discusses the symbolism of the plan, which appealed to the late-nineteenth-century devout. On the sacramental significance of camp meeting layouts in the Victorian era, especially radial plans, also see Cooley, "Manna and the Manual."

25. Plan by Lyman Werst, located in the archives at Highland Park Camp Meeting, Sellersville, PA.

26. Conversation with Merv Werst, January, 1997.

27. Weiss cited a commentator for the *Western Christian Advocate* from 1839 who suggested that the tents themselves were supposed to act like walls of the church. See Weiss, *City in the Woods*, 9–10.

28. On the edges of larger camps, where facing the tabernacle was not possible, the cabins faced one another, perhaps the next best alternative to gazing upon the minister, as at Northeast Nazarene Camp in Northeast, Maryland.

29. Goodrow, "From Sacred Space to Suburban Retreat," 31, and Weiss, *City in the Woods*, 69.

30. Weiss, *City in the Woods*, 30–38 and 70–75.

31. *New York Times* (20 Aug. 1867), 2, as quoted in Weiss, *City in the Woods*, 51.

32. See James Jackson Jarves, "A New Phase of Druidism," *Galaxy* 10 (Dec. 1870): 777–83; quoted in Weiss, *City in the Woods*, 73–74.

33. Unknown artist, *Patterson Grove Auditorium, Patterson Grove Camp Ground, Fairmount Township, Luzerne County, Pennsylvania*, last quarter of the nineteenth century, lithograph, 86.534, Palmer Museum of Art, Pennsylvania State University, partial gift and purchase from John C. O'Connor and Ralph M. Yeager. reproduced in Richard Sharpe Patterson, *Patterson Grove Centennial, 1868–1968* (Harveyville, PA: Patterson Grove Camp-Meeting Association Board of Trustees, 1968), 26–27.

34. Methodist Episcopal Church, Newark Conference, Camp Meeting Association, *Manual of the Denville Camp Ground of the Newark Conference Camp Meeting Association* (Denville, NJ, 1874), 38. Permission to build a fence was granted only after securing written permission from the camp's board.

35. Weiss, *City in the Woods*, 28.

36. Ibid., 9.

37. H. Vincent, *A History of the Wesleyan Grove, Martha's Vineyard, Camp Meeting* (Boston: G. C. Rand & Avery, 1858), 203. Also see Weiss, *City in the Woods*, 28; she claims that this was a traditional rule at many camp meetings.

38. Crystal Spring Camp Meeting Association, *By-Laws, Rules and Regulations of the Crystal Spring Campmeeting Association of Brush Creek, Fulton Country, Pa.* (Everett, PA: John C. Chamberlain's Book and Job Office, 1889), 12. Rules such as these were thought to prevent certain indiscretions, such as drinking and illicit sexual encounters, from occurring on the grounds. On indiscretions and methods to prevent them, see Johnson, *The Frontier Camp Meeting*, 54 and 89–92; Smith, *An Altar in the Forest*, 14; and Weiss, *City in the Woods*, 73.

39. M[ary]. H[arriott]. N[orris], *Camp Tabor: A Story of Child Life in the Woods* (New York: Phillips and Hunt; Cincinnati: Cranston and Sloan, 1874).

40. Ibid., 25.

41. Ibid., 32.

42. See accounts of various camp meetings cited throughout this chapter, as well as Jones, *Perfectionist Persuasion,* which discusses in detail the differences between Methodist and Holiness camps. Also see books that focus on the relation of the Holiness movement to Methodism including Brasher, *The Sanctified South,* 27–30, and Dieter, *The Holiness Revival of the Nineteenth Century.*

43. Adam Wallace, *The Parson of the Islands; A Biography of the Late Rev. Joshua Thomas* (Philadelphia, 1861), between pages 230 and 231.

44. See Gorham, *Camp Meeting Manual.*

45. William Henry Milburn, *Ten Years of Preacher-Life: Chapters from an Autobiography* (New York: Derby and Jackson, 1859), 116–17. The equation of *seeing* with knowledge of God has a long history as a metaphor in Christianity; a good discussion of this tradition may be found in Martin Jay, *Downcast Eyes: The Denigration of Vision in Twentieth-Century French Thought* (Berkeley: Univ. of California Press, 1993), especially chapter 1.

46. Cooley examines this in "Manna and the Manual," though he focuses on the *religious* and *symbolic* contexts for the camp-meeting space as heaven more than on the spatial ramifications of this.

47. Porter, *An Essay on Camp-Meetings,* 22–23.

48. God's Holiness Grove Camp Meeting Association, *Fifty Years of Spiritual Ministry,* n.p. For other statements by holiness advocates of the separateness of holiness camp meetings from everyday society, see George Hughes, *Days of Power in the Forest Temple: A Review of the Wonderful Work of God at Fourteen National Camp-Meetings, 1867 to 1872* (Boston: John Bent, 1873); A. McLean and J. W. Eaton, *Penuel; Or, Face to Face with God* (New York: W. C. Palmer, Jr., 1869), especially x–xvi; and Adam Wallace, *A Modern Pentecost: Embracing a Record of the Sixteenth National Camp-Meeting for the Promotion of Holiness Held at Landisville, Pa., July 23d to August 1st, 1873* (Philadelphia: Methodist Home Journal, 1873), especially 26.

49. God's Holiness Grove Camp Meeting Association, *Fifty Years of Spiritual Ministry,* n.p.

50. Porter, *An Essay on Camp-Meetings,* 20. Other Methodist tracts that talk about the camp-meeting family include countless histories of individual camps, as well as Gorham, *Camp Meeting Manual,* and Mead, *Manna in the Wilderness.*

51. Brown discussed this throughout both editions of his book on camp meetings in *Holy Ground* and *Holy Ground, Too.* Cooley argued for the sacramental and symbolic meanings that the Methodist camp-meeting space was thought to acquire, noting how Methodists in the Victorian period, such as A. P. Mead, emphasized this aspect of the space far more than its usefulness as a site for conversions in "Manna and the Manual," 134–36.

52. Jesse Lee and Minton Thrift, *Memoir of the Rev. Jesse Lee, with Extracts from His Journals* (New York: N. Bangs and T. Mason, 1823), 289.

53. See Mead, *Manna in the Wilderness,* 29–30.

54. Gorham, *Camp Meeting Manual,* 44–45.

55. On how the hierarchy between different levels of campers related to their position on the grounds, see Bruce, *And They All Sang Hallelujah,* 79. Brasher raised the issue of one's religious status determining the space one occupied in the Southern Methodist church, in *The Sanctified South,* 23, although he did not apply this to camp meetings.

56. Wallace, ed., *A Modern Pentecost,* 24–29.

57. McLean and Eaton, *Penuel,* 150–52.

58. The engraving of Wesleyan Grove comes from Vincent, *History of Wesleyan Grove Camp Meeting.*

59. *Interior View of West Branch Camp Meeting, Clinton County, Pennsylvania* (Philadelphia: W. H. Rease, 1872); lithograph may be found in the Prints and Photographs Division, Library of Congress.

60. On the role of appearances in Victorian society, see Halttunen, *Confidence Men and Painted Women,* and Kasson, *Rudeness and Civility.* Some Methodists went so far as to say that one must give up fashion altogether if one wished to be a sanctified Christian; see Rev. E. H. Stokes et al. *The Earnest Minister: A Record of the Life, Labors and Literary Remains of Rev. Ruliff V. Lawrence . . .* (Philadelphia: A. Wallace, 1873), 84.

61. Porter, *An Essay on Camp-Meetings,* 15–16.

62. Ibid., 25.

63. Ibid., 30.

64. Ibid., 78–79.

65. The complicated nature of these hierarchies at holiness camp meetings is discussed by Brasher in *The Sanctified South,* 94–95.

66. Stokes et al., *The Earnest Minister,* 330–31.

67. Ibid., 332–33.

68. Wallace, ed., *A Modern Pentecost,* 16.

69. Ibid., 126. Stories like these appear repeatedly throughout the Holiness camp-meeting literature. See also Stokes et al., *The Earnest Minister,* 63, 164; McLean and Eaton, *Penuel,* 14; and Brasher, *The Sanctified South.*

70. Mead, *Manna in the Wilderness,* 135–36.

71. Gorham, *Camp Meeting Manual,* 151. For more on the necessity of leadership at camp meetings and the role of ministers in it, see Mead, *Manna in the Wilderness,* 84–85.

72. Wallace, *The Parson of the Islands,* 222–23.

73. Conversion stories such as this abound in the literature on camp meetings. See the account of Joshua Thomas's own conversion in Wallace, *The Parson of the Islands*, 88–90. Other examples may be found in Mead, *Manna in the Wilderness,* 286–93; Hughes, *Days of Power in the Forest Temple,* 145–47; McLean and Eaton, *Penuel,* 150–52; and Stokes et al., *The Earnest Minister,* 164.

74. Stokes et al., *The Earnest Minister,* 120–21; 129.

75. Milburn, *Ten Years of Preacher Life,* 118.

76. See B. Carradine, *Graphic Scenes* (Cincinnati, OH: God's Revivalist Office, 1911), 254. For more references to the reciprocal gaze between ministers and worshippers in a holiness context, see Brasher, *The Sanctified South.*

77. Mead, *Manna in the Wilderness,* 239. See also Wallace, *The Parson of the Islands,* 222–23, and John Franklin Grimes, *The Romance of the American Camp Meeting: Golden Jubilee Etchings of the Lancaster Assembly and Camp Meeting, 1872–1922* . . . (Cincinnati: Caxton Press, 1922), 84.

78. Brasher, *The Sanctified South,* 103–04.

79. Mead, *Manna in the Wilderness,* 410.

80. Levy in Wallace, ed., *A Modern Pentecost,* 144.

Conclusion

1. Foucault, *Discipline and Punish,* 217.

BIBLIOGRAPHY

Abu-Lughod, Lila. "The Romance of Resistance: Tracing Transformations of Power through Bedouin Women." *American Ethnologist* 17, no. 1 (February 1990): 41–55.

Aitken, Hugh G. J. *Taylorism at Watertown Arsenal: Scientific Management in Action, 1908–1915.* Cambridge, MA: Harvard Univ. Press, 1960.

Alford, Leon Pratt. *Management's Handbook, by a Staff of Specialists.* New York: Ronald Press, 1924.

American Sunday-School Union. *Parlour and Kitchen; Or, the Story of Ann Connover.* Philadelphia: American Sunday-School Union, 1835.

Ames, Kenneth L. "Meaning in Artifacts: Hall Furnishings in Victorian America." *Journal of Interdisciplinary History* 9 (Summer 1978): 19–46.

Anderson, Arthur G. *Industrial Engineering and Factory Management.* New York: Ronald Press, 1928.

Andrzejewski, Anna Vemer. *"Perspectives in Vernacular Architecture,* the VAF, and the Study of Ordinary Buildings and Landscapes in North America." *Perspectives in Vernacular Architecture* 13, no. 2 (2006/2007): 55–63.

Arthur, T. S. *Trials and Confessions of an American Housekeeper.* Philadelphia: Lippincott, Grambo, 1854.

Austin Company. *Austin Standard Factory-Buildings.* Cleveland, OH: The Company, 1919.

"Automatic Assistant Managers—How Machinery Aids in Supervision." *Factory* 14 (April 1915): 233–34, 288, 290.

Bahr, Betsy W. *New England Mill Engineering: Rationalization and Reform in Textile Mill Design, 1790–1920.* Ann Arbor, MI: UMI Press, 1987.

Barnes, Ralph Mosser. *Industrial Engineering and Management, Problems and Policies.* New York: McGraw-Hill, 1931.

"The Battlefields of Business." *System* 12 (July 1907): 52–55.

"The Battlefields of Business." *System* 15 (January 1909): 29–32.

Baxter, Vern K. *Labor and Politics in the United States Postal Service.* New York: Plenum Press, 1994.

Becker, O.M., and William J. Lees. "Building a Factory V—Plans and Materials for Construction." *System* 11 (January 1907): 28–35.

Beecher, Catharine Esther. *Letters to Persons Who Are Engaged in Domestic Service.* New York: Leavitt and Trow, 1842.

———. *A Treatise on Domestic Economy, for the Use of Young Ladies at Home, and at School.* Boston: Marsh, Capen, Lyon, and Webb, 1841.

Beecher, Catharine Esther, and Harriet Beecher Stowe. *The American Woman's Home; Or, Principles of Domestic Science: Being a Guide to the Formation and Maintenance of Economical, Healthful, Beautiful, and Christian Homes.* New York: J. B. Ford, 1869.

Beecher, Eunice White Bullard (Mrs. Henry Ward Beecher). *The Law of a Household.* Boston: Small, Maynard, 1912.

———. *All Around the House; Or, How to Make Homes Happy.* New York: D. Appleton, 1879.

———. *Motherly Talks with Young Housekeepers: Embracing Eighty-Seven Brief Articles on Topics of Home Interest, and About Five Hundred Choice Receipts for Cooking, etc.* New York: J. B. Ford, 1875.

Bentham, Jeremy. *Panopticon; Or, the Inspection-House: Containing the Idea of a New Principle of Construction Applicable to any Sort of Establishment, in which Persons of any Description are to be Kept Under Inspection: And in Particular to Penitentiary-Houses, Prisons, Houses of Industry . . . and Schools: With a Plan of Management Adapted to the Principle: In a Series of Letters, Written in the Year 1787.* London: Reprinted and sold by T. Payne, 1791. Reprinted as *The Panopticon Writings*, ed. Miran Božovič. London: Verso, 1995.

Bevier, Isabel. *The House: Its Plan, Decoration and Care.* Chicago: American School of Home Economics, 1907.

Bicknell, A. J. *Bicknell's Cottage and Villa Architecture: Containing Sixty-Six Plates of Wooden and Brick Buildings, with Details Showing Plans, Elevations, Views, Sections and Details, of Low Priced, Medium and First Class Cottages, Villas, Farm Houses and Country Seats: Also, Specifications for Frame and Brick Dwellings, etc.: Drawings to Scale.* New York: William T. Comstock, 1881.

Biggs, Lindy. *The Rational Factory: Architecture, Technology, and Work in America's Age of Mass Production.* Baltimore: Johns Hopkins Univ. Press, 1996.

Bluestone, Daniel. "Civic and Aesthetic Reserve: Ammi Burnham Young's 1850s Federal Customhouse Designs." *Winterthur Portfolio* 25 (Summer/Autumn 1990): 131–56.

Boydston, Jeanne, Mary Kelley, and Anne Throne Margolis. *The Limits of Sisterhood: The Beecher Sisters on Women's Rights and Woman's Sphere.* Chapel Hill: Univ. of North Carolina Press, 1988.

Brandes, Stuart D. *American Welfare Capitalism, 1880–1940.* Chicago: Univ. of Chicago Press, 1976.

Brasher, John Lawrence. *The Sanctified South: John Lakin Brasher and the Holiness Movement.* Urbana: Univ. of Illinois Press, 1994.

Braverman, Harry. *Labor and Monopoly Capital: The Degradation of Work in the Twentieth Century.* New York: Monthly Review Press, 1975.

Brennan, Teresa, and Martin Jay eds. *Vision in Context: Historical and Contemporary Perspectives on Sight.* New York: Routledge, 1996.

Brody, David. *Workers in Industrial America: Essays on the Twentieth Century Struggle.* New York: Oxford Univ. Press, 1980.

Brown, Michael. "On Resisting Resistance." *American Anthropologist* 98 (December 1996): 729–35.

Brown, Kenneth O. *Holy Ground: A Study of the American Camp Meeting.* New York: Garland, 1992.

———. *Holy Ground, Too: The Camp Meeting Family Tree.* Hazleton, PA: Holiness Archives, 1997.

Brown, Susan Anna. *Home Topics: A Book of Practical Papers on House and Home Matters.* New York: Century, 1881.

Bruce, Dickson D. *And They All Sang Hallelujah: Plain-Folk Camp-Meeting Religion, 1800–1845.* Knoxville: Univ. of Tennessee Press, 1974.

Brunner, Arnold William, and William Paul Gerhard. *Cottages; Or, Hints on Economical Building, Containing Twenty-Four Plates of Medium and Low Cost Houses, Contributed by Different New York Architects. Together with Descriptive Letterpress, Giving Practical Suggestions for Cottage Building.* New York: W. T. Comstock, 1884.

Bruns, James H. *Great American Post Offices.* Washington, DC: Preservation Press; New York: Wiley, 1998.

Bryson, Norman. *Vision and Painting: The Logic of the Gaze.* New Haven: Yale Univ. Press, 1983.

Buder, Stanley. *Pullman: An Experiment in Industrial Order and Community Planning, 1880–1930.* New York: Oxford Univ. Press, 1967.

Buggeln, Gretchen Townsend. *Temples of Grace: The Material Transformation of Connecticut's Churches, 1790–1840.* Hanover, NH: Univ. Press of New England, 2003.

Bulfinch, Charles. *Report of Charles Bulfinch on the Subject of Penitentiaries.* Washington: Gales and Seaton, 1827.

Campbell, Helen. *Prisoners of Poverty: Women Wage-Workers, Their Trades and Their Lives.* Boston: Roberts Brothers, 1887.

Carradine, B. *Graphic Scenes.* Cincinnati, OH: God's Revivalist Office, 1911.

Carter, Thomas, and Bernard L. Herman, eds. *Perspectives in Vernacular Architecture, IV.* Columbia: Univ. of Missouri Press, 1991.

Caskey, Marie. *Chariot of Fire: Religion and the Beecher Family.* New Haven: Yale Univ. Press, 1978.

Chamberlain, Charles, Jr. *The Servant-Girl of the Period, the Greatest Plague of Life: What Mr. and Mrs. Honeydew Learned of Housekeeping.* New York: J. S. Redfield, 1873.

Chandler, Alfred D., Jr. *The Visible Hand: The Managerial Revolution in American Business.* Cambridge, MA: Belknap Press, 1977.

Chappell, Lodge W., Harry J. Daniels, and John P. Campbell. *Camp Meeting Memories: A Short History of Holiness Camp Meetings in Central Penna.* Sunbury, PA: Sunbury Daily Item, 1951.

Clark, Clifford Edward. *The American Family Home, 1800–1960.* Chapel Hill: Univ. of North Carolina Press, 1986.

Coben, Stanley. *Rebellion Against Victorianism: The Impetus for Cultural Change in 1920s America.* New York: Oxford Univ. Press, 1991.

Collins, D. C. Newman. "The Design and Construction of Industrial Buildings." *Engineering Magazine* 33 (September 1907): 906–30.

Comstock, William T. *American Cottages; Consisting of Forty-Four Large Quarto Plates, Containing Original Designs of Medium and Low Cost Cottages, Seaside and Country Houses. Also, a Club House, Pavilion.* New York: W. T. Comstock, 1883.

———. *Victorian Domestic Architectural Plans and Details: 734 Scale Drawings of Doorways, Windows, Staircases, Moldings, Cornices, and Other Elements.* New York: William T. Comstock, 1881.

Consolidated File, Construction of Federal Buildings. Records of the Public Buildings Service. Record Group 121. National Archives Building at College Park, Maryland—Cartographic Division.

Constable, Nicole. *Maid to Order in Hong Kong: Stories of Filipina Workers.* Ithaca, NY: Cornell Univ. Press, 1997.

Construction of Post Offices, 1885–1925. Records of the Public Buildings Service, Prints, Record Group 121-C. National Archives at College Park, Maryland—Still Pictures Branch.

Cooley, Steven D. "Manna and the Manual: Sacramental and Instrumental Constructions of the Victorian Methodist Camp Meeting during the Mid–Nineteenth Century." *Religion and American Culture* 6 (Summer 1996): 131–59.

Cornelius, Mrs. [Mary H.]. *The Young Housekeeper's Friend.* Revised and enlarged. Boston: Thompson, Brown, 1871.

Crary, Jonathan. *Techniques of the Observer: On Vision and Modernity in the Nineteenth Century.* Cambridge, MA: MIT Press, 1990.

Crawford, Margaret. *Building the Workingman's Paradise: The Design of American Company Towns.* London: Verso, 1995.

Crawford, William. *Report of William Crawford, Esq., on the Penitentiaries of the United States, Addressed to His Majesty's Principal Secretary of State for the Home Department.* London, 1834.

Crystal Spring Camp Meeting Association. *By-Laws, Rules and Regulations of the Crystal Spring Campmeeting Association of Brush Creek, Fulton County, Pa.: Chartered December 6th, A.D. 1886.* Everett, PA: John C. Chamberlain's Book and Job Office, 1889.

Cullinan, Gerald. *The Post Office Department.* New York: F. A. Praeger, 1968.

Cushing, Marshall Henry. *The Story of Our Post Office: The Greatest Government Department in All Its Phases.* Boston: A. M. Thayer, 1893.

Darnton, Robert. *The Great Cat Massacre and Other Episodes in French Cultural History.* New York: Basic Books, 1984.

Davis, Mike. *City of Quartz: Excavating the Future in Los Angeles.* London: Verso, 1990.

Davis, Ralph Currier. *The Principles of Factory Organization and Management.* New York: Harper and Brothers, 1928.

de Beaumont, Gustave, Alexis de Tocqueville, and William B. Sarsfield. *Origin and Outline of the Penitentiary System in the United States of North America.* London: Sold by J. and A. Arch, 1833.

Deetz, James. *In Small Things Forgotten: The Archaeology of Early American Life.* Garden City, NY: Anchor Press/Doubleday, 1977.

Demetz, F. A., and G. A. Blouet. *Rapports . . . sur les Penitenciers des Etats-Unis.* Paris: Imprimerie Royale, 1837.

Denniston, Elinore. *America's Silent Investigators: The Story of the Postal Inspectors Who Protect the Unites States Mail.* New York: Dodd, Mead, 1964.

DePuy, LeRoy B. "The Triumph of the 'Pennsylvania System' at the State's Penitentiaries." *Pennsylvania History* 21, no. 2 (April 1954): 128–44.

———. "The Walnut Street Prison: Pennsylvania's First Penitentiary." *Pennsylvania History* 18 (April 1951): 130–44.

Diemer, Hugo. *Factory Organization and Administration.* 3rd ed. New York: McGraw-Hill, 1921.

———. "The Planning of Factory Buildings and the Influence of Design on Their Productive Capacity." *Engineering News* 50 (24 March 1904): 292–94.

Dieter, Melvin Easterday. *The Holiness Revival of the Nineteenth Century.* Metuchen, NJ: Scarecrow Press, 1980.

Doll, Eugene E. "Trial and Error at Allegheny: The Western State Penitentiary, 1818–30." *Pennsylvania Magazine of History and Biography* 81 (January 1957): 3–27.

Donnelly, Michael. "Foucault's Genealogy of the Human Sciences." *Economy and Society* 11 (November 1982): 363–80.

Downing, A. J. *The Architecture of Country Houses: Including Designs for Cottages, Farm Houses, and Villas, with Remarks on Interiors, Furniture, and the Best Modes of Warming and Ventilating.* New York: D. Appleton, 1850.

———. *Cottage Residences; Or, A Series of Designs for Rural Cottages and Cottage Villas, and Their Gardens and Grounds. Adapted to North America.* New York: Wiley and Putnam, 1842.

Dublin, Thomas. *Women at Work: The Transformation of Work and Community in Lowell, Massachusetts, 1826–1860.* New York: Columbia Univ. Press, 1979.

Dudden, Faye E. *Serving Women: Household Service in Nineteenth-Century America.* Middletown, CT: Wesleyan Univ. Press. Distributed by Harper and Row, 1983.

Edwards, Richard. *Contested Terrain: The Transformation of the Workplace in the Twentieth Century.* New York: Basic Books, 1979.

Ellet, Mrs. E. F., ed. *The New Cyclopedia of Domestic Economy, and Practical Housekeeper Adapted to All Classes of Society, and Comprising Subjects Connected with the Interests of Every Family.* Norwich, CT: Henry Bill Publishing, 1872.

Emerson, Howard P., and Douglas C. E. Naehring. *Origins of Industrial Engineering: The Early Years of a Profession.* Norcross, GA: Industrial Engineering and Management Press, Institute of Industrial Engineers, 1988.

Eslinger, Ellen. *Citizens of Zion: The Social Origins of Camp Meeting Revivalism.* Knoxville: Univ. of Tennessee Press, 1999.

Evans, Robin. *The Fabrication of Virtue: English Prison Architecture, 1750–1840.* Cambridge: Cambridge Univ. Press, 1982.

Finzsch, Norbert, and Robert Jütte. *Institutions of Confinement: Hospitals, Asylums, and Prisons in Western Europe and North America, 1500–1950.* New York: Cambridge Univ. Press, 1996.

Fletcher, Robert. "What Are We Fighting For? Rethinking Resistance in a Pewenche Community in Chile." *Journal of Peasant Studies* 28 (April 2001): 37–66.

Foucault, Michel. *Discipline and Punish: The Birth of the Prison.* 1st American ed. Translated by Alan Sheridan. New York: Pantheon Books, 1977.

———. *The History of Sexuality.* 1st American ed. Translated by Robert Hurley. New York: Pantheon Books, 1978.

———. *Surveiller et punir: Naissance de la prison.* Paris: Gallimard, 1975.

Fowler, C. H., and William De Puy. *Home and Health and Home Economics: A Cyclopedia of Facts and Hints for All Departments of Home Life, Health, and Domestic Economy.* New York: Phillips and Hunt, 1880.

Fowler, O. S. *A Home for All; Or, The Gravel Wall and Octagon Mode of Building.* New York: Fowler and Wells, 1854.

Gandy, Oscar H. *The Panoptic Sort: A Political Economy of Personal Information.* Boulder, CO: Westview, 1993.

Gane, Mike, ed. *Towards a Critique of Foucault.* London: Routledge, 1986.

Gardner, E. C. *The House That Jill Built, After Jack's Had Proved a Failure.* New York: Fords, Howard, and Hulbert, 1882.

———. *Illustrated Homes: A Series of Papers Describing Real Houses and Real People.* Boston: J. R. Osgood, 1875.

———. "Model Homes for Model Housekeeping, IV." *Good Housekeeping* 1, no. 6 (25 July 1885): 1–5.

Garland, David. *Punishment and Modern Society: A Study in Social Theory.* Chicago: Univ. of Chicago Press, 1990.

Garrison, J. Ritchie. *Two Carpenters: Architecture and Building in Early New England, 1799–1859.* Knoxville: Univ. of Tennessee Press, 2006.

Garvin, James L. "Mail-Order House Plans and American Victorian Architecture." *Winterthur Portfolio* 16, no. 4 (Winter 1981): 309–34.

Genovese, Eugene D. *Roll, Jordan, Roll: The World the Slaves Made.* New York: Pantheon Books, 1974.

Gibbons, Herbert Adams. *John Wanamaker.* New York: Harper and Brothers, 1926.

Gibson, Louis H. *Convenient Houses, with Fifty Plans for the Housekeeper Architect and Housewife, a Journey through the House, Fifty Convenient House Plans, Practical House Building for the Owner, Business Points in Building, How to Pay for a Home.* New York: T. Y. Crowell, 1889.

Goddell, R. H. "Saving 42% on Routine Work." *System* 37 (June 1920): 1184–86.

God's Holiness Grove Camp Meeting Association. *Fifty Years of Spiritual Ministry.* Hummel's Wharf, PA: The Association, 1969.

Goldstein, Jan Ellen. *Foucault and the Writing of History.* London: Basil Blackwell, 1994.

Goodrow, Ray McKinzie. "From Sacred Space to Suburban Retreat: The Evolution of the American Camp Meeting Ground." M.A. thesis, Univ. of Virginia, 1994.

Gordon, Robert B., and Patrick M. Malone. *The Texture of Industry: An Archaeological View of the Industrialization of North America.* New York: Oxford Univ. Press, 1994.

Gorham, B[arlow]. W[eed]. *Camp Meeting Manual: A Practical Book for the Camp Ground; in Two Parts.* Boston: H. V. Degen, 1854.

Gospel, Howard F., and Craig R. Littler. *Managerial Strategies and Industrial Relations: An Historical and Comparative Study.* London: Heinemann Educational Books, 1983.

Greif, Martin. *The New Industrial Landscape: The Story of the Austin Company.* Clinton, NJ: Main Street Press, 1978.

Griffith, Nicholas A. [Elizabeth Strong Worthington]. *The Biddy Club: And How Its Members ... Grappled with the Troublous Servant Question to the Great Advantage of Themselves, and, as They Hope, of Many Others.* Chicago: A. C. McClurg, 1888.

Grimes, John Franklin. *The Romance of the American Camp Meeting: Golden Jubilee Etchings of the Lancaster Assembly and Camp Meeting, 1872–1922, Illustrative of the Camp Meeting as an American Institution.* Cincinnati: Caxton Press, 1922.

Groth, Paul Erling. "Making New Connections in Vernacular Architecture." *Journal of the Society of Architectural Historians* 58 (September 1999): 444–51.

Hale, Sarah Josepha Buell. *The Good Housekeeper; Or, The Way to Live Well and To Be Well While We Live: Containing Directions for Choosing and Preparing Food, in Regard to Health, Economy and Taste.* Boston: Weeks, Jordan, 1839.

———. *Keeping House and House Keeping; A Story of Domestic Life.* New York: Harper and Brothers, 1845.

Halttunen, Karen. *Confidence Men and Painted Women: A Study of Middle-Class Culture in America, 1830–1870.* New Haven: Yale Univ. Press, 1982.

Handlin, David P. *The American Home: Architecture and Society, 1815–1915.* Boston: Little, Brown, 1979.

Haviland, John. *A Description of Haviland's Design for the New Penitentiary Now Erecting Near Philadelphia, Accompanied with a Birds-Eye View.* Philadelphia: R. Desilver, 1824.

Herman, Bernard L. *Architecture and Rural Life in Central Delaware, 1700–1900.* Knoxville: Univ. of Tennessee Press, 1987.

———. *The Stolen House.* Charlottesville: Univ. Press of Virginia, 1992.

———. *Town House: Architecture and Material Life in the Early American City, 1780–1830.* Chapel Hill: Published for the Omohundro Institute of Early American History and Culture, Williamsburg, Virginia, by the Univ. of North Carolina Press, 2005.

Herrick, Christine Terhune. *The Expert Maid-Servant.* New York: Harper and Brothers, 1904.

Hess, Henry. "Works Design as a Factor in Manufacturing Economy." *Engineering Magazine* 27 (July 1904): 498–520.

Hexamer, Ernest, and Sons. *Hexamer General Surveys, 1866-1896.* 30 vols. Philadelphia: E. Hexamer and Sons, 1866–95.

Hindle, Brooke, ed. *Material Culture of the Wooden Age.* Tarrytown, NY: Sleepy Hollow Press, 1981.

Hirsch, Adam Jay. *The Rise of the Penitentiary: Prisons and Punishment in Early America.* New Haven: Yale Univ. Press, 1992.

Hoagland, Alison K. *Army Architecture in the West: Forts Laramie, Bridger, and D. A. Russell, 1849–1912.* Norman: Univ. of Oklahoma Press, 2004.

Holly, Henry Hudson. *Modern Dwellings in Town and Country Adapted to American Wants and Climate with a Treatise on Furniture and Decoration.* New York: Harper and Brothers, 1878.

Holst, Nancy Ann. "'The Wise Woman Buildeth Her House': Catharine Beecher and Nineteenth-Century House Pattern Books." M.A. thesis, Univ. of Delaware, 1996.

Hopkins, Alfred. *Prisons and Prison Building.* New York: Architectural Book Publishing, 1930.

Houghton, Walter Edwards. *The Victorian Frame of Mind, 1830–1870.* New Haven: Yale Univ. Press, 1957.

"How Loafing of Employees Was Stopped." *System* 13 (January 1908): 55–56.

"How to Prevent 'Soldiering.'" *System* 8 (December 1905): 572–75.

Howe, Daniel Walker, ed. *Victorian America.* Philadelphia: Univ. of Pennsylvania Press, 1976.

Hubka, Thomas C. *Big House, Little House, Back House, Barn: The Connected Farm Buildings of New England.* Hanover NH: Univ. Press of New England, 1984.

Hughes, George. *Days of Power in the Forest Temple: A Review of the Wonderful Work of God at Fourteen National Camp-Meetings from 1867 to 1872.* Boston: John Bent, 1873.

Hutchins, Catherine E., ed. *Everyday Life in the Early Republic.* Winterthur, DE: Henry Francis du Pont Winterthur Museum, 1994.

Ignatieff, Michael. *A Just Measure of Pain: The Penitentiary in the Industrial Revolution, 1750–1850.* New York: Pantheon Books, 1978.

Interior View of West Branch Camp Meeting, Clinton County, Pennsylvania. Philadelphia: W. H. Rease, 1872.

Jacoby, Sanford M. *Employing Bureaucracy: Managers, Unions, and the Transformation of Work in American Industry, 1900–1945.* New York: Columbia Univ. Press, 1985.

Jarves, James Jackson. "A New Phase of Druidism." *Galaxy* 10 (December 1870): 777–83.

Jay, Martin, ed. *Downcast Eyes: The Denigration of Vision in Twentieth-Century French Thought.* Berkeley: Univ. of California Press, 1993.

Jensen, Derrick, and George Draffan. *Welcome to the Machine: Science, Surveillance, and the Culture of Control.* White River Junction, VT: Chelsea Green Publishing, 2004.

Johnson, Charles A. *The Frontier Camp Meeting: Religion's Harvest Time.* Dallas: Southern Methodist Univ. Press, 1955.

Johnson, H. Thomas, and Robert S. Kaplan. *Relevance Lost: The Rise and Fall of Management Accounting.* Boston, MA: Harvard Business School Press, 1987.

Johnson, Joseph French, and Alexander Hamilton Institute (U.S.). *Office Management,* vol. 19 of Modern Business: A Series of Texts Prepared as Part of the Modern Business Course and Service of the Alexander Hamilton Institute. New York: Alexander Hamilton Institute, 1919.

Johnston, Norman Bruce. *Forms of Constraint: A History of Prison Architecture.* Urbana: Univ. of Illinois Press, 2000.

———. *The Human Cage: A Brief History of Prison Architecture.* New York: Published for the American Foundation, Institute of Corrections by Walker, 1973.

Johnston, Norman Bruce, et al. *Eastern State Penitentiary: Crucible of Good Intentions.* Philadelphia: Philadelphia Museum of Art, 1994.

Jones, Charles Edwin. *Perfectionist Persuasion: The Holiness Movement and American Methodism, 1867–1936.* Metuchen, NJ: Scarecrow Press, 1974.

Jones, Colin, and Roy Porter, eds. *Reassessing Foucault: Power, Medicine, and the Body.* London: Routledge, 1994.

Jones, Edward David. *The Administration of Industrial Enterprises, with Special Reference to Factory Practice.* New York: Longmans, Green, 1916.

Judson, William. "Cashing the Manpower in Business." *System* 13 (January 1908): 4–7.

Kahn, Moritz. *The Design and Construction of Industrial Buildings.* London: Technical Journals, 1917.

Kasson, John F. *Rudeness and Civility: Manners in Nineteenth-Century Urban America.* New York: Hill and Wang, 1990.

Katzman, David M. *Seven Days a Week: Women and Domestic Service in Industrializing America.* New York: Oxford Univ. Press, 1978.

Kerr, Robert. *The Gentleman's House; Or, How to Plan English Residences, from the Parsonage to the Palace; with Tables of Accommodation and Cost, and a Series of Selected Plans.* 2nd ed. London: J. Murray, 1865.

Keve, Paul W. *The History of Corrections in Virginia.* Charlottesville: Univ. Press of Virginia, 1986.

Kincheloe, Joe L., Jr. "Women at Camp Meetings and Political Rallies." *Tennessee Historical Quarterly* 40 (Summer 1981): 158–69.

Kostof, Spiro. *A History of Architecture: Settings and Rituals.* New York: Oxford Univ. Press, 1985.

Kwolek-Folland, Angel. *Engendering Business: Men and Women in the Corporate Office, 1870–1930.* Baltimore: Johns Hopkins Univ. Press, 1994.

Lacan, Jacques. *The Four Fundamental Concepts of Psycho-Analysis.* Translated by Alan Sheridan. Harmondsworth: Penguin Books, 1979.

Lears, T. J. Jackson. *No Place of Grace: Antimodernism and the Transformation of American Culture, 1880–1920.* New York: Pantheon Books, 1981.

Lee, Antoinette J. *Architects to the Nation: The Rise and Decline of the Supervising Architect's Office.* New York: Oxford Univ. Press, 2000.

Lee, Jesse, and Minton Thrift. *Memoir of the Rev. Jesse Lee. with Extracts from His Journals.* New York: Published by N. Bangs and T. Mason, for the Methodist Episcopal Church, 1823.

Lewchuk, Wayne. Review of *The Rational Factory: Architecture, Technology, and Work in America's Age of Mass Production,* by Lindy Biggs. *Economic History Review* 50, no. 4 (November 1997): 845–46.

Lewis, J. Slater. *The Commercial Organisation of Factories: A Handbook for the use of Manufacturers, Directors, Auditors, Engineers, Managers, Secretaries, Accountants,*

Cashiers, Estimate Clerks, Prime Cost Clerks, Bookkeepers, Draughtsmen, Students, Pupils, etc. London: E. and F. N. Spon; New York: Spon and Chamberlain, 1896.

Lewis, W. David. *From Newgate to Dannemora: The Rise of the Penitentiary in New York, 1796–1848.* Ithaca, NY: Cornell Univ. Press, 1965.

Litterer, Joseph A. "The Emergence of Systematic Management as Shown by the Literature of Management from 1870–1900." M.A. thesis, Univ. of Illinois, 1954.

———. "Systematic Management: Design for Organizational Recoupling in American Manufacturing Firms." *Business History Review* 37 (Winter 1963): 369–91.

Littmann, William. "Designing Obedience: The Architecture and Landscape of Welfare Capitalism, 1880–1930." *International Labor and Working-Class History* 53 (Spring 1998): 88–114.

Longstreth, Richard W. *City Center to Regional Mall: Architecture, the Automobile, and Retailing in Los Angeles, 1920–1950.* Cambridge, MA: MIT Press, 1997.

Lynes, Russell. *The Domesticated Americans.* New York: Harper and Row, 1963.

Lyon, David. *The Electronic Eye: The Rise of Surveillance Society.* Minneapolis: Univ. of Minnesota Press, 1994.

———. *Surveillance after September 11.* Cambridge, UK: Polity; Malden, MA: Blackwell, 2003.

———. *Surveillance Society: Monitoring Everyday Life.* Buckingham: Open Univ. Press, 2001.

Makris, John N. *The Silent Investigators: The Great Untold Story of the United States Postal Inspection Service.* New York: E. P. Dutton, 1959.

Markus, Thomas A. *Buildings and Power: Freedom and Control in the Origin of Modern Building Types.* London: Routledge, 1993.

Martin, Ann Smart, and J. Ritchie Garrison, eds. *American Material Culture: The Shape of the Field.* Winterthur, DE: Henry Francis du Pont Winterthur Museum. Distributed by Univ. of Tennessee Press, 1997.

Marx, Gary T. "The Surveillance Society: The Threat of 1984-Style Techniques." *The Futurist* 19 (June 1985): 21–26.

Marx, Karl. *Capital: A Critique of Political Economy.* 3 vols., 1867, 1885, and 1894; reprint, New York: International Publishers, 1967.

Mayhew, Augustus, Henry Mayhew, and George Cruikshank. *The Greatest Plague of Life; Or, The Adventures of a Lady in Search of a Good Servant.* London: D. Bogue, 1847.

Maynard, W. Barksdale. *Architecture in the United States, 1800–1850.* New Haven: Yale Univ. Press, 2002.

McLean, A., and J. W. Eaton. *Penuel; Or, Face to Face with God.* New York: W. C. Palmer, Jr., 1869.

McElwee, Thomas B. *A Concise History of the Eastern Penitentiary of Pennsylvania, Together with a Detailed Statement of the Proceedings of the Committee, Appointed by the Legislature, December 6th, 1834, for the Purpose of Examining into the Economy and Management of That Institution, Embracing the Testimony Taken on That Occasion, and Legislative Proceedings Connected Therewith*. Philadelphia: Neall and Massey, 1835.

McKelvey, Blake. *American Prisons: A History of Good Intentions*. Montclair, NJ: P. Smith, 1977.

McKinley, Blaine Edwards. "'The Stranger at the Gates': Employer Reactions toward Domestic Servants in America, 1825–1875." Ph.D. diss., Michigan State Univ., 1969.

————. "Troublesome Comforts: The Housekeeper-Servant Relationship in Antebellum Didactic Fiction." *Journal of American Culture* 5 (Summer 1982): 36–44.

McMurry, Sally Ann, and Annmarie Adams, eds. *People, Power, Places: Perspectives in Vernacular Architecture, VIII*. Knoxville: Univ. of Tennessee Press, 2000.

Mead, Amos P. *Manna in the Wilderness; Or, The Grove and Its Altar, Offerings, and Thrilling Incidents: Containing a History of the Origin and Rise of Camp Meetings, and a Defence of This Remarkable Means of Grace, Also an Account of the Wyoming Camp Meeting; Together with Sketches of Sermons and Preachers*. Philadelphia: Perkinpine and Higgins, 1859.

Merrill, Horace Samuel. *William Freeman Vilas, Doctrinaire Democrat*. Madison: State Historical Society of Wisconsin, 1954.

Methodist Episcopal Church, Newark Conference, Camp Meeting Association. *Manual of Denville Camp Ground of the Newark Conference Camp Meeting Association*. Denville, NJ, 1874.

Meyer, Stephen. *The Five Dollar Day: Labor Management and Social Control in the Ford Motor Company, 1908–1921*. Albany: State Univ. of New York Press, 1981.

Mikusko, M. Brady. *Carriers in a Common Cause: A History of Letter Carriers and the NALC*. Washington, DC: National Association of Letter Carriers, 1982.

Milburn, William Henry. *Ten Years of Preacher-Life: Chapters from an Autobiography*. New York: Derby and Jackson, 1859.

"The Miseries of Mistresses." *Harpers Monthly* 13 (October 1856): 716–17.

Miyoshi, Masao. *The Divided Self: A Perspective on the Literature of the Victorians*. New York: New York Univ. Press, 1969.

Montgomery, David. *The Fall of the House of Labor: The Workplace, the State, and American Labor Activism, 1865–1925*. Cambridge: Cambridge Univ. Press, 1987.

Moore, Sally Falk, and Barbara G. Myerhoff, eds. *Secular Ritual*. Assen: Van Gorcum, 1977.

Mulvey, Laura. "Visual Pleasure and Narrative Cinema." *Screen* 16 (August 1975): 6–18.

Myerson, Joel, ed. *Antebellum Writers in New York and the South*. Dictionary of Literary Biography, vol. 3. Detroit: Gale Research, 1979.

Nadworny, Milton J. *Scientific Management and the Unions, 1900–1932: A Historical Analysis*. Cambridge, MA: Harvard Univ. Press, 1955.

Neal, Alice B. "Fetch and Carry." *Godey's Lady's Book* 54 (February 1857): 112–17.

Nelson, Daniel. *Managers and Workers: Origins of the New Factory System in the United States, 1880–1920.* Madison: Univ. of Wisconsin Press, 1975.

Nesbitt, Murray B. *Labor Relations in the Federal Government Service.* Washington, DC: Bureau of National Affairs, 1976.

Newton, Craig A. "Of Piety's Pleasure: The Mountain Grove Camp Meeting." *Pennsylvania Heritage* 11 (Spring 1985): 12–17.

N[orris], M[ary] H[arriott]. *Camp Tabor: A Story of Child Life in the Woods.* New York: Phillips and Hunt; Cincinnati: Cranston and Sloan, 1874.

Noyes, Henry T. "Planning for a New Manufacturing Plant." *Annals of the American Academy of Political and Social Science* 85 (September 1919): 66–89.

O'Leary, Elizabeth L. *At Beck and Call: The Representation of Domestic Servants in Nineteenth-Century American Painting.* Washington, DC: Smithsonian Institution Press, 1996.

Ortner, Sherry B. "Resistance and the Problem of Ethnographic Refusal." *Comparative Studies in Society and History* 37 (January 1995): 173–93.

Osborne, Charles Francis. *Notes on the Art of House-Planning.* New York: William T. Comstock, 1888.

Palliser, Palliser, and Company. *Palliser's Model Homes: Showing a Variety of Designs for Model Dwellings.* Bridgeport, CT: Palliser, Palliser, 1878.

Parks, George M., and Roger B. Collins. "200 Years of Industrial Engineering." *Industrial Engineering* 8 (July 1976): 14–25.

Patterson, Richard Sharpe. *Patterson Grove Centennial, 1868–1968.* Harveyville, PA: Patterson Grove Camp-Meeting Association Board of Trustees, 1968.

Peltz, George A. *The Housewife's Library (Many Volumes in One): Furnishing the Very Best Help in All the Necessities, Intricacies, Emergencies, and Vexations That Puzzle a Housekeeper in Every Department of Her Duties in the Home: Household Management, Domestic Cookery, Home Furnishing, Home Decoration, Polite Deportment, Trying Emergencies, Care of Children, Games, Amusements, etc., General Hints.* Boston, MA: E. R. Curtis, 1885.

Perrigo, Oscar E. "Economical Arrangement of Machinery." *System* 8 (September 1905): 261–65.

Pettengill, Lillian. *Toilers of the Home: The Record of a College Woman's Experience as a Domestic Servant.* New York: Doubleday, Page, 1903.

"Piloting a Shop from the 'Bridge.'" *Factory* 14 (April 1915): 244.

Plain Talk and Friendly Advice to Domestics, with Counsel on Home Matters. Boston: Phillips, Sampson, 1855.

Porter, G. Harvey. "The Cost Accountant, an Essential to Management." *Journal of Accountancy* 45 (May 1928): 351–56.

Porter, James. *An Essay on Camp Meetings.* New York: Lane and Scott, 1849.

Post Office Department. *Report of the Postmaster-General of the United States.* 45th Cong., 2d sess., 1877, H.exdoc.1, part 4 (serial set 1799); 45th Cong., 3d sess., 1878, H.exdoc.1, part 4 (serial set 1849); 46th Cong., 2d sess., 1879, H.exdoc.1, part 4 (serial set 1909); 50th Cong., 1st sess., 1887, H.exdoc.1, part 4 (serial set 2540); 51st Cong., 1st sess., 1889, H.exdoc.1 (serial set 2723); 51st Cong., 2d sess., 1890, H.exdoc.1, part 4 (serial set 2839); 52nd Cong., 1st sess., 1891, H.exdoc.1 (Serial 2932); 52nd Cong., 2d sess., 1892, H.exdoc.1 (serial set 3086); 53rd Cong., 2d sess., 1893, H.exdoc.1 (serial set 3208); 54th Cong., 1st sess., 1895, H.exdoc.4 (serial set 3380); 7th Cong., 1st sess., 1901. H.doc.4 (serial set 4288); 63rd Cong., 2d sess., 1913. H.doc.712 (serial set 6629).

Powers, Gershom. *A Brief Account of the Construction, Management, and Discipline of the New York State Prison at Auburn, Together with a Compendium on Criminal Law. Also a Report of the Trial of an Officer of Said Prison for Whipping a Convict.* Auburn, NY: Printed by U. F. Doubleday, 1826.

Prison Discipline Society. *First Annual Report of the Board of Managers of the Prison Discipline Society, Boston, June 2, 1826. Uniform Title: Annual Report, 1826.* Boston: T. R. Marvin, printer, 1827.

———. *Second Annual Report of the Board of Managers of the Prison Discipline Society, Boston, June 1, 1827. Uniform Title: Annual Report, 1827.* Boston: T. R. Marvin, printer, 1827.

Prown, Jules David. "Mind in Matter: An Introduction to Material Culture Theory and Method." *Winterthur Portfolio* 17 (Spring 1982): 1–19.

Prown, Jules David, and Kenneth Haltman, eds. *American Artifacts: Essays in Material Culture.* East Lansing: Michigan State Univ. Press, 2000.

Quimby, Ian M. G., ed. *Material Culture and the Study of American Life.* New York: Published for the Henry Francis du Pont Winterthur Museum, Winterthur, Delaware, by W. W. Norton, 1978.

Records of the Office of the Division of Inspectors, Philadelphia, PA, 1889–93. Office of the Post Master General, Division of Post Office Inspectors. Records of the Post Office Department. Record Group 28. National Archives Building, Washington, DC.

Records of the Inspection Office, Denver, CO, 1879–1907. Office of the Post Master General, Division of Post Office Inspectors. Records of the Post Office Department. Record Group 28. National Archives Building, Washington, DC.

Records of the Inspection Office, Philadelphia, PA, 1896–1909. Office of the Postmaster General, Division of Post Office Inspectors. Records of the Post Office Department. Record Group 28. National Archives Building, Washington, DC.

Records of the Public Building Service. Record Group 121. National Archives at College Park, Maryland.

Roper, Daniel C. *The United States Post Office, Its Past Record, Present Condition, and Potential Relation to the New World Era.* New York: Funk and Wagnalls Company, 1917.

Rosen, Jeffrey. "A Cautionary Tale for a New Age of Surveillance." *New York Times Magazine,* 7 October 2001.

———. *The Unwanted Gaze: The Destruction of Privacy in America.* New York: Random House, 2000.

Rothman, David J. *The Discovery of the Asylum: Social Order and Disorder in the New Republic.* Rev. ed. Boston: Little, Brown, 1990.

Sahlins, Marshall. *Waiting for Foucault.* Cambridge: Prickly Pear, 1993.

Salmon, Lucy Maynard. *Domestic Service.* New York: Macmillan, 1897.

Schlereth, Thomas J. *Material Culture Studies in America.* Nashville, TN: American Association for State and Local History, 1982.

———, ed. *Material Culture: A Research Guide.* Lawrence: Univ. Press of Kansas, 1985.

Schulze, John William. *The American Office: Its Organization, Management and Records.* New York: Ronald Press, 1914.

Schuyler, David. *Apostle of Taste: Andrew Jackson Downing, 1815–1852.* Baltimore: Johns Hopkins Univ. Press, 1996.

Scott, James C. *Weapons of the Weak: Everyday Forms of Peasant Resistance.* New Haven: Yale Univ. Press, 1985.

Semple, Janet. *Bentham's Prison: A Study of the Panopticon Penitentiary.* Oxford: Oxford Univ. Press, 1993.

Simpson, Herbert F. "The Design and Construction of Industrial Buildings, Part II." *Engineering Record* 59 (5 June 1909): 716–18.

Singal, Daniel Joseph. "Towards a Definition of American Modernism." *American Quarterly* 39 (Spring 1987): 7–26.

Sklar, Kathryn Kish. *Catharine Beecher: A Study in American Domesticity.* New Haven: Yale Univ. Press, 1973.

Smith, Darrell Hevenor. *The Office of the Supervising Architect of the Treasury: Its History, Activities, and Organization.* Baltimore: Johns Hopkins Univ. Press, 1923.

Smith, Frederic. *Workshop Management: A Manual for Masters and Men, Comprising a Few Practical Remarks on the Economic Conduct of Workshops, and c.* London: Wyman and Sons, 1879.

Smith, Jeanne Jacoby. *An Altar in the Forest: A History of Mount Lebanon Campmeeting, 1892–1992.* Lebanon, PA: Mt. Lebanon Campmeeting Association, 1990.

Spero, Sterling Denhard. *The Labor Movement in a Government Industry: A Study of Employee Organization in the Postal Service.* New York: George H. Doran, 1924.

Spofford, Harriet Prescott. *The Servant Girl Question.* Boston: Houghton, Mifflin; Cambridge: Riverside Press, 1881.

Standard Sanitary Manufacturing Company. *Factory Sanitation.* Pittsburgh, PA: The Company, 1913.

Stanton, Florence K. *The Practical Housekeeper and Cyclopedia of Domestic Economy: Adapted to All Classes of Society, and Comprising Subjects Connected with the Interests of Every Family . . . and Five Thousand Receipts and Maxims . . .* Philadelphia: Keeler and Kirkpatrick, 1898.

Stevenson, John James. *House Architecture.* London: Macmillan, 1880.

Stevenson, Katherine H., and H. Ward Jandl. *Houses by Mail: A Guide to Houses from Sears, Roebuck and Company.* Washington, DC: Preservation Press, 1986.

Stillman, Damie. *English Neo-Classical Architecture.* London: A. Zwemmer, 1988.

Stockton, Frank Richard, and Marian Edwards Tuttle Stockton. *The Home: Where It Should Be and What to Put in It.* New York: G. P. Putnam and Sons, 1873.

Stokes, E. H., Adam Wallace, and George Hughes. *The Earnest Minister: A Record of the Life, Labors and Literary Remains of Rev. Ruliff V. Lawrence, for Sixteen Years an Itinerant in the New Jersey and Philadelphia Conferences.* Philadelphia: A. Wallace, 1873.

Stradley, Edward M. "Economy by Centralized Control." *Factory* 2 (November–December–January 1908–9): 105–7.

Sutherland, Daniel E. *Americans and Their Servants: Domestic Service in the United States from 1800 to 1920.* Baton Rouge: Louisiana State Univ. Press, 1981.

Sykes, Gresham M. *The Society of Captives: A Study of a Maximum Security Prison.* Princeton, NJ: Princeton Univ. Press, 1958.

Tatum, George Bishop. "Andrew Jackson Downing: Arbiter of American Taste." Ph.D. diss., Princeton Univ., 1949.

Taylor, Frederick Winslow. "A Piece Rate System, Being a Step Toward Partial Solution of the Labor Problem." *Transactions of the American Society of Mechanical Engineers* 16 (1895): 856–903.

———. *The Principles of Scientific Management.* New York: Harper and Brothers, 1911.

———. *Shop Management.* New York: Harper and Brothers, 1911.

Teeters, Negley K., and Albert Gray Fraser. *They Were in Prison: A History of the Pennsylvania Prison Society, 1787–1937, Formerly the Philadelphia Society for Alleviating the Miseries of Public Prisons.* Philadelphia: John C. Winston, 1937.

Teeters, Negley K., and John D. Shearer. *The Prison at Philadelphia, Cherry Hill: The Separate System of Penal Discipline, 1829–1913.* New York: Published for Temple Univ. Publications by Columbia Univ. Press, 1957.

Thayer, Rufus H. *History, Organization, and Functions of the Office of the Supervising Architect of the Treasury Department, with Copies of Reports, Recommendations, etc.* Washington, DC: GPO, 1886.

Tregoning, John. *A Treatise on Factory Management, Being a Comprehensive and Practical Scheme for the Better Management of Factories.* Lynn, MA: Press of Thomas P. Nichols, 1891.

"Trials of an English Housekeeper: High Life below Stairs." *Godey's Lady's Book* 55 (December 1857): 531–33.

Turner, Victor Witter. *The Ritual Process: Structure and Anti-Structure.* London: Routledge and K. Paul, 1969.

Turner, Victor Witter, and Edith L. B. Turner. *Image and Pilgrimage in Christian Culture: Anthropological Perspectives.* New York: Columbia Univ. Press, 1978.

Tyrrell, Henry Grattan. *A Treatise on the Design and Construction of Mill Buildings and Other Industrial Plants.* Chicago: Myron C. Clark Publishing, 1911.

United States Bureau of Prisons. *Handbook of Correctional Institution Design and Construction.* Washington: GPO, 1949.

United States Post Office Department. *Manual of Instructions for Post Office Inspectors.* Washington, DC: GPO, 1941.

United States Public Buildings Administration. *United States Post Offices.* July 1, 1948, edition. Washington, DC: The Administration, 1948.

Upton, Dell. *Architecture in the United States.* Oxford: Oxford Univ. Press, 1998.

———. *Holy Things and Profane: Anglican Parish Churches in Colonial Virginia.* New York: Architectural History Foundation; Cambridge, MA: MIT Press, 1986.

———. "Pattern Books and Professionalism: Aspects of the Transformation of Domestic Architecture in America, 1800–1860." *Winterthur Portfolio* 19, no. 2/3 (Summer-Autumn 1984): 107–50.

———. "The Power of Things: Recent Studies in American Vernacular Architecture." *American Quarterly* 35 (Bibliography 1983): 262–79.

———. "The VAF at 25: What Now?" *Perspectives in Vernacular Architecture* 13, no. 2 (2007): 7–13.

———. "Vernacular Domestic Architecture in Eighteenth-Century Virginia." *Winterthur Portfolio* 17 (Summer/Autumn 1982): 95–119.

Van Slyck, Abigail Ayres. *Free to All: Carnegie Libraries and American Culture, 1890–1920.* Chicago: Univ. of Chicago Press, 1995.

Vaux, Calvert, et al. *Villas and Cottages. A Series of Designs Prepared for Execution in the United States.* New York: Harper and Brothers, 1857.

Vincent, H. *A History of the Wesleyan Grove, Martha's Vineyard, Camp Meeting: From the First Meeting Held There in 1835 to That of 1858.* Boston: G. C. Rand and Avery, 1858.

Walker, Perley F. *Management Engineering: The Design and Organization of Industrial Plants.* New York: McGraw-Hill, 1924.

Wallace, Adam. *A Modern Pentecost: Embracing a Record of the Sixteenth National Camp-Meeting for the Promotion of Holiness Held at Landisville, Pa., July 23d to August 1st, 1873.* Philadelphia: Methodist Home Journal, 1873.

———. *The Parson of the Islands; A Biography of the Late Rev. Joshua Thomas; with Sketches of Many of His Contemporaries, Remarkable Camp Meeting Scenes, Revival Incidents, and the Reminiscences of the Introduction the Islands of the Chesapeake and Eastern Shores of Maryland and Virginia.* Philadelphia, 1861.

Weiss, Ellen. *City in the Woods: The Life and Design of an American Camp Meeting on Martha's Vineyard.* New York: Oxford Univ. Press, 1987.

Westinghouse Electric Corporation, Power Generation Division, Lester, Pennsylvania. Photographic Collection. Acc. No. 69.170. Hagley Museum and Library, Wilmington, Delaware.

"What's the Matter with the Employer, III—Overworking Men—Result: Under-Production." *System* 11 (May 1907): 491–94.

Wheeler, Gervase. *Homes for the People, in Suburb and Country: The Villa, the Mansion, and the Cottage, Adapted to American Climate and Wants. With Examples Showing How to Alter and Remodel Old Buildings. In a Series of One Hundred Original Designs.* New York: C. Scribner, 1855.

White, George Alan. "Issues and Answers: The Post Office Observation Gallery Controversy." M.A. thesis, George Washington Univ., 1965.

Whitmore, John. "Factory Accounting as Applied to Machine Shops." *Journal of Accountancy* 2 (October 1906): 430–41.

Wright, Gwendolyn. *Building the Dream: A Social History of Housing in America.* New York: Pantheon Books, 1981.

Yanni, Carla. *The Architecture of Madness: Insane Asylums in the United States.* Minneapolis: Univ. of Minnesota Press, 2007.

Yarns, Cloth Rooms, Mill Engineering, Reeling and Baling, Winding. International Library of Technology: A Series of Textbooks for Persons Engaged in Engineering Professions, Trades, and Vocational Occupations or for Those Who Desire Information Concerning Them, vol. 78. Scranton, PA: International Textbook Company, 1906.

Yentsch, Anne Elizabeth, and Mary C. Beaudry, eds. *The Art and Mystery of Historical Archaeology: Essays in Honor of James Deetz.* Boca Raton: CRC Press, 1992.

Zimmerman, T. J. "The Chalk Line of Business, I. The System of General Inspection." *System* 10 (October 1906): 353–60.

———. "The System of the Armours." *System* 5 (April 1904): 234–47.

Zunz, Olivier. *Making America Corporate, 1870–1920.* Chicago: Univ. of Chicago Press, 1990.

INDEX

Building Power was designed and typeset on a Macintosh OS 10.4 computer system using InDesign CS 3 software. The body text is set in 10.5/13.5 Garamond and display type is set in Impact. This book was designed and typeset by Stephanie Thompson and manufactured by Thomson-Shore, Inc.